ENCOUNTERS WITH OTHERS
Interpersonal Relationships and You

Don E. Hamachek
Michigan State University

Holt, Rinehart and Winston

New York   Chicago   San Francisco   Philadelphia
Montreal   Toronto   London   Sydney
Tokyo   Mexico City   Rio de Janeiro   Madrid

Library of Congress Cataloging in Publication Data

Hamachek, Don E.
   Encounters with others.

   Includes bibliographical references and index.
   1. Interpersonal relations.   2. Self-perception.
I. Title.
HM132.H329   158'.2   81–6696
ISBN 0–03–088411–X   AACR2

CBS COLLEGE PUBLISHING
Holt, Rinehart and Winston
The Dryden Press
Saunders College Publishing

To Alice . . .
For pleasant encounters
past and future

CONTENTS

3 HOW WE INFLUENCE OTHERS— HOW OTHERS INFLUENCE US

96

PREFACE

This is a book that focuses on human behavior in an interpersonal context. It is an effort to comprehend more fully the underlying dynamics that may be involved when two or more people relate to one another. Included in this volume are discussions about how and why our self-perceptions are related to our perceptions of others, how we form impressions of people and attribute certain characteristics to each other that may or may not be correct, why people are attracted to each other (or not, as the case may be), how self-esteem works as an intervening variable in the attraction process, and some of the specific behavioral components that influence our decision to move away from or toward certain people. Also included are discussions about interpersonal influence—in terms of how it works, when we are most susceptible to it, and what we can do to enhance our own chances of being successfully persuasive with others. In addition, there is a discussion about some of the various ways that we may unwittingly sabotage healthier interpersonal relationships with unrealistic expectations for either others or ourselves, along with some ideas about what we might do to avoid these possibilities. In relation to ways of developing healthy interpersonal connections, there is also an intensive examination of communication processes, which includes a look at how we communicate through the language of behavior, how we communicate with words, and some specific suggestions for developing better communication skills. All in all, it is a look at some of the possible reasons why relationships develop and evolve the way they do, and an overview of what might be done to encourage better interpersonal connections, both personally and professionally.

One of the objectives of this book is to try to encourage a greater sense of awareness of how our own self-perceptions and feelings of self-esteem influence our perceptions of others and, hence, the ebb and flow of our ongoing daily encounters. Sometimes our problems with others originate not so much "out there" as they do "in here," and what needs to be fixed may be something not in the other person, but in ourselves.

A second objective for this volume is to involve you—the reader—not just intellectually, but also personally. I think there is no easy way to do this, but to encourage your involvement, there are opportunities for "Reflections" of a more

vii

personal sort scattered throughout the book. Sometimes the "Reflections" simply raise questions in relation to a particular discussion; other times they may suggest some ideas that you may find interesting to try out on some aspect of your own interpersonal relationships; in some instances, they present opportunities for you to respond to certain questions or situations so that you can compare how you respond with how others are known to have responded. The "Reflections" exercises will, I hope, give you both opportunity and reason to relate what is addressed in the book to the laboratory of your own daily living and your personal experience.

A third objective I hope to accomplish is to promote a greater consciousness about the idea that how we behave has a great influence on how others behave toward us, and that, unless we are aware of the implications of our own behavior, we may unwittingly behave in ways that stir negative feelings and lead to unhappy consequences. My overall goal is to encourage a deeper sense, not only of awareness, but of appreciation for how and why our interpersonal encounters work the way they do.

There is no magic involved in developing healthy, positive interpersonal relationships. There is no single way to achieve these relationships; no *single* way is better than the others. Rather, there are *many* better ways. I hope that this book can be a helpful reading experience for you and that it will enable you to understand more about the nature of interpersonal relationships and what some of the "better" ways might be for you.

I would like to extend a very large thank-you to Professors Joel S. Dill (University of Evansville), Jerry D. Freezel (Kent State University), George M. Gazda (The University of Georgia), Walter F. Johnson (Michigan State University), and W. Larry Osborne (The University of North Carolina) for their constructive, critical reviews of the manuscript and very helpful suggestions for its improvement.

Don E. Hamachek

We cannot live only for ourselves. A thousand fibers connect us with others; and along those fibers, as sympathetic threads, our actions run as causes, and they come back to us as effects.

Henry Melville (1742–1811)

Chapter 1

HOW WE PERCEIVE OTHERS AND HOW OTHERS PERCEIVE US

OVERVIEW

PROLOGUE

How I perceive you and how you perceive me is a complex happening. We may see each other, we may hear each other, and we may even touch each other. With such rich sensory inputs, we might think that getting to know each other would be a relatively easy matter. But that's not usually the case, is it? Why? Well, for one thing, it's not likely that we see each other as we really are. Actually, what we end up seeing in each other is a complex mix of what we choose to see, what we want to see, and what we expect to see. Indeed, through an interesting and largely self-serving process called "attribution," it is possible for us literally to "attribute" certain behaviors and dispositions to each other, which enhances the likelihood that we will see in each other pretty much what we put there. The old maxim, "Seeing is believing," is somewhat misleading. When it comes to interpersonal perceptions, it may be truer to say, "Believing is seeing," for what we see appears to be strongly shaped and limited by our preconceptions and prior convictions. Indeed, as we shall see in this chapter, our beliefs about others are even related to our beliefs about ourselves. Perhaps it's this idea that Oscar Wilde had in mind when he suggested that "All criticism is a form of autobiography."

How and why do we perceive each other the way we do? What are the relationships between our self-perceptions and our perceptions of others? To what extent does our "implicit" or private theory of personality influence how we behave toward others? What factors play a part in determining what we attribute to causing our own or another person's behavior under certain conditions? In what ways are self-concept and self-esteem related to how we see others and how we think others see us? How can we recognize a sincere person when we see one? We will direct our attention to these related questions in this chapter.

Since we probably know most about how we see ourselves, a look at how our self-perceptions influence how we perceive others seems a good place to begin.

RELATIONSHIPS BETWEEN SELF-PERCEPTIONS AND PERCEPTIONS OF OTHERS

Ralph Waldo Emerson insightfully observed that "What we are, that only can we see." As both common sense and research have demonstrated, this simple aphorism stands as the cornerstone upon which are built our most important principles of how we see others. Psychoanalyst Erich Fromm was one of the first to notice the close relationship between a person's feelings toward himself and his feelings toward others. As Fromm expressed it, "Hatred against oneself is inseparable from hatred against others."[1] Summarizing from his more than forty years of experience as a psychotherapist, Carl Rogers[2] has noted a somewhat similar phenomenon in many of his clients. Those who feel least capable of reaching their goals are also inclined to be most rejecting of the people around them. On the other hand, he has also noted that as persons move toward accepting themselves as worthy individuals, they are also inclined to move toward accepting others more uncritically. This is quite consistent with the research of N. A. Kuiper and T. B. Rogers,[3] who concluded from their investigation of how people encode personal information about others that "how we summarize information about other people is bound up with our own view of self."

What we seem inclined to see "out there" in the behavior of other people is quite frequently a projection of our own drives and needs and fears. The person who tells us that people are basically untrustworthy and cruel—ignoring the plain fact that they are also dependable and kind—may be saying more about himself than about the world. Early research by Elizabeth Sheerer[4] and by D. Stock,[5] and Ruth Wylie's[6] review of later research generally support the idea that if an individual thinks well of him- or herself, he or she is more likely to think well of others. Conversely, if one disapproves of oneself, one is more likely to disapprove of others. Perhaps another way of saying this is that what we find "out there" is what we put there with our unconscious projections. When we think we are looking out a window, it may be, more often than we realize, that we are really gazing into a looking glass.

Frank Barron offers some tantalizing evidence to support this looking glass idea. While doing research related to the nature and meaning of psychological health, he and his colleagues first had to develop some operational conceptions about what a healthy person would probably be like. They then studied subjects chosen for their general effectiveness as persons. Following this, each staff member described each subject on an adjective checklist. The intention was to derive from these checklists a composite staff description of each subject's so-called "soundness as a person." The results were surprising. As it turned out, individual staff members used quite different adjectives to describe the same person. The most revealing aspect of this was the great consistency with which staff members described highly effective persons with exactly the same adjectives that in private moments of good will toward themselves they could use to characterize themselves. Barron went on to add:

> Moreoever, they tended to describe clearly *ineffective* persons as possessing traits which in themselves they most strongly denied . . . Thus, one staff member noted for his simple and clear thought processes most frequently described an ineffective person as *confused:* another staff member who is especially well-behaved in matters of duty checked the adjectives *conscientious* and *responsible* most frequently in describing highly rated subjects . . . another staff member who has subsequently been interested professionally in independence of judgment saw effective subjects as independent and *fairminded. Each of us, in brief, saw his own image in what he judged to be good.*[7]

The inclination to see in others what is in oneself is true as early as adolescence. Morris Rosenberg,[8] for example, found that adolescents who thought poorly of themselves tended to think poorly of others and to feel that others felt poorly of them. Those in high self-regard, on the other hand, thought well of others and believed others thought well of them.

Psychiatrist Harry Stack Sullivan once said: "It is not as ye judge that ye shall be judged, but as you judge yourself so shall you judge others."[9] Clinical and empirical research generally supports Sullivan's observation. We do tend to see others as we see ourselves, particularly if we are not aware that this is what we are doing. Seeing others as a projection of our own images may serve several functions: (1) it may tend to make others seem more like us than they really are and therefore more compatible, and (2) it may help perpetuate the feeling that the way we are is really the "right" way.

It seems to be generally true that our own view of ourselves and of our particular life situation serves as a filter through which we view the world around us. The angry person sees hostile intentions, the friendly person sees relationship possibilities; the suspicious individual sees ulterior motives, the trusting individual sees positive outcomes; the fearful person focuses on the scary aspects of being close, the courageous person concentrates on life's exciting possibilities. And so it goes. The way we interpret the world may have a great deal to do with making it become more that way for us. It may indeed be that our perception of what is reality becomes, for better or worse, a self-fulfilling prophecy. And it starts, it seems, with our own self-picture. Whereas as our self-image influences how we evaluate others, our self-esteem influences how we think others are evaluating us —an idea we turn to next.

OUR LEVEL OF SELF-ESTEEM AFFECTS HOW WE THINK OTHERS FEEL ABOUT US

When we talk about how we feel about ourselves, we're talking about the extent to which we admire or value or esteem ourselves—hence, the term self-esteem. Whereas self-concept is the cognitive portion of the self, self-esteem refers more directly to the affective part of the self. That is, not only do we have certain *ideas* about who we are, but we have certain *feelings* about who we are. These feelings reflect our level of self-esteem, and this, in turn, affects how we think others may perceive and evaluate us. What does research say about this? Consider the following:

1. Penny Baron[10] and Elaine Walster[11] found that not only do high-self-esteem people expect more acceptance and less rejection than low-self-esteem people, but they are also inclined to view others in a more favorable light.
2. People with generally high self-esteem tend to evaluate their *own* performance on a task they've failed more favorably than do those with low self-esteem.[12]
3. People with low self-esteem tend to perform more poorly on particular tasks when they know they are being watched—they are more sensitive to possible negative feedback—than is the case for people with higher self-esteem.[13]
4. Low-self-esteem people are apt to work harder for a person they perceive as being relatively undemanding and uncritical. (This maximizes possibilities for positive feedback.) High-self-esteem people, on the other hand, are inclined to work harder for a person they view as difficult to satisfy. (Since they already have high self-esteem, expending greater rather than less effort is the only way to maintain, and perhaps enhance, self-esteem.)[14] Perhaps another way of stating this is to say that high-self-esteem people tend to be spurred on when feedback is more demanding and critical, while low-self-esteem people tend to remain motivated and involved when feedback is more supportive and positive. (We should note, however, that no person is likely to be much affected by feedback that is indiscriminately negative or positive *all the time.* Being more demanding of a high-self-esteem person, for example, may get him or her started, but it's not likely to keep that person going if that's all the input he or she receives.)
5. Low-self-esteem people are more inclined to feel threatened in interactions with someone they view as in some way superior to them than are high-self-esteem people.[15]
6. Research on the relationship between personality and persuasibility has highlighted the general importance of self-esteem as a determinant of an individual's responsiveness to influence both mass media and social interaction. For example, Irving Janis and Peter Field[16] have found that low-self-esteem people seem more influenced by persuasive communication (strong arguments, fear-arousing appeals, prestigious endorsements, and the like) than high-self-esteem people.
7. On a more interpersonal level, Arthur Cohen[17] found that high-self-esteem people are not very likely to be influenced by low-self-esteem persons. In addition, high-self-esteem individuals are more active in their attempts to influence others and better able to protect themselves against negative feedback from their social group than those with lower self-esteem.

What do these research results suggest? For one thing, they suggest that a person's self-esteem—his perception of worth—is like an emotional filter through which he screens the evaluations and perceptions that he feels others have of him. People whose self-esteem is somewhat shaky are more apt to be influenced, persuaded, and bamboozled by others, precisely because their own feelings of self-acceptance depend largely on whether others accept them or not. The process probably works something like this: If my self-esteem is low, it is likely that my self-acceptance is, too. If *I* have problems accepting me, chances are very good that I will wonder how you could accept me. Since my self-esteem is not high enough to allow me to do what I really want to do or say for fear of its being wrong or unacceptable, I may end up living what sociologist Frank Riesmann[18] called an *other directed* life, and developing what psychologist Julian Rotter[19] has termed an *external locus of control.* In other words, I will be more concerned with trying to figure out what *you* want me to do (external locus of control) and very much less concerned with trying to figure out what it is that *I* want to do (internal locus of control). In the process, I reinforce the life position that psychiatrist Eric Berne[20] has described as "I'm not OK—you're OK."

You may begin to see why it is that low-self-esteem people are likely to be more easily influenced, more quick to believe that others may not like them, more motivated to work harder for someone who is less critical and more positive, and more inclined to feel threatened when interacting with people in authority positions. So long as I perceive you as OK and myself as not OK, I have little chance of being the master of my own fate. The question is, why?

Low Self-Esteem May Lead to Indirect Self-Acceptance and Heightened Self-Consciousness

When people lack self-approval, it usually means that their self-doubts outweigh their self-esteem. These people learn to seek self-acceptance indirectly, a process involving the substitution of the good opinion of others for self-approval. In this way, some people grow to be excessively other-directed.

Ultimately, the search for indirect self-acceptance is self-defeating. Why? There are at least two explanations that may help us understand this.

For one thing, if our motivation for presenting ourselves to others in an appealing way is primarily to commandeer their acceptance and to gain their good will, then we are in the position of having to give up who we are in order to become who we think *they want us to be.* Some people become quite chameleon-like in their encounters with others. During one of our therapy sessions, a young man, who was working through a deep sense of inferiority and low self-worth, expressed one of the basic problems involved in the search for indirect self-acceptance:

It's such a pain in the neck living as I do. It seems like I'm constantly wondering what other people want and whether other people will like me. Sometimes I say to myself that I don't care whether others like me or not, but damn it, I know that's not true. It just seems to me that I work so hard at getting others to like me and doing what I think others want that I don't even know what the hell it is I want. Isn't that awful? I don't even know what I want. And do you know what's even worse? Even when others do seem to accept me and like me, *I can't believe it.*

You can probably see the self-defeating aspects of his behavior. *We can believe what others say about us—particularly if it is positive—only when we believe that others see us as we really are.* Ironically, the more successful we are in achieving indirect self-acceptance, the more difficult it is to take credit for any favorable feedback we may get. Inside we realize that the applause we receive is simply the consequence of a successful performance: the friendly attitude we convey, but only act; the helping hand we offer, but without caring; the smile we flash, but without sincerity; the agreements we offer, but without conviction.

Paradoxically, others may be quite aware and tolerant of certain characteristics that an individual is trying to conceal. For example, a man who conceals from others the fact that he has had little formal schooling may never realize that others recognize that he is largely self-educated, admire and respect him for it, and make allowances for whatever gaps there may be in his academic background. However, as long as he is afraid of being himself and accepting his limited academic training, he will never be in a position to believe that he is acceptable to others. This idea has been nicely expressed by sociologists Snell and Gail Putney:

> Inevitably, the pursuit of indirect self-acceptance produces an exaggerated concern for outward appearance. It leads a man to feign a friendliness he does not feel, rather than to develop a capacity for warmth. It leads a woman to feel that her grooming, but not her self is acceptable. It leads to anxious conformity and a tense struggle for recognition. . . . It leads to the fake, to a mode of existence that, like a Hollywood set, is only an elaborate front with nothing but a few props to shore it up.[21]

There is a second, but related, explanation for why it may be self-defeating to go after self-acceptance via indirect means. It has to do with the fact that if my encounter with you is based primarily on gaining your approval, I may end up being so self-conscious that I stumble over my best (more likely my worst) efforts to appear as the likable or competent guy I would like you to see me as. In addition, I am even more sensitive to your appraisal of me. Erving Goffman argues persuasively in *The Presentation of Self in Everyday Life*[22] that when we are attending to and involved in an ongoing encounter, that encounter usually flows smoothly and naturally. However, if we are engaged in an undue amount of self-focused thought during that encounter, then concern shifts away from what is being said toward whether what we are saying will be evaluated positively or negatively. Hence, when we are primarily concerned with impressing our friend, we may find ourselves in a heightened state of self-consciousness. Social psychologist Michael Argyle[23] suggests that when this happens two events usually follow: (1) there is a decreased concern with evaluating the behavior of others, and (2) there is an increased concern with how others are evaluating our behavior. It makes sense—if I'm concerned about making a good impression, I probably am not too worried about the sort of impression you are making.

An important underlying assumption is that heightened self-consciousness results in an increased concern about how the self is presented and the reactions of others to that presentation. Research[24, 25, 26] indicates that this does indeed tend to happen. That is, people high in self-consciousness, by virtue of their greater awareness of how others may be perceiving them, are inclined to be more sensitive and to react more negatively to rejection and disapproval than people low in self-consciousness.

You may begin to see a pattern emerging. If my self-esteem is low, I become increasingly dependent on your good feelings about me as a substitute for my own lack of positive self-regard. As my dependency on your good will increases, so too does my self-consciousness around you.

All in all, it seems clear that self-esteem, depending on whether it is high or low, can have either a positive or negative influence on interpersonal relationships and encounters with others. When self-esteem is low and seems to be causing a problem, is there something that can be done about it? Good question. Let's turn our attention to it.

Ways to Deal Constructively with the Self-Esteem Problem

Low self-esteem usually means low self-approval, low self-regard, and low self-acceptance. If I am low on these counts, I am probably more sensitive to your evaluation of me and, as a consequence, more self-conscious when I interact with you. What can I do to reduce my sensitivity and self-consciousness? Some suggestions:

1. Avoid prolonged eye contact. Allan Fenigstein's[27] research suggests that eye contact has the effect of increasing self-consciousness because it intensifies one's awareness of being observed. So, if I want to be a bit less self-conscious as I talk to you, it may help if my eye contact with you is not prolonged. I may even want to tell you what I am doing so that you know that I am working on a problem of mine and not avoiding something about you.
2. Learn to be a good listener. This is perhaps the single most common characteristic shared by persons who are communicators. They know how to listen, and they do so in such a way as to convey to others that they are interested, involved, and accepting. When I listen, I accomplish at least two things: (1) I tell you with my behavior that I think you're important, and (2) I tell you that I want to know you better. An excellent book by David W. Johnson, *Reaching Out: Interpersonal*

Effectiveness and Self-Actualization, [28] is very helpful in developing listening skills. (We'll look more deeply at ways of doing this in Chapter 5.)

3. Learn to be a better conversationalist. One of the reasons people may feel inadequate in encounters with others is that they either don't know what to say or how to say what they want to say. Both of these states encourage an "I'm not OK" feeling and increase my self-consciousness when I try to talk to you. If I really want to get out of this "not OK" state, I can choose to be a better conversationalist. I can do this in at least two ways: (1) I can pay close attention to people who already are good at this; I can make a deliberate effort to model myself after those who are skilled conversationalists. (2) I may want to combine the first suggestion with some relevant reading. For example, a book by James Morris, Jr., *The Art of Conversation,* [29] is full of helpful hints on how to talk to others in a more fluid, easy manner.

4. Learn to be "real." This is a tough one because being real has different meanings for different people. Nonetheless, it's important, because being real, however it is interpreted, is the opposite of being phony, which is how any one of us may feel when we find ourselves trying to win the approval of others. However we learn this, being real is a helpful way to reduce self-consciousness in interpersonal relationships, because it means turning more of our attention inward to find out what has meaning for us rather than focusing so much attention outward to find out what others want. Being real, whatever else it means, implies giving up trying to impress people. There is an immediate self-esteem payoff in being more authentic in relationships. If I'm real and you accept me, I have good reason to feel good about me. If I'm phony and you accept me, I underscore what I suspected in the first place: I'm a successful phony.

Two books that would be helpful in trying to gain a deeper understanding of interpersonal authenticity are *The Search for Authenticity* by James Bugental[30] and *On Becoming a Person* by Carl Rogers.[31]

So far, we have seen that how people view one another is influenced by their self-perceptions and levels of self-esteem. To what extent do first impressions play a part in our perceptions of one another? Are first impressions lasting impressions? Or can they change? Let's turn our attention to these questions.

THE PSYCHOLOGY OF IMPRESSION FORMATION

If you and I were to meet for the first time, each of us would very likely come away from our encounter with certain impressions of each other. And these impressions would have a strong influence on the sorts of expectations we would have for each other and also on the way we felt about each other. A remarkable aspect of the psychology of impression formation is that people are quite capable of drawing conclusions about each other in a very short time span and with relatively little information.

What Characteristics Most Influence
Our Impressions of Others?

You may know from your own experience that when you meet a person for the first time, you do not see that person as a collection of individual characteristics. Rather, there is a tendency to see the whole person as a totality; we see that person and not each part. And from this totality we form a more general impression, which tends to color any specific impressions we may have.

Social psychologist Solomon Asch[32] has nicely demonstrated this point. He prepared two lists of adjectives that described two different people. He presented these lists to two different groups of respondents and asked them to check, on a form provided, any additional characteristics or qualities that they thought the person described might be likely to have. The two lists the respondents were given looked like this:

PERSON A	PERSON B
Intelligent	Intelligent
Skillful	Skillful
Industrious	Industrious
Warm	Cold
Determined	Determined
Practical	Practical
Cautious	Cautious

As you can see, the lists are identical, with the exception of the fourth word, which on one is *warm* and on the other, *cold*.

Reflections

Before reading further, pause a moment. Suppose you knew two individuals, one of whom was pretty much like Person A and the other pretty much like person B. How would you respond to the following questions?
1. Who would you rather have as a friend? Why?
2. What other adjectives come to mind that might further describe each person?
3. Which person would you be likely to avoid? Why?

It may be interesting for you to compare your responses to Person A and Person B with the responses given by the respondents in Asch's research. The differences between the ways Persons A and B were seen were quite dramatic. Person A, whose description included the word *warm*, was more likely to be described as generous, wise, happy, good-natured, humorous, sociable, popular, and altruistic. Person B, whose description included the word *cold*, was much more apt to be rated as unhappy, ungenerous, unstable, humorless, and even ruthless. In other words, there seems to be a strong inclination to develop certain overall expectations and to form more general impressions of how "warm" and "cold" people are likely to behave. This leads us to an important observation.

A Person's Central Traits Strongly Affect Our Impressions

Is it true that certain perceived behaviors are so powerful that they influence our impressions and subsequent behavior toward others? Is it true that certain traits are so central in our eyes that they color all else we may see in another person's behavior? When particular *central traits* are involved, for example, being *warm* or *cold,* can our perceptions be swayed to such an extent that we see most other aspects of that individual in terms of his or her being warm or cold, as the case may be? There is evidence to suggest that this does indeed happen.

Harold Kelley[33] found supporting evidence for this idea in an ingenious study. He presented a guest lecturer to a psychology class. Before the lecturer's appearance, students were given a brief biographical sketch of him, which, among other items, included the statement: "People who know him consider him to be a rather (cold/warm) person, industrious, critical, practical, and determined." (You will note that these adjectives come directly from Asch's original list.) All students read the same biographical sketch, except that the word *cold* was included in half the copies and the word *warm* in the other half. Then all students heard the same lecture from the same instructor.

Were there differences between the two groups' responses to him? There were indeed. For example, students who had been told that the instructor was warm tended to rate him as much more informal, sociable, considerate, popular, and likable than did those students who had been told that the man was cold. Their respective impressions of him were not only reflected in their feelings about him, but in their behavior toward him as well. For example, some 56 percent of the students who were told that he was warm interacted with him in class, but only 32 percent who believed that he was cold entered into the discussion.

Reflections

Think of someone you regard as "cold." To what extent to do you feel that that characteristic colors your perception of him/her? Do you have trouble seeing that person's redeeming qualities? Why? How do you suppose people might rate you on a warm–cold continuum?

You can see that perceived characteristics such as warm and cold are examples of central traits, aspects of an individual that are potent enough to affect the interpretation of other traits, thus influencing how others see that person. Other traits are more peripheral than central and do not particularly influence our judgment of others one way or the other. For example, when Asch[34] substituted the words *polite/blunt* in place of *warm/cold* in the lists given to his subjects, he found that it made little difference in their reported impressions. Characteristics such as polite or blunt are examples of traits that are only peripherally important and, as such, probably have only secondary status when it comes to our impressions of others. Hair color would probably not be central for most of us in judging others, but intelligence would be.

Research by Charles Osgood and his colleagues[35, 36] has shown that we can characterize most experiences and people in terms of where they fall in each of three central dimensions: (1) an evaluation dimension, represented mainly by the adjective pair *good/bad* (*warm/cold* is highly related to *good/bad*); (2) a potency dimension—*strong/weak*; and (3) and activity dimension—*active/passive*. This means that our impressions of another person can be strongly affected once we recognize—from our own perceptions or from having been told—that a particular individual has one or more of these characteristics. The meaning of a particular characteristic, however, depends on its context. Let's say you meet a person who has previously been described to you as a "warm but somewhat shallow individual." For the sake of contrast, imagine that you meet another person who has previously been described as a "warm and fairly strong, self-sufficient individual."

©1978 United Feature Syndicate, Inc.

Our impressions of others are frequently determined by certain central features.

Reflections

What would your impressions likely be of a person you see as "warm but somewhat shallow" and of another person who is "warm and fairly strong and self-sufficient"? How are your impressions different? Why?

Central traits are important insofar as they serve as useful "perceptual organizers" that help us to give another person's behavior primary meaning. The emotional meaning we give any particular central characteristic can be greatly influenced by the peripheral traits that are associated with it. Although this is largely an unconscious process, it is one over which we can exercise more control by simply being aware of how it operates. I remember an instance of how this awareness was helpful to a 26-year-old man in one of my therapy groups, who had problems with women he viewed as assertive. During one of the group sessions, he shared an insight that he found particularly useful in helping him to resolve the difficulties he had been having with his girl friend, whom he had previously described as "rather pushy." In his words:

> You know, a remarkable thing has happened since I talked to you all last week about the conflict that I was having with Mary about her pushiness. Or at least that's what I thought it was. Anyway, Angie, I remember what you said about a woman being assertive. I think it was something like, "Just because a woman is assertive doesn't mean that she's a negative person." You know, that rang a bell somewhere in my head. I remember lots of times my mother would try to voice her opinion about something and my dad would usually say something like, "Shut up, you don't know what you're talking about." I think without knowing it, I think I had negative ideas about a woman who assertively expressed her opinion, just as my dad no doubt did about my mother when she spoke up. When Mary speaks her mind now, I just don't see that as an awful thing. I see it as all right and my whole feeling about her is beginning to change.

Without knowing it, he viewed a woman's assertiveness negatively, as something to be defensive about, no doubt just as his father had done. What he once saw as a negative characteristic he now sees as a more positive trait. As his perception of a dominant characteristic has changed, his idea of what an assertive woman is like has changed, too. (P.S. His relationships with women who speak their minds are much better.)

All in all, it appears that certain behavioral characteristics are so dominant or "central" to what we see in another person that much of what else we perceive in that individual is filtered through that dominant trait. For example, once Richard Nixon had established, of his own doing and with the help of the press, his central "Tricky Dick" image, there was very little he could do, particularly in the eyes of those who saw him that way, that was not seen as having some ulterior or self-serving motive behind it.

Several questions invariably arise in relation to impression formation. Are first impressions lasting impressions? Or can they change? Let's turn our attention to this important question.

How Strong and Lasting Are First Impressions?

Even though we may meet someone for the first time and talk to that person for only minutes, chances are very good that we will come away from the encounter with some reasonably strong first impressions. Consider the following exercise.

Reflections

Meet Jim. This is a thumbnail sketch of what might be one of his typical days.

Jim left the house to get some stationery. He walked out into the sun-filled street with two of his friends. . . . Jim entered the stationery store, which was full of people. Jim talked with an acquaintance while he waited to catch the clerk's eye. On his way out, he stopped to chat with a school friend who was just going into the store. Leaving the store, he walked toward school. On his way, he met the girl to whom he had been introduced the night before. They talked for a short while, and then Jim left for school. After school, Jim left the classroom alone. Leaving school, he started his long walk home. . . . Coming down the street toward him, he saw the pretty girl whom he had met on the previous evening. Jim crossed the street and entered a candy store. . . . Jim waited quietly until he caught the counterman's eye and then gave his order. Taking his drink, he sat down at a side table. When he had finished his drink, he went home.[37]

How does Jim come across to you? Do you see him as a friendly, outgoing type? Or do you have the impression that he is somewhat shy and introverted?

If you think Jim is more accurately described as friendly than unfriendly, you are in agreement with most people (78 percent) who read this description. If you look carefully at the description of Jim, you can see that it reflects two very different pictures of his personality. Until the sentence that begins "After school, Jim left . . .," Jim is characterized as a fairly friendly guy; after that point, however, he is portrayed as a more introverted loner. In fact, in psychologist Abraham Luchins's original research, 95 percent of the people shown only the first half of the description rated Jim as friendly, whereas only 3 percent who were shown only the second half did so. However, reading the combined description that you read in the preceding exercise, more people had the impression that he is friendly rather than unfriendly. How can we explain this? Is there something intrinsically positive about the trait of friendliness, or does it have more to do with whether Jim's "friendliness" or "unfriendliness" is placed first or second? To test this out, Luchins had individuals read the same description, but this time with the unfriendly, more introverted half presented first. What were the results?

Under this condition, Jim's unfriendly behavior left the major impression, with only 18 percent of the readers judging him as friendly. This result squares with what we may sense from our everyday experiences: the initial information we receive about another person has the greatest impact on our overall impressions. This is known as the *primacy* effect. Table 1–1 gives you a quick overview of the results of Luchins's study.

The primacy effect is a very real phenomenon and has been observed under more real-life conditions, too. For example, in a study by Edward Jones and his associates,[38] subjects were asked to observe a student taking a college entrance test and to rate his or her intelligence. All students who took the test got fifteen of the thirty questions right, but it was rigged in such a way so that some got most of their right answers at the beginning of the test and others got most of their correct responses toward the end of the test.

What were the findings? Again, a strong primacy effect was noted. Students who had done better near the beginning of the test were rated as more intelligent. Indeed, not only were they judged as more intelligent, but they were also credited by the observers as having made more correct responses than was actually the case. For instance, when asked to recall each student's score, observers who had seen the fifteen correct answers bunched at the beginning of the test "remembered," on the average, that the student had achieved a score of 20.6 out of the thirty questions. On the other hand, observers who saw students do their best work toward the end of the test recalled only 12.5 successes out of the thirty questions.

Earlier research by Asch[39] provides other evidence for the impact of the primacy effect. Before we look at what he found, pause a moment.

Reflections

1. Consider person A, who is described in the following way: *intelligent, industrious, impulsive, critical, stubborn, envious.* What is your impression of this person? Favorable? Unfavorable? Why?
2. Consider person B, who is described as: *envious, stubborn, critical, impulsive, industrious, intelligent.* What is your impression of this person? Positive? Negative? Why?

TABLE 1–1.   Primacy Effects in Impression Formation

ORDER OF PRESENTATION	PERCENTAGE RATING JIM AS FRIENDLY
Friendly description only	95
Friendly first—unfriendly last	78
Unfriendly first—friendly last	18
Unfriendly description only	3

Asch gave one group of subjects a list of adjectives describing person A and another group a list of adjectives describing person B, which, as you see above, is Person A's list in reverse order. As Asch expected, the subjects in his experiment evidenced a marked primacy effect. That is, subjects tended to see a person more favorably when the *positive* adjectives were presented first. On the other hand, they were more likely to dislike a person if the *negative* adjectives were presented first. How do these findings square with your own impressions of persons A and B?

What causes the primacy effect? There may be several explanations. In the first place, there is evidence to indicate that we are more apt to pay attention to information about a person when we are in the initial phase of forming an impression of him or her. And, as suggested by the research findings of Norman Anderson,[40] Mark Snyder, and William Swann, Jr.,[41] *once an intial impression is formed, there is an inclination—alas, an unfortunate one—to pay less attention to subsequent information.* In addition, there is also evidence to suggest that most of us think that what we find out first is more apt to reveal the "real" person. Later, discrepant information is then seen as not representative.

What Does First Impressions Research Teach Us?

A very important lesson: namely, what we see in others, initially, and what others see in us, initially, tends to stick. Unconsciously, most of us have an inclination to give greater weight to our first impressions of a person than to our later impressions. The implications of this primacy effect are rather far-reaching. We should be aware that the impact of this effect will play an important part in job interviews, first dates, or establishing an image when running for public office. There is a large body of research[42,43,44] to suggest that teachers' first impressions of their students can significantly—for better or worse—influence their expectations for their students. This is an important observation, particularly in light of conclusions reached in several large-scale reviews,[45,46] which indicate that teacher expectations are strongly linked to student achievement. In fact, Robert Rosenthal's[47] review of the teacher expectancy research added even more support for the primacy effect when he found cases where students who *surpassed* their teachers' original expectations were viewed *negatively,* rather than more positively. Could it be that we don't like to find out that our first impressions are wrong?

Reflections

You might like to try a simple research project. In the next day or so, make a deliberate effort to find out more about a particular person(s) who, for one reason or another, has left you with a somewhat negative impression. Find out about that person. Get to know him or her. Check your assumptions. Do your initial impressions stand up? Are you able to modify those impressions if they're wrong?

If the primacy effect works because we pay less attention to later information, then it should be possible to minimize the effect by warning people about the hazards of making early judgments and telling them to take *all* information into account before drawing their conclusions. A warning of this sort seems to work. For example, Luchins[48] found that he could reduce the primacy effect and, in some cases, even reverse it, simply by warning subjects to withhold final judgments until they had read all the information about Jim (this refers to the description you read several pages ago). Moreover, he found that the warning was particularly effective when it was given *between* the two inconsistent blocks of information about Jim's behavior. If, after you read the description, you came out with a lower primacy effect, you may have been responding like the subjects who were warned. Perhaps the earlier material in this chapter alerted you to the dangers of premature judgment. In any case, when *later* information has a greater impact on our judgments of others, it is called the *recency* effect.

When we process conflicting information about a person all in one block, we are inclined to assign more importance to information that comes first. We form a first impression and then either ignore later conflicting information as unimportant or reinterpret it as a fluky deviation from the person's "real" personality. Hence, whether it be a student's first day in class, a teenager's first date, a job candidate's first few minutes in an interview, or a boxer's first minute in a round, each would be advised to remember that it is how they start and not *necessarily* how they finish that will most likely influence others' impressions of them. On the other hand, recency effects—the things that happen subsequent to first meetings—are more influential in ongoing relationships, in which there are more opportunities for intervening experiences and new information to correct or modify erroneous first impressions. Given enough time, first impressions certainly can and do change, but not easily.

Reflections

It may be interesting to compare first impression notes with someone you're close to—someone you've known for a long time. What impressions did each of you start out with? How, if at all, have those impressions changed? What caused the changes? How do you see each other now?

What we see in another person and what that person sees in us can be significantly influenced by our impressions of each other. We develop these impressions through inferences about each other's underlying traits or dispositions, which we base on observable behavior. This process is called *attribution,* an idea that will help us further understand how people see each other.

THE ATTRIBUTION PROCESS: KNOWING OTHERS THROUGH THEIR BEHAVIOR

An important part of getting to know another person is our ability to make inferences about that person's underlying traits and deeper dispositions. We do this by considering what we know about an individual from first- or secondhand observations, then drawing some inferential conclusions about "the sort of person" he or she is. Using what social psychologist Fritz Heider[49] called the *attribution process*, we attribute to others motives that make their behaviors more understandable (predictable) to us. This helps us "size people up," so we can begin to understand what they're really like. We do this in order to make other people more knowable, and it enables us to do two things: (1) make predictions about how others may behave in the future (which helps us feel more secure about them) and (2) gauge our own behavior so that we know how to behave around others or respond to them (which helps us feel more secure about ourselves). In short, when we interact with others, our initial task is to understand their behavior. Is this an easy process? Apparently not. Consider some examples of behaviors we might see in our everyday lives:

1. A man volunteers to give blood to a local Red Cross drive, which pays 15 dollars for each pint. Is he an altruistic person committed to helping others? Or is he an expedient individual who would do anything for money?
2. An Olympic decathlon champion endorses Wheaties as a fine breakfast cereal. Does he really believe Wheaties is the "breakfast of champions"? Or is he saying those things primarily for the dollars he receives?
3. A woman kisses her male companion at the end of a date. Does she see him as someone special, or does she allow most men to kiss her because she feels that it is the thing to do? Or are both of these factors involved?
4. A couple go to church every Sunday. Are they religiously devout people deeply interested in enhancing their spiritual lives? Or are they socially conscious people primarily interested in creating a good image?
5. A salesperson greets you warmly and speaks highly of her product. Does she really like you or is that an expedient gesture? Is her product really that good or does she talk glowingly only to make a sale?

The examples could go on and on—no doubt you can think of many—but you can see the problems involved in trying to decide what any particular behavior really means. We are faced with a certain "attribution problem." That is, we have an awareness of some behavior—in many cases our own—and must decide to which of many possible causes and motivations the behavior should be attributed. At first glance, it may appear that our task of making inferences about the underlying intentions and deeper motivations would be a relatively straightforward one. Not so. Two important factors greatly complicate our attribution efforts. Let's turn our attention to these factors.

Two Factors that Complicate the Attribution Process

First, there is the *deception* factor. People sometimes seek to mislead, deceive, and hoodwink each other in their interpersonal relationships as a way of masking their real feelings and camouflaging their true behavior. That is, they may say things they don't mean, act in ways inconsistent with their actual beliefs and values, and in other ways disguise who they really are. In cases like this, there is little to learn about such people except, perhaps, that they are fraudulent. Even worse, we may actually be seduced into forming erroneous impressions of them.

Second, there is the *external pressure* factor. Our behavior is sometimes moderated and shaped not so much by our internal states or personal dispositions, but rather by powerful external factors. How many times, for example, can you recall plodding through dreary and dull assignments not because of a deep intrinsic interest, but because they were part of the course requirements—something you had to do? How often have you been polite and kind to another individual you've strongly disliked—perhaps your boss or an in-law or an instructor or a co-worker—because the consequences of acting otherwise were too fruitless or painful or risky to permit? Each of us can probably see ourselves in these simple examples. Indeed, there are times when all of us—perhaps more often than we'd like to admit—find ourselves behaving more in response to what is going on around us (external factors) than in resonse to what we feel within us (internal factors). This is not to say that it is wrong to respond to external factors. Sometimes it is both appropriate and necessary to put aside our personal whims and inclinations in order to avoid fruitless confrontations and needless hassles. The point is, when the behavior of other people is determined primarily by various external factors, it cannot be used as a valid basis for making inferences about their personal characteristics.

Together these two factors comprise a major attribution task we face daily. That is, does the behavior we observe tell us something unique about a person —his values, her attitudes—or something about the situation? Can we, for example, infer something about an athlete's real attitude toward Wheaties from his TV endorsement of the cereal, or do we conclude that he is pushing the product primarily because he's getting paid? If we infer that there is something about a person that is primarily responsible for his or her behavior, then our inference is termed a *dispositional attribution*. On the other hand, if we conclude that some external factor is responsible for his or her behavior—such as money, social pressure, threats, and so on, then this is a *situational attribution*. Which leads us to an important question.

Personal Dispositions or Situational Factors: How Do We Tell Which Is Causing the Behavior?

As suggested by Fritz Heider's seminal work on attribution processes, when we seek to determine *why* a person is behaving in a particular way, we usually look for a situational or dispositional cause. This is largely an unconscious process; somewhat universally we use certain attribution "rules" without being aware of them. Edward Jones and Keith Davis[50] have developed a theoretical framework of person perception that may help us understand this process.

Two Aspects of Behavior Influencing Our Attributions of Others

According to these investigators, the secret to making reasonably accurate attributions about why people behave the way they do is embedded in our tendency to focus on two specific aspects of behavior.

First, Jones and Davis suggest that we pay particular attention to those underlying reasons that seem to stand out most as explanations for other people's behavior. For instance, imagine that you have just heard that a top male college basketball player is considering signing a contract which (1) requires him to move to a warm west-coast city, (2) involves a no-cut clause and guaranteed playing time in his first year, and (3) pays $100,000 for the season. Aside from the fact that he must be a very fine basketball player, are you able to determine anything conclusive about the personal dispositions of this person if he signs? Probably not. There are so many good reasons for signing that contract (favorable climate, guaranteed job and playing time, lots of money) that it is not possible to determine which reason would be instrumental in motivating his signing. All you can infer is that there are some very compelling situational reasons for him to sign on the dotted line. But now imagine something different. Let's say that about a week later you read that this same person has signed a contract that (1) places him on a last-place team in an unattractive part of the country, (2) involves a no-cut contract, but not guaranteed playing time in his first year, and (3) pays $200,000 for the season. This is a different situation because there is a more apparent and telling reason for signing, namely, more money. Now you're in a better position to make some reasonable inferences about the basketball player's personal dispositions. For example, you might conclude that he values money more than an attractive location, and you may even have a hunch that he is sufficiently confident in his ability that he doesn't need a guaranteed playing time clause. Perhaps you can begin to see why we can generally obtain more revealing information about others' personal dispositions from behavior for which there may be one, or at most a few, underlying reasons that we can from behavior for which there may be many underlying reasons.

Second, Jones and Davis suggest that we are inclined to attribute *situational* dispositions to behavior that we see as common, ordinary, and expected, but that we are more apt to attribute *personal* dispositions to behavior that is uncommon, extraordinary, and unexpected. Hence, the more any particular behavior is caused by situational or environmental factors, the less informative or revealing it is. For example, behaviors that have high social desirability, such as being polite, exchanging opinions about the weather, or saying, "Hello, how are you?," do not reveal much about a specific person, because nearly everyone does these things. These are common and more or less expected. But imagine knowing a middle-aged man who lives by himself, runs fifteen miles five mornings a week, and keeps two Doberman pinschers tied to the front of his house. You can quickly see how such information provides rich clues for attributing personal dispositions to him. (For example, he may be divorced or separated or widowed or gay, or perhaps he just enjoys living alone and has never lived with anyone; he is a physical fitness fanatic or is preparing for a marathon; he loves dogs or he's wary of robbers.) We have many possibilities to consider, because the way he lives and what he does is somewhat unusual. Thus, we're able to make attributions about the possible personal dispositions behind his behavior. The principle is this: The more we focus on the behavior of others that is different from most people's behavior, the more certain we can be that it may reflect something about the individual rather than the situation.

You can see that an important preliminary task we face in our efforts to "size people up" is *causal attribution*—that is, figuring out whether others' behaviors spring primarily from internal or external causes. The work of psychologist Harold Kelley can help us further understand how we do this.

Three Criteria to Consider When Making Causal Attributions

Kelley's[51, 52] contributions to our understanding of attribution processes are directly descended from the work of Fritz Heider and from the work of Edward Jones and Keith Davis. In order to determine whether the behavior of others is attributable to situational or dispositional factors, Kelley suggests that we rely (not always consciously) on three criteria: (1) *distinctiveness*—the extent to which a person behaves in more or less the same manner in many other situations or only in this one, (2) *consistency*—the extent to which a person behaves in more or less the same manner in this situation as on other, similar occasions, and (3) *consensus*—the extent to which other people behave in somewhat the same manner as the individual in question. Figure 1–1 may help you understand how we distinguish between dispositional and situational attributions.

Figure 1–1 shows that we are most likely to attribute another person's behavior to situational causes under conditions of high distinctiveness, high consistency, and high consensus, but to dispositional causes under conditions of low distinctiveness, high consistency, and low consensus. Take an example of how these attribution processes work in actual behavior.

First, imagine that one of your classmates gets into a heated argument with the instructor over the issue of how the grading was done on a particular test. Further, imagine that (1) she does not have similar disagreements with other instructors (distinctiveness is high); (2) she has challenged the same instructor

FIGURE 1-1. Factors Influencing the Kind of Attributions We Make

We are inclined to attribute a person's behavior to situational (external) factors
when there is:
1. *High Distinctiveness* The person behaves differently in other situations.
2. *High Consistency* The person behaves in the same manner in this situation
   on other occasions.
3. *High Consensus* Many other people behave in the same manner in this
   situation on other occasions.
On the other hand, we are inclined to attribute a person's behavior to dispositional
(internal) factors when there is:
1. *Low Distinctiveness* The person behaves in the same manner in other situations.
2. *High Consistency* The person behaves in the same manner in this situation
   on other occasions.
3. *Low Consensus* Few persons behave in the same manner as this person.

several times previously about his grading policies (consistency is high); and (3)
other students have also argued with the instructor about his grading policies
(consensus is high). Under conditions like this, Kelley's theory predicts that we
would be most likely to attribute your classmate's behavior to situational or
external factors. That is, the arguments seem to have more to do with situational
factors outside your classmate's control (the instructor's shaky grading practices)
than to dispositional factors inherent in your classmate (an argumentative or
negative nature).

That's one example. But now imagine that you observe another student in one
of your classes getting embroiled in a head-on argument with the instructor about
how grades were distributed on a test. In addition, imagine that (1) he also argues
about grading practices with other instructors (distinctiveness is low); (2) he has
had similar run-ins with this instructor in the past (consistency is high); and (3)
none of the other students in class argue with the professor over this issue
(consensus is low). Under conditions like these, Kelley's attribution theory predicts that we would be most likely to infer that the student's behavior is related
more to dispositional factors (the student's quarrelsome and perhaps suspicious
nature) than to situational factors (unfair grading practices).

As mentioned earlier, these are criteria that we use more or less unconsciously
in our efforts to size people up and make sense of their behavior. The simple
examples cited above provide some informal evidence for the everyday usefulness
of Kelley's attribution criteria, but a significant body of research[53, 54, 55] has more
thoroughly documented their validity and the underlying processes in more
controlled conditions. Indeed, there is even evidence to suggest that horse race
bettors unknowingly apply the criteria of distinctiveness, consistency, and con-

sensus when trying to figure out whether a particular horse won or lost because of its own characteristics, or because of external factors such as the field in which it ran![56]

Sometimes,however, we fail in our efforts to size people up, because we fail to perceive others accurately, which brings us to an important topic.

ATTRIBUTION ERRORS THAT MAY DISTORT OUR PERCEPTIONS OF OTHERS

If, while taking a stroll one day, you observed the person in front of you trip over a bump in the sidewalk and take an ungraceful pratfall, how do you suppose you might explain this behavior? Although we can't say with certainty, the chances are rather good that you would interpret it in terms of the characteristics of the person. That is, you might perceive that person as uncoordinated or clumsy or even careless. In short, you might be inclined to attribute the pratfall largely to dispositional (internal) factors. But let's say that a block later precisely the same thing happened to you. Would you be likely to account for your mishap in the same manner? Again, it's hard to know for sure, but the probability is that you would not. More likely, you would explain your tumble in terms of various situational (external) factors, such as the sidewalk's not being level or a hole in the cement or a banana peel, and so on. Which brings us to one of our most common attribution errors.

We Tend to Underestimate Situational Causes of Others' Behavior and Overestimate Dispositional Causes of Our Own

Fritz Heider[57] was the first to note our general inclination to take another person's behavior at face value and underestimate the possible situational causes contributing to it. Lee Ross[58] has dubbed this the "fundamental attribution error."

Reflections

When Gerald Ford was President, there were innumerable newspaper accounts of the various "accidents" he experienced; for example, tripping as he came off an airplane, bumping his head on a low doorframe, slicing a golf ball off a spectator, and so on. It wasn't long before Mr. Ford was seen as a somewhat bungling, clumsy person whose awkward moments were attributed more to personal characteristics than to situational considerations. (It would be interesting to know if there were differences in attributions among Republicans and Democrats.) Can you think of other examples of attributions derived from the behavior of persons who are in the public eye that may illustrate how we tend to underestimate situational causes of behavior?

The idea that we tend to see our own behavior as occurring largely in response to situational conditions and that we perceive the behavior of others as stemming primarily from personal dispositions is supported by a convincing and impressive array of research.[59, 60, 61, 62]

A study by Richard Nisbett and his colleagues[63] nicely illustrates this phenomenon. They asked a group of male college students to write out brief statements about why they liked their girl friends and why they (the male students) had chosen their college major. Then they were asked to write short statements about why their best friends liked *their* girl friends, and why they had chosen *their* college majors. What were the findings? (1) Describing *their own choice* of a girl friend or field of study, respondents tended to emphasize *external* factors (their women's looks or personality, the opportunities afforded by their field of study, and so forth). (2) Describing *their friends' choices,* however, they tended to emphasize personal dispositions (the need for a particular kind of woman, the suitability of a particular field of study, and so on).

In a second, related study by the same researchers, participants were asked to choose from a series of paired characteristics (quiet/talkative, lenient/firm) those traits that they saw as true for themselves and for four other persons: their father, their best friend, a casual acquaintance, and Walter Cronkite. On each item, they could also choose a third alternative, which was "depends on the situation." The prediction was that they would choose this third option more frequently when describing themselves than when describing the others—that is, they would more frequently claim that their own behaviors were due to external situational factors, while the behaviors of others were more a result of internal dispositional factors. The research findings confirmed this, which further supports the idea that we tend to look *outside* ourselves to explain our own behavior, but *inside* others to explain theirs. Why do we do this? Good question. Jones and Nisbett[64] have suggested two possible reasons that may help us understand the underlying dynamics.

First of all, they suggest that since we are not able to observe our own behavior directly, we seem to focus our attention on the external factors that surround us, which encourages our inclination to see these factors as the major causes of our behavior. The second part of their explanation has to do with the idea that, since we cannot know for sure what factors in an external situation are causing another person's behavior, we more readily attribute the causes of that person's behavior to personal dispositions. But not always. For example, Susan Eisen's research[65] suggests that the better we know a person, in the sense of having more information about him, the less likely we will be to attribute personal dispositions to his or her behavior arbitrarily. The implications of this research are surely a strong vote of confidence in the common-sense wisdom of getting to know a person before judging him or her.

Reflections

Perhaps you can test the validity of Eisen's findings in a more personal way. I wonder what would happen, for example, if you were to make an effort to really get to know several persons about whom you have some definite opinions (either positive or negative), but who you know only casually. Let me suggest you start out with three research questions: (1) Will my attributions change regarding the kind of person he or she is? (2) How (if at all) have they changed? (3) Why (if at all) have they changed?

There is another attribution error we're inclined to make in our perception of others.

We Tend to Give More Weight to Negative Information About Others than to Positive Information

Our inclination to be swayed more by the negative information we have about a person is another one of those attribution processes that happens frequently without our being aware of it. For example, Kanouse and Hanson's[66] review of research related to this phenomenon indicates that even when people are knowledgeable about both the positive and negative aspects of another person's behavior, they are likely to be more influenced by that individual's negative qualities than by his or her positive virtues. Elizabeth Webster[67] found this to be particularly true in situations in which people were being interviewed for various jobs. Negative information was found to be more highly related to the decision to hire or not to hire than was positive information. Indeed, Webster found that negative information, particularly if it was received early in the interview, was likely to lead to a candidate's rejection *even when the total amount of information was overwhelmingly positive.*

There are at least three explanations that may help us understand this negativity bias: (1) Unconsciously, we may stay alert to another person's negative qualities as a means of protecting ourselves from unfavorable comparisons. A client of mine, in a moment of insight during one of our therapy sessions, expressed this idea with the following observation: "I know I look for the bad in other people. Sometimes I'm really obsessed with it. And I usually manage to find a flaw or two. You know, I think I just figured out why I do that. When I find something bad in the other person, I don't feel so bad about myself." And then he added, "You know, I'm not sure I like what I just discovered—it seems a cheap way for me to feel good about me." He was right. It was a cheap way, because his good feelings about himself depended on uncovering the shortcomings in other people. It's a kind of psychological pulley system operation. We go up when

someone else goes down. (2) Another reason behind the negativity bias may be the defensive function it serves. That is, we may unwittingly be more sensitive to others' negative qualities, because a person's negative characteristics and not his or her positive characteristics could be hurtful or damaging to us. Imagine, for example that you are going to take a class from a professor who is described to you as intelligent, well-prepared, witty, entertaining, and sarcastic. Which of those adjectives stands out for you? If you're like most people, *sarcastic* will probably be the most telling, because it is your behavior in response to this aspect of the professor's personality that will be most crucial to getting along with him. By preparing yourself for the possibility that he is a cold person, you reduce the possibility of being disappointed and let down by his lack of warmth. Being alert to another person's negative aspects may be adaptive, in the Darwinian sense, insofar as we are able to protect ourselves from being damaged by that person's negative behavior. (3) A third possible reason behind the negativity bias (according to Kanouse and Hanson[68]) is our inclination to avoid negative outcomes rather than seek positive outcomes, because we learn that the pursuit of highly positive outcomes in life is good but not *that* good (for instance, we don't win grand prizes or lotteries every day), and that extremely bad outcomes (say, the death of a loved one) are more frequent than extremely good outcomes. Hence, for many, happiness depends on a large number of nonnegative outcomes rather than on a few highly positive ones. "Staying out of trouble" is more important than "trying to make it big." Thus, any sign of "trouble," whether we sense it about an experience or see the potential for it in another person, may be something that is both unconsciously and consciously avoided.

There is a third attribute that we are prone to make, and it has to do with our inclination to perceive others in a way that is more or less consistent with the labels we've given them.

We Tend to Label People and Sometimes We're Wrong

A major attribution task involves indentifying the major motives and characteristics of others. The final step in this process is usually the assignment of descriptive labels, representing various traits, to people to whom we relate. For example, we may label one person as friendly and cheerful, another as bossy and stubborn, and still another as cynical and gloomy. When accurate, this helps us relate appropriately to different people, insofar as such labels provide us with a kind of summary of their core characteristics.

We run into trouble, either because we've jumped to early conclusions or have been given erroneous information, when our labels do not accurately reflect the true nature of a particular individual. You may recall from an earlier discussion in this chapter that once we have decided—however rightly or wrongly—that another person is a certain *kind* of person, we usually find it difficult to alter our perceptions. Indeed, when a person behaves differently from what we might have expected, we may be inclined to pass off such an occurrence as an exception to the rule.

A common means of hanging on to the label we've attached to a person is a process called *discounting,* which is a way of negating the possibility that it is the person himself who is causing the behavior. For example, if a person whom we've labeled as intellectually dull gets an A on an exam, we might find ourselves maintaining the label by attributing his success to various external factors such as luck or perhaps an especially "good day." We discount the possibility that he may have been personally responsible. Similarly, if we have labeled another person as cold and distant, then friendly, warm overtures on her part will usually serve to arouse our suspicions. In the back of our minds we may be wondering, "What is she up to? What does she really want?" We discount the idea that she may really be friendly and warm. Since our perceptions can be so dramatically shaped and limited by our expectations and preconceptions, you can begin to see why the old maxim, "Seeing is believing," would be stated more accurately as "Believing is seeing."

One of the most striking demonstrations of how labels can severely limit and narrow our perceptions of others has been documented in a bold and ingenious field study by David Rosenhan, which he wrote up and titled, appropriately, "On Being Sane in Insane Places."[69] Here's what happened. Rosenhan and seven of his colleagues began by feigning certain mental illness symptoms (they heard voices) in order to get themselves admitted for treatment in mental hospitals. The ploy worked and they ended up being diagnosed as schizophrenic (the label) and being admitted to twelve different hospitals.

Once in these institutions, Rosenhan and his fellow pseudopatients, according to plan, dropped all pretense of being mentally disturbed and acted in a completely normal manner. Did this change the perceptions of the psychiatric staffs and orderlies? Not at all. Indeed, the staffs frequently interpreted perfectly normal actions on the part of these "patients" as further evidence of their illness. For example, during their hospitalization, Rosenhan and his colleagues took copious notes concerning their experiences. It didn't take long for the *real* patients to notice that Rosenhan and friends were not inmates, but members of the hospital staffs reached a quite different conclusion; note-taking was simply perceived as further evidence of their patients' unstable mental condition. One nurse, for instance, saw the note-taking as a manifestation of an abnormal compulsion.

In short, once they had been labeled as mentally ill, there was hardly anything that they could do that was not interpreted to be consistent with this label. As a footnote to this story, we might add that even when they were released, they were described as "recovered schizophrenics" rather than as normal individuals.

Obviously, all the labels we assign to others do not have such negative or potentially harmful effects. The important point is that, whether our labels are positive or negative, accurate or inaccurate, the findings reported by Rosenhan are consistent with other research mentioned in this chapter, namely, that once we assign a trait or a label to another person, it tends to stick. There is a simple rule that, if followed, would probably enhance our interpersonal relationships immeasurably: Don't jump to conclusions!

Reflections

How do you and your friends perceive each other? What sorts of labels have you given each other? How have those labels influenced your interactions with each other? Perhaps if you talked about questions like this with people you know and who know you, you might develop a greater consciousness of how labels affect interpersonal relationships and contribute to attribution errors.

We Tend to Be Influenced by What Seems Most Obvious

Another way we can unknowingly make attribution errors is by tending to be unduly swayed by the salience or conspicuousness of certain features of a person or situation. What this means is that we have a tendency, it seems, to choose the causes of a particular behavior from those aspects of a situation that are most obvious to us. For example, there is research to show that if a person's attention is deliberately directed to a particular member of a dyad during a conversation, the chances are good that that person will be perceived as being the most central and the most causative in directing the conversation.[70] Michael Storms[71] found that it was possible to change the usual pattern of causal attributions markedly when he induced one group of people—the participants in his study—to focus upon their own behavior, and another group of people—observers—to focus on the situation. Contrary to what we would ordinarily expect, the participants no longer saw their own behavior as rooted primarily in situational causes, and the observers no longer perceived the behavior of the participants as stemming primarily from internal dispositions.

Together, these findings and the conclusions of other related research[72, 73] suggest that when there are several possible causes for an event or behavior, *the one on which we focus our attention will be viewed more often than not as the most important.* This helps explain how and why we sometimes have incorrect, or at least incomplete, perceptions of events we witness. For example, we may blame the quarterback for an interception, failing to see that a breakdown in blocking caused him to hurry his throw; we may accuse certain members of a class of being overly dominant and verbose, failing to see that the passive silence of many others not only encouraged the dominant ones, but made it possible for them to be that way in the first place; we may accuse the President of incompetency when our favorite piece of legislation doesn't pass, failing to see that certain key legislators did not support it because they were too busy representing special interest groups who opposed it. And so it goes. We tend to see what is most available to our perceptions. If we were to extract from this a working principle, it might be something like this: Since what is most dominant in our perceptions is not necessarily the most accurate, we would be well advised to look both events and people over carefully before leaping to hasty conclusions.

Another cause of attribution errors has its foundation in a rather common egocentric bias.

We Tend to Judge Others on the Assumption that Most People Are Like Us

We expect that if we behave in a certain way, others will, too—a conclusion based on the assumption that everyone else is more or less like us. When we discover that others are not like us, then we fell we have learned something about them. When we see behavior that is different from our own, our inclination is to perceive it as less socially desirable, in the sense that it is unusual. And given that it is unusual we seem more prepared to make certain inferences about the person who behaves in such a way.

Psychologist Lee Ross and his colleagues[74] demonstrated this egocentric bias in a novel research project. They asked a group of college students if they would be willing to work around campus wearing a large sign that read, "EAT AT JOE'S." Of the eighty students asked, forty-eight accepted. Then all eighty were asked if they believed their peers would wear the sign. Those who agreed to wear the sign believed that most of their peers (62 percent) would also tote the sign, while students who refused to carry the sign estimated that only 33 percent of their peers would wear it. The interesting finding was that students who agreed to wear the sign were more likely to make inferences about the disposition of those who refused (their behavior was viewed as unusual) than about those who agreed. On the other hand, those who refused to carry the sign were more likely to make inferences about those who did wear them. (In this case the sign-bearers were seen as unusual.)

Rather than judge a person who behaves or believes differently from us as "odd" or "wrong," we might be better off—and a lot more accurate—if we simply accepted that person as he or she is, namely, different from us. When we do this, the normal attribution processes discussed earlier in this chapter—distinctiveness, consistency, and consensus—have a chance to operate fully and give us the necessary data for making reasonably accurate attributions.

There is another possible attribution error that we have a tendency to make.

We Tend to Blame Innocent Victims for Their Suffering

Closely connected to our penchant for perceiving the causes of others' behavior as largely internal is another common attributional bias or "error," and that is our tendency to blame innocent victims for their misfortunes. We seem to do this basically for two reasons: (1) Since we're inclined to believe that others' behavior is due primarily to their dispositional characteristics, it is only a small step to the assumption that somehow they must be responsible for their own unhappy circumstances. Thus, we sometimes erroneously perceive others as resonsible for negative outcomes they couldn't possibly have caused or foreseen. (2) Another possible reason for blaming innocent others may be related to what Melvin Lerner[75] has described as our need to believe that we live in a world where good things happen to good people and bad things happen only to bad people. We unconsciously develop what social psychologists call a "Just World" hypothesis, where good is rewarded and evil is punished. This may enhance our own feelings of personal control. If, for example, some tragedy befalls a best friend or the neighbor across the street and we attribute it to a chance happening, it is only a short step away from thinking that the same thing could happen to us. If, on the other hand, we can find some shortcoming in our friend's behavior or some flaw in our neighbor's character that may possibly explain their unhappy circumstances, then we can feel less threatened by the possibility of similar misfortunes crashing down on our own heads. We do this by assuming that we are different from such careless people and would never do such foolish things.

Reflections

There are countless everyday examples of how we may blame innocent others for their misfortunes. Do the following sound familiar?

We see on the news that a family was flooded out of their home: "They didn't show good sense by building so close to the river."

We read that a young man was killed by a hit-and-run driver when he was out for an evening run: "He should have known better than to be running at night."

We hear that a young woman was raped: "She was pretty stupid to be out by herself."

We read that a stereo cassette set was stolen from a car: "It was his own fault —he never locked his car."

Can you think of other examples?

There is an impressive array of research evidence[76, 77, 78] to support the idea that we become much less impartial observers of another person's misfortune when we feel that an unfortunate accident could just as easily happen to *us*. In fact, Elaine Walster[79] showed that the greater the harm people suffer or the more serious the consequences, the more likely it is that we will hold people personally responsible for their fate. This was vividly illustrated in a novel research project. Walster told the saga of Lennie, who left his car parked at the top of the hill. Unfortunately, the brake cable snapped and the car rolled down the hill. In one version of her story, there was minimal damage to the car and other people, while in another version, the car and other people were harmed more severely. Sure enough, the more damage there was to the car and other people, the more Lennie was held responsible by those who were asked to evaluate the accident. You can see the reasoning here. If we can imagine ourselves in the same predicament as Lennie, there may be some solace in perceiving him as responsible for what happened; otherwise we may have to live with the disconcerting idea that we could just as easily be victims of the same fickle finger of fate.

The evidence from both research and our everyday experiences seems clear; we have a strong tendency to attribute to others responsibility and blame for events and outcomes that are beyond their control. This is usually an unconscious process and is activated primarily to protect our sometimes wavering feelings of personal security. If we work on being aware of our inclination to do this, we are in a much better position to perceive others more accurately and to give innocent victims of fate, injustice, crime, nature, or war our sympathy and compassion rather than our criticism and blame.

We have now had an overview of six of the more common attribution errors that we may make, which, singularly or in combination, can cause us to misperceive others' behavior. Is there something we can do to help ourselves perceive others more accurately?

PRACTICING EMPATHY CAN HELP DECREASE ATTRIBUTION ERRORS

Empathy refers to that special capacity for putting ourselves in another person's shoes and trying to feel how things are from that person's perspective. It isn't always easy to do—particularly with persons we may not like anyway—but it is possible. And it works. For example, research[80, 81] related to this idea suggests that practicing empathy can affect us in two ways: (1) It helps us to understand the other person better, and (2) it aids us in perceiving the possible situational causes contributing to a particular behavior. You will recall that our usual inclination is to attribute dispositional causes to others' behavior because we fail to see the possible situational inputs. Practicing empathy helps give us a more balanced view.

Dennis Regan and Judith Totten[82] nicely demonstrated the power of empathy in an interesting two-part study. In one phase of the study, college students were asked to give their impressions of a person shown in videotaped discussion. In the second phase of the study, students gave their judgments of a person in a short story. Half of the students in each of these studies were instructed to empathize with the person as deeply as possible and to try to picture in their minds how that person was feeling. The remaining students received no special instructions about empathy. The results were clear. Students who did not practice empathy were much more apt to attribute the person's behavior to personality characteristics such as character, mood, and personal traits. On the other hand, those who did practice empathy were more appreciative of *how elements in the situation* may have contributed to the person's behavior.

Practicing empathy, then, is a way to understand better how things seem from another person's point of view and to perceive more accurately how dispositional *and* situational factors can influence behavior.

In our interactions with others, the following important question is frequently raised.

HOW CAN WE RECOGNIZE A SINCERE PERSON WHEN WE SEE ONE?

The basic question here is whether other people mean what they say or are merely using words glibly in an effort to mislead and deceive us—will the car really run as well as he says? Does she really love me more than anyone else? Will he really lower taxes if elected? Being able to discern whether a person is sincere or not can help us avoid both disappointment and heartache. Given some people's remarkable ability to be dishonest and deceitful, this is a challenging task. But it *is* a possible one. We *can* separate truth from fiction, sincerity from insincerity. Some ideas on how we do this are provided in a theoretical framework offered by psychologists Edward Jones and Keith Davis.[83] Specifically, the theory suggests that our judgments of sincerity are based in part on (1) the extent to which others' statements depart from popular or widely accepted views and (2) the degree to which others stand to profit from our acceptance of their remarks.

When we look at the first point, research does, in fact, support the idea that we are apt to have greater confidence that a person really means what he says when there is a high degree of disparity between that person's own statements and those that would probably be made by most other people.[84, 85] For example, not long ago, a well-dressed and seemingly intelligent middle-aged man wandered through our campus community proclaiming the impending doom of the planet Earth. Although such a proclamation was somewhat bizarre and far-fetched, its very extremity and rarity lead us to believe that it probably did represent his true beliefs and sincere viewpoint. As another example, if we should hear one of our friends wax on about the charms of someone of the opposite sex—someone who is seen as somewhat unattractive by most others—we probably would not question the sincerity of his or her statements (although we might question his or her taste). One way we judge people's sincerity is by considering their willingness to "stick their necks out"—to risk being unpopular for expressing a different point of view. If they do "stick their necks out," we seem more willing to believe they're doing it because they "really mean it" rather than for some expedient ulterior motive.

Recognizing a sincere person is not always easy.

A second way we assess others' sincerity is by scrutinizing the extent to which they stand to gain personally from our acceptance of their remarks. For example, most of us are somewhat skeptical of salespeople's claims because we realize that they stand to gain a great deal by convincing us that their products are superior to others'. On the other hand, when a representative of our local consumer protection agency endorses a particular product, we are probably more willing to listen because we understand that that person has nothing to gain from such an endorsement.

Extending this idea a step further, you can understand why we are even more likely to judge others as sincere when they endorse positions *contrary* to their own best interests. Research confirms this;[86] it supports our everyday experiences of being more willing to trust the truthfulness of others when we know for sure that they do not have ulterior motives. For example, we would probably attribute a high degree of sincerity to lawyers who argued in favor of "no fault" insurance, or to a politician who recommended strict limitations on political contributions, or to a medical doctor who supported a crackdown on Medicare payments to physicians. I think this idea was unwittingly reflected in something an old college buddy of mine said during a moment of insight about whether his girl friend *really* loved him: "I'm skinny, broke, have a wart on my nose, carry a C average, and she says she really loves me. Now how in the world could I possibly doubt that?"

WE TEND TO PERCEIVE EACH OTHER HOLISTICALLY

Making sense of the flood of information we have about others, although a staggering task, is something we're able to do without much conscious thought and with remarkable efficiency. But how, exactly, do we go about it?

When we perceive another person, in terms of evaluating or sizing him or her up, we do not view that person as a simple summation of his or her individual traits and characteristics. Rather, research indicates that we tend to perceive others holistically and use what amounts to a kind of psychological averaging process to do so.[87, 88]

Norman Anderson[89] illustrated how we do this in an interesting study in which subjects were asked to indicate how well they liked a person who was described as having two highly favorable traits (truthful and reasonable) and another person who was described as having two highly favorable characteristics *and* two moderately favorable ones (truthful and reasonable; painstaking and persuasive). If the information about each of these individuals were simply added together, we might expect that the second person would be liked better than the first, since he had a greater number of positive characteristics. However, if the information about each person was integrated through a psychological averaging process, then we might expect that the first person would be liked better. Why? The reason has to do with the idea that the average of two highly favorable characteristics is necessarily higher than the average of two favorable *and* two moderately favorable traits. Take a look at Figure 1–2. When we assign the highly favorable traits a value of (+3) and the moderately favorable traits a value of (+2), you can see how this works.

The results of Anderson's experiment clearly support the idea that our attributions and impressions of others are the result of an averaging process. That is, subjects responded more positively to the individual who was described by only two highly favorable traits than they did to the one described by two highly favorable and two moderately favorable characteristics.

How we see others is more complicated, however, than a simple averaging process. It seems that our impressions of others actually reflect a weighted average of (1) all of our available input about these people (each piece of information weighted by its own importance), and (2) our own inclination to evaluate them positively or negatively (this, too, weighted by its relative importance). When we say that information about others is weighted according to its relative importance, it means that all the different things we know about a particular person do not exert equal influence on our final impressions. Quite literally, some kinds of information carry greater weight than other kinds of information. For example, if you were considering hiring a particular person for a job and received a highly laudatory letter of recommendation from his friend and a somewhat more negative letter from his former employer, do you think you would assign equal importance to these two sources of information in forming your impression of this person? Probably not. In this case, you would very likely give greater weight to

ADDING

Two pieces of information		Four pieces of information	
Truthful	= (+ 3)	Truthful	= (+ 3)
Reasonable	= (+ 3)	Reasonable	= (+ 3)
		Painstaking	= (+ 2)
		Persuasive	= (+ 2)
Total values	= (+ 6)	Total values	= (+ 10)

AVERAGING

Two pieces of information		Four pieces of information	
Truthful	= (+ 3)	Truthful	= (+ 3)
Reasonable	= (+ 3)	Reasonable	= (+ 3)
		Painstaking	= (+ 2)
		Persuasive	= (+ 2)

$$\text{Average values} = \frac{(+\,6)}{2} = (+\,3) \qquad \text{Average values} = \frac{(+\,10)}{4} = (+\,2.5)$$

FIGURE 1–2.   The Effects of Adding or Averaging Information About Others

the former employer's letter. In short, what we seem to do is weigh the information we have about others according to the credibility of its source.

This tendency to differentially weigh various pieces of information about others seems to be a basic aspect of how we form impressions of others and attribute certain traits to them. As you might suspect, the information we weigh most heavily has the greatest impact on our final impressions. Four factors play important parts in helping us determine how much importance to attach to information we receive about others.

First of all, the credibility of the source makes a difference. The less reliable or credible the source, the less weight the information is given. Second, we are inclined to give greater weight to information about others that is received first. This, you will recall, is called the *primacy effect* and helps us understand why our first impressions of others are so hard to shake and why, too, we may try so valiantly to make a good first impression on others. Third, we weigh information about others according to its relevancy to us. For example, when choosing a roommate, we may give most importance to characteristics such as compatibility and neatness; when choosing a work partner, we might give more weight to traits such as dependability and reliability, and so on. Fourth, we seem inclined to assign greater weight to information about a person's negative characteristics than to information about the positive ones. An unpleasant relationship can cause pain and disappointment, which may be why we remain alert to traits in others that may cause such pain and disappointment.

All in all, the evidence suggests that our overall impressions of others stem from a weighted average of our information about them. We perceive each other, it seems, as total persons and not simply as the sums of individual parts.

IN PERSPECTIVE

We began with the observation that how we perceive each other is a complex happening. It is indeed. How we feel about others and how we think others feel about us depend to some extent on the level of our self-esteem. Research suggests that people with higher levels of self-esteem are inclined to perceive others more positively than are individuals with lower levels of self-esteem. Low-self-esteem people feel somewhat more threatened by others, particularly those who they view as superior in some way, and they seem to have a greater need for others' approval, in order to feel acceptable to themselves. It appears that our self-esteem functions very much like an emotional filter through which we screen our perceptions of others and our expectations for our behavior toward others.

The way we perceive each other is strongly influenced by our impressions of each other. There is a large body of evidence to suggest that our first impressions of each other are strong and lasting. Furthermore, they can be made in very little time and can be based upon relatively little information. In addition, there appear to be certain "central traits" in others' behavior that have a rather significant influence on the sorts of impressions we develop. Indeed, research indicates that once we have identified a certain dominant or "central" characteristic in a person, whatever else we perceive in that person is filtered through that trait.

An important part of the process of getting to know another person is our ability to make inferences about that person's underlying traits and deeper dispositions. This helps us size people up so we can begin to understand their behavior —at least as we see it. One of the ways we do this is by attributing certain meanings and interpretations to the behavior we see in others. This is not an easy process because of certain attribution problems we face. First of all, we have to decide whether a person's behavior is caused primarily by situational (external) or dispositional (internal) factors. (More often than not, we attribute others' behavior to dispositional causes and our own behavior to situational factors.) Another attribution problem is the deception factor. That is, we don't always mean what we say or say what we mean, which could lead us to false impressions of each other.

Still other attribution errors that may bias our perceptions of others include tendencies to give more weight to negative information than to positive information about others, to label people and then to look for ways to justify the label, to attribute causality to that which we see first, and to judge others on the assumption that they are like us. All of these factors, either singularly or in combination, can contribute to possibly wrong initial impressions of others.

Practicing empathy, listening more carefully, and not jumping to hasty conclusions are useful ways to help to see others in their true light. Just being aware of the various factors and influences that, for better or worse, affect how people see each other can help us to be more humane and fair in our perceptions and evaluations of each other. Awareness is the first step. Putting that awareness into practice is the important, necessary next step.

How we perceive each other is very closely related to what types of people we are, and are not, attracted to, an idea we will explore in Chapter 2.

REFERENCES

1. E. Fromm, "Selfishness and Self-Love," in C. Gordon and K. J. Gergen (Eds.), *The Self in Social Interaction,* Vol. I, New York: Wiley, 1968, p. 331.

2. C. R. Rogers, *On Becoming a Person,* Boston: Houghton Mifflin, 1961, pp. 163–176.

3. N. A. Kuiper and T. B. Rogers, "Encoding of Personal Information," *Journal of Personality and Social Psychology,* 37 (1979): 499–514.

4. E. T. Sheerer, "An Analysis of the Relationship Between Acceptance of and Respect for Self and Acceptance of and Respect for Others in Ten Counseling Cases," *Journal of Consulting Psychology* 45 (1949): 169–175.

5. D. Stock, "An Investigation into the Interrelationships Between Self-Concept and Feelings Directed Toward Other Persons and Groups," *Journal of Consulting Psychology* 13 (1949): 176–180.

6. R. C. Wylie, *The Self-Concept: Theory and Research on Selected Topics, Vol. 2,* Lincoln, Nebr.: University of Nebraska Press, 1978.

7. F. Barron, *Creativity and Personal Freedom,* New York: Van Nostrand Reinhold, 1968, p. 12.

8. M. Rosenberg, *Society and the Adolescent Self-Image,* Princeton, N.J.: Princeton University Press, 1965.

9. H. S. Sullivan, *Conceptions of Modern Psychiatry,* Washington, D.C.: William Alanson White Psychiatric Foundations, 1947, p. 17.

10. P. Baron, "Self-Esteem, Ingratiation, and Evaluation of Unknown Others," *Journal of Personality and Social Psychology* 30 (1974): 104–109.

11. E. Walster, "The Effect of Self-Esteem on Romantic Liking," *Journal of Experimental and Social Psychology* 1 (1965): 184–197.

12. E. Stotland, S. Thorley, E. Thomas, A. R. Cohen, and A. Zander, "The Effects of Group Expectation and Self-Esteem Upon Self-Evaluation," *Journal of Abnormal and Social Psychology* 54 (1957): 55–63.

13. J. S. Shrauger, "Self-Esteem and Reactions to Being Observed by Others," *Journal of Personality and Social Psychology,* 23 (1972): 192–200.

14. H. Sigall and R. Gould, "The Effects of Self-Esteem and Evaluation Demandingness on Effort Expenditure," *Journal of Personality and Social Psychology* 35 (1977): 12–20.

15. C. W. Ellison and I. J. Firestone, "Development of Interpersonal Trust as a Function of Self-Esteem, Target Status, and Target Style," *Journal of Personality and Social Psychology* 29 (1974): 655–663.

16.   I. L. Janis and P. B. Field, "A Behavioral Assessment of Persuasibility: Consistency of Individual Differences," in C. I. Hovland and I. L. Janis (Eds.), *Personality and Persuasibility*, New Haven and London: Yale University Press, 1959, pp. 29–54.

17.   A. R. Cohen, "Some Implications of Self-Esteem for Social Influence," in C. I. Hovland & I. L. Janis, *Personality and Persuasibility*, New Haven and London: Yale University Press, 1959, pp. 102–120.

18.   D. Riesmann, *The Lonely Crowd*, New Haven: Yale University Press, 1950.

19.   J. Rotter, "External Control and Internal Control," *Psychology Today*, June 1971: pp. 37–42, 58–59.

20.   E. Berne, "Classification of Positions," *Transactional Analysis Bulletin*, 29 (July 1962): 23.

21.   S. Putney and G. J. Putney, *The Adjusted American: Normal Neuroses in the Individual and Society*, New York: Harper and Row, 1974, p. 74.

22.   E. Goffman, *The Presentation of Self in Everyday Life*, Garden City, N.Y.: Doubleday, 1959.

23.   M. Argyle, *Social Interaction*, Chicago: Aldine, 1969.

24.   S. Duval and R. A. Wicklund, *A Theory of Objective Self-Awareness*, New York: Academic Press, 1972.

25.   A. Fenigstein, "Self-Consciousness, Self-Attention, and Social Interaction," *Journal of Personality and Social Psychology*, 37(1979): 75–86.

26.   N. A. Kuiper, "Depression and Causal Attributions for Success and Failure," *Journal of Personality and Social Psychology* 36 (1978): 236–246.

27.   A. Fenigstein, "Eye Contact, Self-Attention, and the Processing of Relevant Feedback," Unpublished manuscript, Dept. of Psychology, Kenyon College: Gambier, Ohio, 1978.

28   D. W. Johnson, *Reaching Out: Interpersonal Effectiveness and Self-Actualization*, 2d ed., Englewood Cliffs, N.J.: Prentice-Hall, 1981.

29   J. A. Morris, Jr., *The Act of Conversation*, New York: Cornerstone Library, 1977.

30.   J. F. T. Bugental, *The Search for Authenticity*, New York: Holt, Rinehart and Winston, 1965.

31   C. R. Rogers, *On Becoming a Person*, Boston: Houghton Mifflin, 1961.

32.   S. E. Asch, "Forming Impressions on Personality," *Journal of Abnormal and Social Psychology* 41 (1946): 258–290.

33.   H. H. Kelley, "The Warm-Cold Variable in the First Impression of Persons," *Journal of Personality* 18 (1950): 431–439.

34.   S. E. Asch, "Forming Impressions on Personality," *Journal of Abnormal and Social Psychology* 41 (1946): 258–290.

35.   C. E. Osgood, "The Nature and Measurement of Meaning," *Psychological Bulletin*, 49 (1952): 197–237.

36.   C. E. Osgood, G. J. Suci, and P. H. Tannenbaum, *The Measurement of Meaning*, Urbana, Ill.: University of Illinois Press, 1957.

37.   A. Luchins, "Primacy-Recency in Impression Formation," in C. I. Hovland, W. Mandell, E. Campbell, T. Brock, A. Luchins, A. Cohen, W. McGuire, I. Janis, R. Feiera-

bend, and N. Anderson (Eds.), *The Order of Presentation in Persuasion,* New Haven: Yale University Press, 1957.

38.   E. E. Jones, L. Rock, K. G. Shaver, G. R. Goethals, and L. M. Ward, "Pattern of Performance and Ability Attribution: An Unexpected Primacy Effect," *Journal of Personality and Social Psychology* 9 (1968): 317–340.

39.   S. E. Asch, "Forming Impressions on Personality," *Journal of Abnormal and Social Psychology* 41 (1946): 258–290.

40.   N. H. Anderson, "Cognitive Algebra: Integration Theory Applied to Social Attribution," in L. Berkowitz (Ed.), *Advances in Experimental Social Psychology,* Vol. 7, New York: Academic Press, 1974.

41.   M. Snyder and W. B. Swann, Jr., "Hypothesis-Testing in Social Interaction," *Journal of Personality and Social Psychology* 36 (1978): 1202–1212.

42.   R. Rosenthal and L. F. Jacobson, *Pygmalion in the Classroom,* New York: Holt, Rinehart and Winston, 1968.

43.   P. M. Insel and L. F. Jacobson (Eds.), *What Do You Expect: An Inquiry into Self-Fulfilling Prophecies,* Menlo Park, Calif.: Cummings, 1975.

44.   D. E. Hamachek, *Encounters With the Self,* 2d ed. New York: Holt, Rinehart and Winston, 1978, pp. 191–241.

45.   C. Braun, "Teacher Expectation: Sociopsychological Dynamics," *Review of Educational Research,* 46 (Spring, 1976): 185–213.

46.   S. R. Luce and R. D. Hoge, "Relations Among Teacher Rankings, Pupil-Teacher Interactions, and Academic Achievement: A Test of the Teacher Expectancy Hypothesis," *American Educational Research Journal* 15 (Fall, 1978): 489–500.

47.   R. Rosenthal, "The Pygmalion Effect Lives," *Psychology Today,* September 1973: pp. 56–60.

48.   A. Luchins, "Experimental Attempts to Minimize the Impact of First Impressions," in C. I. Hovland et al. (Ed.), *The Order of Presentation in Persuasion,* New Haven, Conn.: Yale University Press, 1957.

49.   F. Heider, *The Psychology of Interpersonal Relations,* New York: Wiley, 1958.

50.   E. E. Jones and K. E. Davis, "From Acts to Dispositions: The Attribution Process in Person Perception," in L. Berkowitz (Ed.), *Advances in Experimental Social Psychology,* New York: Academic Press, 1965, pp. 219–266.

51.   H. H. Kelley, "Attribution Theory in Social Psychology," in D. Levine (Ed.), *Nebraska Symposium on Motivation,* Vol. 15, Lincoln, Nebr.: University of Nebraska Press, 1967.

52.   H H. Kelley, "Processes of Causal Attribution," *American Psychologist* 28 (1973): 107–128.

53.   L. A. McArthur, "The How and What of Why: Some Determinants and Consequences of Causal Attribution," *Journal of Personality and Social Psychology* 22 (1972): 171–193.

54.   E. E. Jones, D. E. Kanouse, H. H. Kelley, R. E. Nisbett, S. Valins, and B. Weiner (Eds.), *Attribution: Perceiving the Causes of Behavior,* Morristown, N.J.: General Learning Press, 1972.

55. T. M. Gilmore and H. L. Minton, "Internal vs. External Attribution of Task Performance as a Function of Locus of Control, Initial Confidence, and Success-Failure Outcome," *Journal of Personality.* 41 (1974): 159–174.

56. V. Karaz and D. Perlman, "Attribution at the Wire: Consistency and Outcome Finish Strong," *Journal of Experimental Social Psychology,* 11 (1975): 470–477.

57. F. Heider, *The Psychology of Interpersonal Relations,* New York: Wiley, 1958.

58. L. Ross, "The Intuitive Psychologist and His Shortcomings: Distortions in the Attribution Process," in L. Berkowitz (Ed.), *Advances in Experimental Social Psychology,* Vol. 10, New York: Academic Press, 1977.

59. L. R. Goldberg, "Differential Attribution of Trait-Descriptive Terms to Oneself as Compared to Well-Liked, Neutral, and Disliked Others: A Psychometric Analysis," *Journal of Personality and Social Psychology* 36 (1978): 1012–1028.

60. J. H. Harvey, B. Harris, and R. D. Barnes, "Actor-Observer Differences in the Perceptions of Responsibility and Freedom," *Journal of Personality and Social Psychology* 32 (1975): 22–28.

61. E. E. Jones and R. E. Nisbett, *The Actor and the Observer: Divergent Perceptions of the Causes of Behavior,* New York: General Learning Press, 1971.

62. R. M. Arkin and S. Duval, "Focus of Attention and Causal Attribution of Actors and Observers," *Journal of Experimental Social Psychology* 11 (1975): 427–439.

63. R. E. Nisbett, C. Caputo, P. Legant, and J. Maracek, "Behavior as Seen by the Actor as Seen by the Observer," *Journal of Personality and Social Psychology* 27 (1973): 154–164.

64. E. E. Jones and R. E. Nisbett, *The Actor and the Observer: Divergent Perceptions of the Causes of Behavior,* New York: General Learning Press, 1971, pp. 10–14.

65. S. V. Eisen, "Actor-Observer Differences in Information Inference and Causal Attribution," *Journal of Personality and Social Psychology,* 37 (1979): 261–272.

66. D. E. Kanouse and L. R. Hanson, "Negativity in Evaluations," in E. E. Jones, D. E. Kanouse, H. H. Kelley, R. E. Nisbett, S. Valins, and B. Weiner (Eds.), *Attribution: Perceiving the Causes of Behavior,* Morristown, N. J.: General Learning Press, 1972.

67. E. C. Webster, *Decision Making in the Employment Interview,* Montreal: Industrial Relations Center, McGill University, 1964.

68. D. E. Kanouse and L. R. Hanson, "Negativity in Evaluations," op cit., 1972.

69. D. L. Rosenhan, "On Being Sane in Insane Places," *Science* 179 (1973): 250–258.

70. S. E. Taylor and S. T. Fiske, "Point of View and Perceptions of Causality," *Journal of Personality and Social Psychology* 32 (1975): 439–445.

71. M. D. Storms, "Videotape and the Attribution Process: Reversing Actors' and Observers' Points of View," *Journal of Personality and Social Psychology,* 27 (1973): 165–175.

72. E. T. Higgins, W. S. Rhodes, and C. R. Jones, "Category Accessibility and Impression Formation," *Journal of Experimental Social Psychology,* 13 (1977): 141–154.

73. J. B. Pryor and M. Kriss, "The Cognitive Dynamics of Salience in the Attribution Process," *Journal of Personality and Social Psychology* 35 (1977): 49–55.

74. L. Ross, D. Greene, and P. House, "The False Consensus Effect: An Egocentric Bias in Social Perception and Attribution Process," *Journal of Experimental Social Psychology* 13 (1977): 279–301.

75. M. J. Lerner, "The Desire for Justice and Reactions to Victims," in J. Macaulay and L. Berkowitz (Eds.), *Altruism and Helping Behavior,* New York: Academic Press, 1970.

76. P. Brickman, K. Ryan, and C. B. Wortman, "Causal Chains: Attribution of Responsibility as a Function of Immediate and Prior Causes," *Journal of Personality and Social Psychology* 32 (1975): 1060–1067.

77. A. L. Chaikin and J. M. Darley, "Victim or Perpetrator?: Defensive Attribution of Responsibility and the Need for Order and Justice," *Journal of Personality and Social Psychology* 25 (1973): 268–275.

78. M. J. Lerner, D. T. Miller, and J. G. Holmes, "Deserving Versus Justice: A Contemporary Dilemma," in L. Berkowitz and E. Walster (Eds.), *Advances in Experimental Social Psychology,* Vol. 12, New York: Academic Press, 1975.

79. E. Walster, "Assignment of Responsibility for an Accident," *Journal of Personality and Social Psychology* 3 (1966): 73–79.

80. M. D. Storms, "Videotape and the Attribution Process: Reversing Actors' and Observers' Points of View," *Journal of Personality and Social Psychology* 27 (1973): 165–175.

81. D. M. Wegner and K. Finstuen, "Observers' Focus of Attention in the Simulation of Self-Perception," *Journal of Personality and Social Psychology,* 35 (1977): 56–62.

82. D. T. Regan and J. Totten, "Empathy and Attribution: Turning Observers into Actors," *Journal of Personality and Social Psychology* 32 (1975): 850–856.

83. E. E. Jones and K. E. Davis, "From Acts to Dispositions: The Attribution Process in Person Perception," in L. Berkowitz (Ed.), *Advances in Experimental Social Psychology,* New York: Academic Press, 1965.

84. R. Eisinger and J. Mills, "Perception of Sincerity and Competence of a Communicator as a Function of the Extremity of His Position," *Journal of Experimental Social Psychology,* 4 (1968): 224–232.

85. E. E. Jones, S. Worchel, G. T. Goethals, and J. F. Grumet, "Prior Expectancy and Behavioral Extremity as Determinants of Attitude Attribution," *Journal of Experimental Social Psychology* 7 (1971): 59–80.

86. E. Walster, E. Aronson, and D. Abrahams, "On Increasing the Persuasiveness of a Low Presige Communicator," *Journal of Experimental Social Psychology* 2 (1966): 325–342.

87. N. H. Anderson, "Cognitive Algebra: Integration Theory Applied to Social Attribution," in L. Berkowitz (Ed.), *Advances in Experimental Social Psychology,* Vol. 7, New York: Academic Press, 1974.

88. M. F. Kaplan, "Information Integration in Social Judgment: Interaction of Judge and Informational Components," in M. Kaplan and S. Schwartz (Eds.), *Human Judgment and Decision Processes,* New York: Academic Press, 1975.

89. N. H. Anderson, "Averaging Versus Adding as a Stimulus Combination Rule in Impression Formation," *Journal of Experimental Psychology* 70 (1965): 394–400.

Chapter 2

WHY PEOPLE ARE ATTRACTED TO EACH OTHER: DETERMINANTS AND OUTCOMES

OVERVIEW

PROLOGUE

It seems like such a simple question. Why do people like each other? Or sometimes love each other? Or why don't they? Why do we feel such a positive affinity for one person, but react so negatively to another person? Why would we like to know more about Robert, but couldn't care less about Richard? What enables us to share our deepest secrets with Sally, when we have trouble sharing even the time of day with Marlene? Why draws people together? Or keeps them apart? Why are your friends *those* particular friends? Why is your loved one *that* particular loved one?

We could go on and on, but inevitably we would return to the same basic question: Why are we attracted to certain people, but not to others? Is it something in ourselves or is it something in the other person? Or, for that matter, is it something about the situation in which we find ourselves? If you were to ask a sample of your friends why they like some of their acquaintances more than others, no doubt you would get a variety of responses. Most, however, would probably say that they tend to like more (1) those with pleasant personalities or admirable qualities, such as kindness, loyalty, and reasonableness, (2) those whose interests and values are similar to their own, (3) those who have special skills or competency, and (4) those who like them in return.

These are good reasons. They make sense. When we choose friends who are pleasant, competent in some way, and who are more like than unlike us, we increase our chances for interpersonal survival. Indeed, these simple ingredients in interpersonal attraction are the very ones that Dale Carnegie, over 40 years ago, took and mixed into a million-dollar recipe for *How to Win Friends and Influence People.*[1] His advice for insuring interpersonal success was disarmingly uncomplicated. If you want to impress, persuade, or sell to others, then give them the appearance of liking them and of being someone who is pleasant, agreeable, and interested in what they're doing. The fact that Carnegie's book has been translated into thirty-five different languages and is still being published so many years after its introduction suggests that a great many people around the world have a strong need to relate, and present themselves favorably, to others and are anxious to learn how to do so better.

I've mentioned the Carnegie book at this point because its incredible sales record is a dramatic example of the importance of interpersonal attraction variables in human relationships. The question of who likes whom and why is a crucial one for many of us. And the problem of how to be a likable, acceptable person is one that apparently concerns a vast number of people.

The question of who likes whom and why is also a complex one. There is no simple Carnegie-like solution. Whom we're attracted to and who's attracted to us results from a complex interplay of many personal and situational factors. Our task in this chapter is to try to sort out those factors. Some of the questions we look at include: How do one's own levels of self-esteem and personal security influence interpersonal attraction? What part does physical attractiveness play? Are there hazards in being *too* physically attractive? Is it true that opposites are attracted to each other? Or is it the similarity between two people that draws them together? What are some of the ways that our behavior can be influenced by those we are or are not attracted to? What is this thing called love? What causes love? Why do we always seem to hurt the one we love?

These are but a few of the issues and questions that we'll turn our attention to in this chapter. There are others. For openers, let's begin with an overview of four major theoretical positions, each of which focuses on a particular aspect of why people may be attracted to each other.

THEORETICAL VIEWPOINTS RELATED TO WHY WE LIKE THE PEOPLE WE LIKE

In order to do research, whether it is related to interpersonal attraction processes or anything else, it is necessary to have a theoretical frame of reference to help interpret, explain, and integrate the research findings. The psychology of interpersonal attraction is so complex that no single theory is able to predict or explain the vast array of behavioral outcomes associated with the question of who likes whom and why. Hence, there are sometimes many theories generated to help us interpret what we see and what we find in everyday behavior. We examine briefly four different theories, each of which has its own slant regarding interpersonal attraction processes. It would probably be helpful for you to keep in mind that these are not competing theories—in the sense that each tries to prove itself right and the others wrong—but, rather, complementary viewpoints offering alternative and even overlapping ways of describing and predicting interpersonal attraction. Our intent here is to develop an overview of each position and then, in the remainder of the chapter, to point back to each of the theories as it is illustrated by a particular research finding or the discussion at hand.

Reinforcement Theory (We Like Those Who Reward Us)

Reinforcement models of attraction have their historical roots in learning theory, and in this sense they treat the issue of who likes whom as simply a matter of learned responses. That is, our attraction to people is based on the feelings we have associated with them. People who arouse positive feelings in us, who are, in other words, rewarding, will be liked. Conversely, people who trigger more negative feelings in us, whose interactions are more punishing, will be disliked.

According to the reinforcement models developed by Donn Byrne and Gerald Clore[2] and by Albert and Bernice Lott,[3] the reward idea can be extended even further. For example, it frequently happens that, along with liking those who reward us directly, we're also inclined to feel positively toward those who may be present when we receive rewards, even though they are not the source of them. It's the kind of thing, for instance, that may happen at banquets or ceremonies when persons who are the honored (rewarded) recipients feel warmly and positively toward the entire audience and not just toward the award committee. In reinforcement terms, the people in attendance become associated with the good feelings and become conditioned reinforcers. In a similar way, we have an inclination to dislike people who are simply associated with our more negative feelings, even when they may not be at all directly involved. For example, adolescents who have had unrewarding, punishing experiences at school are inclined to dislike *all* teachers and school personnel, not just certain ones (although they may indeed have more intense feelings toward certain ones).

The overall picture, then, reveals that we're inclined to like those who are rewarding to us in some way and to dislike those who are punishing.

Exchange Theory (We Like Interactions that Profit Us)

Social psychologists George C. Homans[4] and John Thibaut and Harold Kelley[5] have proposed a theory of human interaction or *exchange* that borrows from the language and conceptual framework of economics. For example, Homans suggests that in the "interpersonal marketplace" you attempt to "give the other man behavior that is more valuable to him than it is costly to you and to get from him behavior that is more valuable to you than it is costly to you."[6] An essential idea behind the theory is that whenever we interact with others, we tend to analyze (but not in these terms) both the rewards and costs of the interaction. When we feel that the rewards of a particular interpersonal exchange are greater than the costs, in the sense of making a psychological "profit," we are likely to want to continue the interaction. Conversely, when we feel that the costs are greater than the rewards, which could lead to psychological bankruptcy, we may be motivated to discontinue the interaction. (You can sometimes see the dynamics of this idea reflected in the underlying reasons behind two lovers breaking up or a couple going through a divorce.)

An advantage of exchange theory over pure reinforcement theory is that it recognizes that there are many rewards (profits) and costs (punishments) available in most interactions. In addition, it continually reminds us that it is the relationship between these rewards and costs—their sum total—that ultimately determines the nature and degree of attraction between two people. For example, you may receive very little attention or affection from a particular person, but still remain attracted to that person because you expend very little time and effort to get what you get. Your costs roughly approximate your rewards.

Exchange theory is somewhat similar to reinforcement theory in the sense that it emphasizes the reward aspects of a relationship. It goes beyond reinforcement models, however, by stressing that what we get from another person, in the way of rewards or punishments, is weighed against what we give to that person. Hence, the emphasis on the exchange aspects of an interaction.

Both reinforcement and exchange theories have limitations. One is that neither of them can adequately explain such common occurrences as altruistic behavior or unrequited love. In addition, neither of them deals very well with the broad range of individual differences regarding what constitutes a reward or a cost.

Equity Theory (We Like Relationships that Are Fair and Equitable)

According to Elaine Walster, G. William Walster, and Elaine Berscheid,[7] equity theory deals with two basic questions: (1) what do people think is fair and equitable?, and (2) how do they respond when they feel they are getting far more or far less from their relationships than they deserve? Equity is defined in terms of relative outcomes, which means that our outcomes are proportional to our inputs. Or, another way to look at it, the more you put into a relationship, the more you should get from it. It is somewhat similar to reinforcement and exchange theories (you can see how theories build on each other) in that it talks about rewards and costs, but it is different in that it focuses on the rewards inherent in an equitable or fair division of rewards and costs between people or among group members.

The practical implication of the theory is that when we find ourselves in an inequitable relationship, our primary response is to restore equity to the relationship so it feels more balanced and fair. Restoration of equity can take one of two routes: actual or psychological. That is, we can: (1) directly change the amount we put into a relationship (for example, by reducing the number of times we write or call someone who is critical of us and gives us little attention), or (2) we can distort reality and convince ourselves that we really *are* getting what we deserve (for example, by reinterpreting criticism and lack of attention as expressions of caring from someone who is just shy and fearful of talking about positive feelings).

Equity theory has also spawned the "matching hypothesis" idea, which suggests that equitable romantic relationships will be the most successful, and thus people will try to find partners who "match" them in terms of their level of physical attractiveness and social skills. Sometimes the match is based on a similar characteristic (highly attractive people tend to choose highly attractive partners); sometimes it is based on a complex weighting of different characteristics (someone who is plain but intelligent might match someone who is beautiful but not so smart).

Evidence for the matching hypothesis is somewhat mixed.[8] Although it is true that people tend to choose partners of approximately the same social worth, the fact is that most people try to attract partners who are far more socially attractive than they may consider themselves. Perhaps another way of saying this is that we strive for the ideal, but in the final analysis our choices are tempered by the reality of what we have to offer the other person and what the other person has to offer us so that the relationship can be fair and equitable.

Gain-Loss Theory (We Like Those Whose Liking for Us Increases with Time)

Over 300 years ago, long before there were psychologists around to worry about such things as who likes whom or who loves whom and why, Dutch philosopher Benedict Spinoza observed:

Hatred which is entirely conquered by love passes into love, and love on that account is greater than if it had not been preceded by the hatred.[9]

And that, in somewhat poetic terms, is what gain-loss theory is all about. Basically, it is a theoretical position developed by Elliot Aronson,[10] that suggests that *changes* in one's evaluation of us will have a greater impact on our liking him or her than if his or her evaluation is constant and unchanging. This means that we may be inclined to *like* a person whose opinion of us increases over time (a *gain* situation) more than a person who has always liked us. Conversely, we may be inclined to *dislike* someone whose opinion of us becomes more negative over time (a *loss* situation) more than someone who has always disliked us.

How can we explain this strange happening? One possible explanation is that we're more likely to interpret a change in the person's opinion about us as being related to something *we* did ("He feels more positively about me because he's gotten to know me better"), while we interpret an unchanging attitude as being more related to the person's disposition ("She always feels that way about people —it's just the way she is and has nothing to do with me"). In ways like this, we feel changes in a person's attitude toward us more personally. Another possible explanation has to do with anxiety arousal and reduction. For example, if we hear a person say negative things about us, this may make us feel anxious. If, later, we hear that person say positive things (a gain), these evaluations will probably not only be rewarding in themselves, but will also reduce our previous anxiety about the negative comments. Hence, the positive things we hear may be doubly rewarding. That is, we are not only pleased, but relieved. If, on the other hand, we hear a person say positive things about us, this may make us feel good. Then, if we later hear this person say negative things (a loss), these evaluations may seem to us even worse because we compare them with the positive things we heard at first. The loss, in other words, may seem more apparent and real.

Reflections

How would you use each of these four positions to explain your relationship with, and your attraction to, your very best friend? Your loved one? Which theory or theories seem to fit your situation best? Do you like those persons primarily because they are in some way rewarding to you? To what extent are your relationships with them fair and equitable? Do you see yourself as being pretty evenly "matched" to your friend and loved one? In what ways?

This, then, in an overview of four theoretical positions related to attraction. They will serve as our backdrop, and we will refer to them from time to time.

Let's continue our look at the dynamics of interpersonal attraction by examining an important issue—not one that focuses on what it is about others, but on what it is about ourselves that affects this process.

SELF-ESTEEM AS A FACTOR AFFECTING WHOM WE'RE ATTRACTED TO AND WHOM WE LIKE

As we saw in Chapter 1, how we view ourselves has a considerable influence on how we perceive others and how we think others perceive us. Inasmuch as our self-concept includes ideas about how attractive we are—to others and ourselves, personality-wise and physically—you can see how our level of self-esteem in these matters can affect not only whom we're attracted to, but also who we think could be attracted to us.

Self-esteem is the emotional barometer inside us that reflects the degree to which we admire or value the self. When we feel reasonably secure about who we are and confident about our talents and abilities, our self-esteem is likely to be high. We are more apt to like ourselves and to feel equal to others when our emotional barometer is up. What happens, however, when the barometer is down, when we don't feel secure, and when our sense of being equal to others is shaky?

For one thing, low self-esteem can directly influence how much we like and are attracted to others. For example, it has been shown that the greater a person's feelings of self-doubt and insecurity, the more he will be attracted to a person who likes him. We can see how this works in a study by Elaine Walster[11] with female university students. First, each of these students filled out personality questionnaires; then, while waiting to be told what to do next, each was approached by a rather smooth, nice-looking young man who was, unbeknown to the women, an accomplice in the experiment. He struck up a conversation with each student, indicated that he liked her, and after 15 minutes asked her for a date. After he left, the experimenter showed each subject an evaluation of certain aspects of her personality. Half of the women in the study read descriptions of themselves that were highly positive, designed purposely to raise their self-esteem temporarily. The other women read descriptions of themselves that were quite negative, designed to lower their self-esteem temporarily and, thus, to cause them to feel a greater sense of insecurity. As the concluding part of the study, the women were asked to rate how much they liked a wide range of people, including the young man who had asked for a date. The results were interesting. Women who received *unfavorable* evaluations about themselves from the personality test—whose self-esteem was temporarily lower—reacted much more positively to their male admirer than did those who received favorable evaluations about themselves. Indeed, those who received the positive feedback—whose self-esteem was temporarily higher—were quite neutral in their feelings about the smooth-talking young man. What we can extract from these results is the idea that when our self-esteem is low and our insecurity is high, we may be more receptive to others' opinions of us, whether they are sincere or not.

Men are no more immune to this vulnerability than women. For example, Lawrence Jacobs and his co-workers[12] conducted a study in which the dating skills of male subjects were evaluated positively or negatively by a woman as a way of temporarily raising or lowering their self-esteem. Then each man was asked to rate his attraction for the woman who evaluated him. The results? The men with lowered self-esteem were much more apt to like accepting women more and rejecting women less than the men whose self-esteem had been experimentally raised. (You can see reflected in both of these studies evidence for the reinforcement model of attraction. That is, we like those who like us, which is rewarding, and it's even more rewarding, it seems, if someone likes us when our self-esteem is low.)

One of the implications of these two studies is that the approval and acceptance of others is particularly important to people whose self-esteem is low and who feel, therefore, more "needy." A client of mine, a young man working through his deep feelings of inadequacy and low self-esteem, expressed the essence of this idea when he said:

> Sometimes when I'm around others I just keep hoping that someone will come over and talk to me. I don't much care who it is. And then when someone does talk to me, I get two feelings—one is that I'm very nervous, but the other is that I'm feeling very relieved. I really like it when people like me. When I know that someone likes me, I feel more worthwhile.

Yes, he did feel more worthwhile when he felt liked by someone, but he was so hungry for acceptance that his emotional starvation caused him to be indiscriminately attracted to any sign of attention from others. Until he discovered some of his own inner strengths and found ways to raise his own self-esteem, he was the kind of person who so lacked a sense of self-worth that his grasping, clinging manner frequently stifled precisely those who might have been able to fulfill his needs.

Self-esteem can influence the attraction process in still another way. For example, a low-self-esteem person may be attracted to a less physically attractive person as a way of reducing the possibility of being rejected. Psychologists Sara Kiesler and Roberta Baral[13] tested this idea by leading a group of male college students to believe that they had performed either very well or very poorly on an intelligence test. Each subject was then taken to the cafeteria for a coffee break during which the experimenter "just happened" to recognize a female student seated alone at a table. The subject was introduced to this student and then he was left alone with her as the experimenter left on a pretense. Of course, the female student was a confederate of the experimenter, intentionally planted there. Half of the time she was made up to look quite attractive and the other half of the time she appeared generally unkempt and unattractive. The investigators looked for evidence of romantic interest on the part of the male subjects: did they pay for her coffee, did they ask for a phone number, did they delay leaving, did they ask for a date, and so on? There were interesting differences between the behavior of males who had been led to believe that they had done very well on the intelligence test and those who believed that they had done very poorly.

Subjects who thought that they had done well—more secure, higher in self-esteem —showed more romantic interest toward the attractive woman. Those who thought that they had done poorly—more insecure, lower in self-esteem—showed more romantic interest toward the "unattractive" woman. (We see here some support for the matching hypothesis in equity theory, in the sense that a low-self-esteem person may, in fact, feel quite unattractive and so choose someone who more or less matches that self-perception. High-self-esteem people, on the other hand, may try to match themselves with persons who are at least as attractive as themselves, if not more so. It may well be that an adequate level of self-esteem is the inner quality that frees one to not only be attracted to, but *attractive* to, a person of equal or superior personal assets and physical features.

How Understanding Self-Esteem Dynamics Can Be Helpful

When it comes to interpersonal attraction processes, low-self-esteem people seem responsive to positive feedback, but reluctant to take the initiative. This understanding can be helpful to us in two ways.

In the first place, when we realize that another person's self-esteem is low— a loved one, a friend, one of our students, or perhaps one of our staff members or employees—we can take remedial steps to help improve his or her shaky self-worth by emphasizing personal strengths and positive gains. This is a tricky issue because, on the one hand, there is research[14, 15] to show that low-self-esteem people have a readiness to believe negative feedback. The reason for this readiness seems to be related to the idea that the negative feedback is consistent with what they already feel about themselves. On the other hand, the research we've reviewed in this section indicates that low-self-esteem people are not only attracted to those who give them positive input, but quite responsive to them, a fact that wise teachers and bosses can put to good use.

There is a point worth keeping in mind regarding the use of positive feedback to bolster a person's sagging self-esteem: it has to be real. That is, it has to be an accurate evaluation of that person's performance. Morton Deutsch and Leonard Solomon,[16] for example, found that when a low-self-esteem person fails at a particular task and is praised by one person and criticized by another, he or she is more apt to be attracted to the critic than the admirer. For instance, if a man tells a woman she is beautiful when she may be feeling *and* looking unattractive, she may be somewhat suspicious about his motives. *Evaluation accuracy,* then, is an important aspect of giving feedback to low-self-esteem people or, for that matter, to anyone else. A helpful rule of thumb might be to praise things that are truly praiseworthy; however, for those aspects of behavior or performance that are not praiseworthy, giving constructive feedback about how to improve might be the best and the most honest thing we can do for another person.

There is a second way that understanding self-esteem dynamics can be helpful. If low self-esteem is something we recognize in ourselves, either as a chronic or a temporary feeling, we can perhaps be more watchful of our inclination to be indiscriminately attracted to those who show us the slightest signs of approval. It is helpful to get recognition and positive input when self-esteem is low, but it is self-defeating to be so excessively needy that we turn off the very people from whom we want to get positive feedback.

Reflections

You may find it particularly instructive if, say, for the next several weeks you pay special attention to your own level of self-esteem. Does your self-esteem affect whom you're attracted to? When your self-esteem feels high, how does this influence how you relate to others? What happens when your self-esteem feels low, as far as whom you relate to and how? An interesting (and no doubt helpful) task you could take on would be to make a special effort to give positive input and feedback to someone you know whose self-esteem seems low. Note for yourself whether the ideas we've discussed in this section seem to fit what you find.

FACTORS ABOUT OTHERS THAT INFLUENCE WHOM WE'RE ATTRACTED TO

Whom we do or do not feel attracted to is very much affected by certain behaviors and personal attributes we see in others. This is not necessarily a conscious process; that is, we are not always aware of why we seem to be drawn to this person or feel somewhat negative toward that person. Most of the time we simply find ourselves liking certain people and not liking others, but not knowing very much about the underlying reasons.

Our purpose in this section, then, will be to develop an awareness and understanding of what some of the factors in others are that influence, for better or worse, how we feel about them. One factor that affects us is a person's ability or competence. Let's look at this idea.

We Like Competent People— Particularly When They're "Human"

This is a tricky idea. We like competent people, yet we don't. We like being around them, because their skills or abilities may rub off on us by association. Yet we are somewhat hesitant to be around them because we may not look as good by comparison. Perhaps this helps to explain why sociologist Robert Bales[17] found evidence in his research to suggest that even though we want competent people and people with good ideas as members of our groups, we are not likely to include them among those we like best. Competent, able people may make us feel uncomfortable; they may seem too unapproachable, too "perfect," and too unlike us for us to identify with them. Of course, if this is true, then the other side of this logic is that we could like competent people more if we saw evidence indicating that they were mere mortals like ourselves, fully capable of falling on their faces now and then. There is some interesting evidence in "real life," as it were, to support the possible validity of this logic. Consider some examples.

In 1961 John F. Kennedy was a highly regarded and popular President, a fact consistently reflected in Gallup polls. He was young, handsome, athletic, a war hero, and he had a beautiful wife and two cute children—all the ingredients necessary to be one of the supermen of that era. Then, an amazing thing happened; at the peak of his public popularity, he made one of the monumental blunders of all time when, at the last possible moment, he withdrew support from what had been a United States-supported invasion of Cuba—an event now commonly referred to as the "Bay of Pigs" fiasco. He neither made excuses for it, nor did he try to pass the buck; rather, he accepted the full responsibility and told the American people that he had, in fact, goofed. This both startled and dismayed many of his advisors, who, looking ahead to the 1964 election, feared that his image would be hurt. But, remarkably, a Gallup poll taken soon thereafter showed that his personal popularity had actually increased; in fact, the ratings were as high as he was ever to receive during his presidency. A national leader —a superman of the times—had blundered, and people seemed to like him more for it. Could it be that he was seen as somewhat more "human" and therefore more like the rest of us?

One has to wonder if somewhat the same dynamics may have been involved in Senator Edward Kennedy's case following the tragedy at Chappaquiddick Island in June 1969, when the car he was driving plunged off humpbacked Dike Bridge into Poucha Pond, trapping and drowing his passenger, Mary Jo Kopechne. In his public confessional, he assumed responsibility for what happened; in his words, the accident was "irrational and indefensible and inexcusable and inexplicable." Although not everyone believed (or believes) his account, the numbers who did were apparently sufficient enough to elect him to another 6-year term as a Massachusetts senator, and to encourage him to run for the Democratic nomination for President of the United States. For Edward Kennedy, Chappaquiddick was a grievous error of colossal proportions; nonetheless, his political career grew and flourished. (It is tempting to compare the Kennedys' open admissions to Richard Nixon's rigid stonewalling during the Watergate affair. Although Nixon and the Kennedys blundered terribly, one has to wonder whether the difference in public acceptance of their blunders was the fact that the Kennedys admitted their errors, while Nixon persisted in covering up his errors in an effort to appear as an unassailable and impeccable leader interested only in "protecting our national security." It may be that a blunder has to be as evident to the blunderer as it is to the observer, if one is to feel attracted to that person.)

Elliot Aronson, Ben Willerman, and Joanne Floyd[18] designed an ingenious experiment to find out more about the effect of blunders on interpersonal attractiveness under more controlled conditions. They had a group of subjects listen to tape recordings of people who were candidates for the "College Quiz Bowl" and then rate each candidate in terms of the kind of impression he or she made, how likable he or she was, and so forth. On one tape, the candidate was a virtually perfect person reflecting a high degree of competence; he answered 92 percent of the questions correctly, admitted modestly that he had been editor of the yearbook, an honor student, and a member of the track team. The candidate on the second tape was someone of more average ability. He answered only 30 percent of the questions correctly, he received average grades in school, he had been on the proofreading staff of the yearbook, and he had tried out for the track team but not made it.

On half of the tapes, the "superior" and "average" candidates committed an embarrassing blunder near the end of the interview—there were sounds of commotion and clatter, a chair scraping, and an anguished voice saying, "Oh my goodness, I've spilled coffee all over my new suit." In the other half of the cases, this "pratfall"—so dubbed by the investigators—did not occur. Thus, there were four experimental conditions involving: (1) a person of superior ability who blundered, (2) one who did not, (3) a person of average ability who blundered, and (4) one who did not.

What were the final ratings? What follows is the order in which they finished, from most to least attractive: (1) superior person who blundered; (2) superior person who did not blunder; (3) average person who did not blunder; (4) average person who blundered. Lo and behold, the superior person who committed a blunder was rated as *most* attractive (supporting equity theory, in that people may see blundering superior people as more like themselves). On the other hand, the average person committing the same blunder was rated *least* attractive. Whereas a pratfall serves to "humanize" a superior person, it seems to have the effect of making a mediocre person seem more mediocre and, as a consequence, less attractive.

The working hypothesis of Aronson's study was that a "pratfall" makes a superior person more attractive because he becomes more like us. But what if we think of ourselves as superior? In this case, a blundering person may seem less like us (in terms of our self-image), and hence less likable. Or there is another possibility. What if we have rather low self-esteem and are very much attracted to the "superpersons" who serve as ego ideals for us? Under this condition, blunders may blemish our idols and, hence, they may seem less likable.

To test these questions, Robert Helmreich[19] and his co-workers expanded Aronson's original blunder experiment to see if there was a relationship between self-esteem and attraction for those who either blundered or didn't. Once again, spilling coffee enhanced the attractiveness of the superior person, but only in the eyes of men with average self-esteem. For those men with very high or very low self-esteem, the superior person was *less* liked after his blunder. Subsequent research findings by Kay Deaux[20] suggest that men are more attracted to the highly competent man who blunders than seems to be the case for women, who show a tendency to like the highly competent nonblunderer better—whether male or female.

All in all, it appears that if you are perfect, you can expect to impress more women than men, perhaps some other infallible souls like yourself, or those inferiors who are looking for someone to model those noble qualities that they themselves lack. However, it should be pointed out that no sizable proportion of people—regardless of their level of self-esteem—preferred the mediocre person. The evidence suggests that we are not drawn to the so-called "perfect" person, but rather to the person who is good at what he or she does, who makes mistakes now and then, who admits them, and who goes on from there.

Reflections

How would you explain Kay Deaux's finding that more women than men are attracted to a competent nonblunderer? If you see yourself as the sort of person who has to be more or less perfect to be liked, you might want to try a little experiment. For the next several weeks, make a deliberate effort to be more open about your shortcomings and faults, particularly among those who know you well. What happens when you are less perfect and more "human"?

We Like Physically Attractive People

On a conscious level, most of us are in tune with the cultural dictum that says that we should not be influenced by a nice body, dazzled by a pretty face, or swayed by a handsome profile. It is as though we would like to be free of the effect of these surface considerations in order to see more clearly the "real" person who resides at a deeper level. If, for instance, you ask a sampling of your friends what it is that attracts them to certain other people, you will very likely discover that they list qualities such as character, personality, sincerity, and honesty ahead of physical attractiveness. Indeed, there is research[21] to indicate that if you ask people to rank those qualities that they are attracted to in another person, they will place physical attractiveness somewhere in the middle. Most of us agree that it probably isn't such a good idea to judge a book by its cover. That's what we say.

But that's not necessarily what we do. As it turns out, covers are important. Although on one level we say that physical attractiveness shouldn't play a big part in our feelings toward others, it appears to be more crucial than we care to admit or even realize. For example, when a group of 376 men and 376 women, who had allegedly been matched for a "computer dance," were asked whether they would date the same person again, both men and women gave significantly more preference to dates who had previously been rated (unknown to the participants) by the researchers as physically attractive.[22] In fact, the more physically attractive the date, the more he or she was liked. It is worth noting that, although the investigators looked hard for other factors that might possibly predict attraction, they could find none. Men and women with exceptional social skills and intelligence levels, for example, were no better liked than those less fortunately endowed. The primary finding was basic and consistent—both men and women preferred the most attractive dates. Subsequent research[23,24,25] lends strong support to the idea that physical appearance is one of the most powerful determinants of attraction.

Before you conclude that being influenced by physical appearance is something that goes on only between men and women, consider the following study by Karen Dion and her colleagues.[26] They showed a group of young adults photographs of three college-age people—one was physically attractive, the second was average, and the third was unattractive. The subjects were then asked to rate each of the people in the photographs on twenty-seven different personality traits, and also to assess their probability for future happiness. The results? Physically attractive people were assigned by far the most desirable traits and given the greatest chance for happiness, and this was true whether men were rating men, men were rating women, women were rating men, or women were rating women. You can see that our penchant for liking physically attractive people cuts across sex boundaries. We are inclined, it seems, to like attractive people regardless of our sex *or* theirs.

Although it's difficult to know for certain why we seem drawn to physically attractive people, one possible reason may be that we unconsciously associate certain positive personality traits with an attractive appearance. For example, in the Dion study mentioned above, respondents thought that good-looking people were generally more sensitive, kind, interesting, strong, poised, modest, sociable, outgoing, and exciting than less attractive people.

Associating certain personality traits with certain physical characteristics is a process that apparently begins early in life. For example, Karen Dion and Ellen Berscheid[27] found that, as early as nursery school, children are responsive to the physical attractiveness of their classmates. In their study, the children were first of all rated on a physical attractiveness scale by independent judges, and then they were administered a sociometric test to find out who liked whom among the children themselves. The clearest results were among the males, and they showed that physically unattractive boys were viewed as more aggressive and were not liked as well as physically attractive boys; in fact, unattractive boys were more frequently mentioned when the children were asked to name classmates that "scared them."

Other evidence supports the idea that stereotyping certain personality traits with certain physical features begins at a tender age. For instance, J. Robert Staffieri[28] found that boys as young as six to ten years of age were already in close agreement when it came to associating certain behaviors to particular body types. For example, overweight boys were seen by their peers as socially offensive and delinquent, while those who were tall and thin were seen as retiring, nervous, shy, and introverted. On the other hand, those who were more muscular and athletic —in other words, more attractive—were perceived as outgoing, active, popular, and they were more frequently chosen as leaders. Other research with five- and six-year-olds also supports this finding.[29] Indeed, this is a process that continues on into the adult years as well. For example, Gerald Adams and Ted Huston[30] found in their research with middle-aged adults that those who were perceived as attractive were apt to be judged as more socially outgoing, more pleasant, and enjoying higher social status than less physically attractive people of the same age. (In these findings, we can see support for both the reinforcement theory of attraction—association with physically attractive people may be rewarding—and the exchange theory of attraction—association with attractive persons may provide interactions that profit us.)

Of course, our inclination to associate positive qualities with physically attractive people may work something like a self-fulfilling prophecy; that is, we see in an attractive person what we expect to see and then behave toward that person in a manner that is consistent with the expectation, which makes it come true. For example, Mark Snyder[31] and his associates found in their research that men who were led to believe that they were talking to an attractive woman behaved quite differently from men who thought they were talking to an unattractive woman. In one half of the study, a group of college-age men were each given a biographical information form with a picture of an attractive woman attached to it. In the second half, another group of men were also each given a biographical information form, but this time with a picture of an unattractive woman attached to it. After examining the information, each man filled out a questionnaire designed to assess the extent to which his impression of the woman reflected general stereotypes linking physical attractiveness and personality characteristics. Then each man engaged in an unstructured conversation over an intercom system (mike and earphones) with the woman he thought corresponded to the biographical form and picture given to him. Remember, this woman and the woman in the picture were different—he only thought they were the same. Consider the results. To begin with, men who thought they would be talking to an attractive woman were more apt to have preconceptions and expectations about her being more sociable, poised, sexually warm, and outgoing than men who thought they were going to talk to the unattractive woman. An interesting and telling finding emerges. Men who interacted with women whom they considered to be physically attractive were more sociable, sexually warm, interesting, bold, outgoing, and socially adept than men interacting with supposedly unattractive women. And even more important, the women who were perceived (unbeknown to them) to be physically attractive *actually behaved in a more friendly, likable, and social manner than the women perceived as unattractive.* In other words, the stereotypes that the men had derived from the pictures truly functioned as self-fulfilling prophecies. The men behaved toward each woman in a manner that was consistent with how they expected attractive or unattractive women to behave, thus encouraging each woman to behave as expected, and in turn, helping the expectations to come true.

The disturbing aspect of this evidence is that such preferential treatment could be the beginning of a cycle of a negative self-fulfilling prophecy. That is, if people are treated poorly, it affects how they perceive themselves and how they perceive their personal qualities. Thus, unattractive children (adults, too) may come to perceive themselves as less than desirable if they are continually treated in negative, rejecting ways. Ultimately, they may begin to behave in a style that is consistent with the self-concept, reflecting how they were treated in the first place. As professional people or as parents, we need to keep a watchful eye on our preferences for this or that individual so that we aren't caught in the trap of believing, either consciously or unconsciously, that only that which is beautiful is good.

The evidence points strongly to the idea that physical appearance and physical attractiveness stereotypes are learned by an early age. It is a subtle process of absorbing certain cultural standards about appearance and the alleged personal characteristics that go with certain physical shapes and features. No doubt much of this is learned from picture books, comics, television, and movies. How often, for example, do we see a dumpy-looking hero or a plain-looking heroine? How frequently is the villain in comic books or television or movies a pleasant, handsome man or a warm, beautiful woman? From childhood through adulthood, we're surrounded by a culture that says, in a variety of ways, that if something is beautiful it must be good.

You may be wondering at this point what constitutes "beauty" or "attractiveness?" Do people agree on the criteria used to rate these subjective judgments? Good question—let's examine this for a moment.

Factors Affecting Whom We See as Physically Attractive　For the most part, people generally agree on standards of beauty. A culture transmits effectively, and fairly uniformly, criteria for labeling others as physically attractive or unattractive, a fact well-documented in Ellen Berscheid and Elaine Walster's[32] monumental review of research related to physical attractiveness.

As long ago as 1883, Sir Francis Galton found out what it took to make a pretty face by superimposing a large number of faces on a single photographic plate. He ended up with a face that averaged the features of all the faces, thus eliminating individual differences and peculiarities. He did this with both men and women, and, as reported in an interesting book by Wilson and Nias,[33] the end result was an artistically striking face. With his photographic trickery, Galton was able to show that what we regard as a nice-looking face is one with regular, typical features. A less attractive face is more apt to be one with surprises.

When it comes to sex appeal, physical attractiveness tends to be based largely on differences in appearance between men and women. The greater those differences, up to a certain point, the more attractive a person generally appears to the opposite sex. Cosmetics, for example, help exaggerate the differences. Lipstick helps make a woman's lips appear fuller, and many women pluck their eyebrows to avoid the bushy look sported by some men. In general, then, men have a better chance to be judged as attractive if they don't look like women, and women are more attractive if they don't look like men.

Although there is general agreement about what physical attractiveness is and what it is not, there is some disagreement—or at least some different ideas—between the sexes and among those of the same sex about particulars. For example, Sally Beck[34] and her associates found that, although the majority of a group of college-age women chose the moderate-size man—as opposed to the "Atlas type"—with small buttocks to be most physically attractive, there were some women who found the large Atlas-like body to be most attractive, and still others who favored overall male smallness. You may find it interesting to know that women who enjoyed physical activity and participated in sports most preferred the large male body, while the moderate-size man was most favored by women who had more "traditionally feminine" interests in home and family. Male smallness was favored more by socially reserved women. All in all, this and other research[35] points to the general conclusion that most women tend to equate male physical attractiveness with overall moderate size coupled with small buttocks. This is also true, by the way, in women's opinions as to what makes a woman attractive. The message seems clear to both men and women: If you're interested in being physically attractive to the greatest number of women, you may want to spend less time expanding your chest and more time reducing your "derrière."

Jerry Wiggins[36] and his colleagues found evidence to support the old idea that, when it comes to judging the attractiveness of women, some men are "breast" men, "buttocks" men, or "leg" men. Different men have different criteria for what constitutes female physical attractiveness, and this seems to have as much—if not more—to do with a man's psychology as with female physiology. For example, men who tend to be extroverted and exhibitionistic, and who have a greater need to be the center of attention, are the ones who are most likely to prefer large-busted women.

We might be reassured to know that we don't necessarily have to meet the usual standards of beauty to be seen as physically attractive. There is evidence, for instance, to suggest that an otherwise plain-looking person with a pleasing, engaging personality can also be perceived as physically attractive.[37] A beautiful personality is apparently seen as belonging to a beautiful person—even when the beautiful person is quite plain. I suspect we can all think of people who we see as quite physically attractive, but it is an attractiveness that radiates more from the inside than from the outside. This helps explain why we often perceive people whom we love as being beautiful, regardless of what anyone else might think.

The influence of physical attractiveness, it seems, is greatest when we first meet someone. As we no doubt know from our personal experiences, physical considerations recede in their importance as a relationship progresses and as people come to know one another in deeper ways. Attractive physical features may open doors but, apparently, it takes more than physical beauty to keep them open.

We Like People Who Are Similar To Us—Usually

You may recognize the following scenario: You're at a social gathering; people are milling about, getting to know one another, and in the process you find yourself talking with someone who grew up in a town of about the same size as yours, who feels more or less the same as you do about the use of nuclear energy, the value of strenuous exercise on a daily basis, and the superior taste of white wines over red wines. When the gathering is over, you tell a friend of yours that you had a chance to meet and talk to a very interesting and engaging person— someone you would like to know better. This sort of everyday personal experience confirms what Donn Byrne[38] has demonstrated time and again under more controlled conditions, namely, that the more similarity Joe Dokes's opinions and attitudes have to our own, the more we will like Joe Dokes.

You may be wondering at this point just *how* similar Joe Dokes's opinions and attitudes have to be to yours for you really to like him.

Reflections

Stop a moment and consider two interesting possibilities. Let's say in one instance you find yourself talking to Acquaintance A, who agrees with you on three issues and disagrees with you on none at all. In a second instance you and Acquaintance B agree on six issues and disagree on three. What's your prediction—who would you and most people like better? Acquaintance B, with whom you agree more often than with the first person—but with whom you also disagree a few times; or Acquaintance A, with whom you agree fewer times, but with whom you have no disagreements?

If you predicted that most people would tend to like Acquaintance A better than Acquaintance B, you would be right on target in terms of what has been discovered in social science research. For example, Byrne and Nelson[39] found that the *absolute number* of issues on which two people agree is less important than the *proportion* of issues on which they agree. This fact helps explain why we may end up liking a person who agrees with us on three issues and disagrees on none better than we do a person who agrees with us on six issues and disagrees on three. And it tends to support the reinforcement theory of interpersonal attraction; that is, we generally seem more responsive to what is rewarding in a relationship (agreement) than to what may be viewed as punishing (disagreement). It may also help explain why, in the course of, say, an hour's conversation, we suddenly may feel a bit irritated and defensive when our friend who essentially has been in agreement with us, unexpectedly disagrees on a single issue. Knowing this may not alleviate our irritation, but being aware of *why* we feel this way may enable us to handle our reaction better.

Actually, similarity in and of itself is not the crucial issue. If you find out that a stranger agrees with you about your favorite brand of toothpaste or your favorite meal of the day, you might not be terribly motivated to get together with that person. However, if that person shares your views on vegetarianism and religion, then the chances are much greater that you might want to know that individual better. Gerald Clore and Bill Baldridge,[40] for example, found much greater attraction between two people when they agreed on mutually important issues and disagreed on trivial issues than when the reverse was true. You may have found in your own experiences that marriages and other love relationships are particularly vulnerable when agreement on basic core issues is missing. As suggested in Henry Bowman and Graham Spanier's[41] review of literature related to marital adjustment, marriages sometimes break down precisely because there is agreement on any number of *trivial* issues, but *lack* of agreement on matters that really count in a deeper way.

The research linking attraction to similarity is strong and persuasive. Generally speaking, the more two people agree on issues that are crucial and important to both of them, the more likely it is that they will be attracted to each other, at least initially. Indeed, there is evidence to indicate that this effect holds true not just for the college-age population that is so frequently studied, but also for children in elementary school[42] and senior citizens.[43] Still other research has examined the result of similarity of economic conditions[44] and of ability.[45] In all cases, the similarity–attraction effect holds up rather well.

Why is similarity or agreement important? There are at least three possibilities: (1) The person who thinks like we do on core issues helps us feel like we want to feel anyway, namely, more right than wrong, (2) agreement helps us avoid the needless hassles that grow naturally from disharmonious relationships, and (3) on a far less conscious level, agreement reduces the chances of our having to face the possibility that not only are we wrong, but that we may have to change our attitude or behavior or both. This third possibility may have more to do with our attraction for those who are similar to us than with any other possibility. There is probably no aspect of human behavior that has been more thoroughly documented and demonstrated in social psychology[46] and therapeutic psychology[47, 48] than our stubborn resistance to change. Perhaps these reasons help explain why we sometimes see a greater similarity between ourselves and certain others in our lives than may actually exist. For example, two independent research efforts involving a group of married couples[49] and pairs of college-age friends[50] found a moderate degree of similarity in the attitudes of the spouses and friends. However, when each person was asked to predict the attitudes of his or her partner, the similarity of the scores increased markedly! In other words, our *perceptions* of similarity may sometimes be more imagined than real, which tends to underscore the idea that similarity is an important aspect of why people like each other, or don't, as the case may be. There is, however, a complicating factor we need to consider for a moment.

Sometimes We Don't Like People Who Are Similar to Us—Some Reasons Why

We don't have to go any further than our own life experiences to recognize that we do not like all people who share our basic values and attitudes.

Reflections

Muse for a moment. Think about a couple of people who seem to have attitudes quite similar to yours and who, on top of that, are fine individuals. Now think of people who may be similar to you in terms of attitudes and values, but who are somewhat obnoxious in one way or another. What effect does the character of a person have on your feelings about being similar to him or her?

Research evidence suggests that when people who are similar to us—in terms of general background and attitudes—behave in strange or socially offensive ways, we tend to dislike them. For example, David Mettee and Paul Wilkins[51] found from their research that people of superior intellectual ability *disliked* a superior-ability person significantly more if he or she committed a blunder than did average-ability individuals reacting to that same person. Other research shows that when groups of subjects were told that their attitudes and general backgrounds were similar or dissimilar to those of a mental patient, those people who found that they were similar to the mental patient liked him less than those who found that they were dissimilar to him.[52] Along this same line, there is evidence to show that an obnoxious person is apt to be disliked more if he is similar to, rather than dissimilar to, another individual,[53] and there is still other research to indicate that people will go to great lengths to dissociate themselves from obnoxious people whose attitudes are similar to their own.[54]

Why do we tend to dislike certain people with undesirable characteristics, who may otherwise be similar to us in basic ways? There are at least two possible reasons: (1) Disliking certain similar *negative others* may be a way of keeping them at a distance, so that neither we nor others will see that we have that much in common. It is a way of preserving and protecting one's self-image. It is a way of saying, "Other people are like that (stupid, mentally ill, obnoxious, etc.), but I'm not." (2) Disliking similar *negative others* may be a way of reducing the disturbing anxiety that we may have more in common with stupid or mentally ill or obnoxious persons than we care to admit. For example, the existence of a similar, emotionally disturbed person may be threatening because it implies that one harbors the seeds of mental illness oneself. Or if someone similar to us does something stupid or behaves obnoxiously, we may have a lingering fear that we could act similarly. Not liking certain similar *negative others* may help a person reduce these fears by enabling him or her to feel somewhat superior or at least above the sort of undesirable behavior seen in others.

All in all, research findings related to why we like or don't like persons similar to us indicate that similarity cuts both ways; that is, similar others are evaluated more positively *and* more negatively than dissimilar others. We welcome with open arms those fine and noble persons who are similar to us because they remind us of our own real or imagined good qualities and virtuous characteristics. We are somewhat wary, however, of intellectually, emotionally, or socially flawed individuals who are attitudinally similar to us, because they may remind us of real or imagined shortcomings in ourselves that we may prefer not to see.

Reflections

Can you think of people or groups of people with whom, although you share certain common attitudes, you would not care to be associated? Why? Your response to this question may help you to understand, in a deeper way, what we've just been talking about.

From what's been stated so far, you might reasonably conclude that birds of a feather *do* flock together. And you would be right—for the most part, they do. But what about the old idea that opposites are attracted to each other? The answer to that is probably best expressed along the following lines.

Opposites Do Attract—But It Depends on How They Are Opposite

When we hear that two people complement each other, we usually understand this to mean that, when they bring their different needs or characteristics together, they help each other to feel, and to appear, more complete, more rounded. To the extent that this happens, opposites may indeed be attracted to each other. But it isn't all that simple, because whether opposites attract or birds of a feather flock together very likely depends on the personality characteristics under consideration. For example, an outgoing, high-energy person may not get along too well with an inward, low-energy individual whose idea of excitement is to watch TV. Or a person who places a premium or orderliness and neatness may be disinclined to live with someone who is generally unkempt and sloppy. Being opposite in ways like these is not apt to draw people together, but rather to keep them at a distance—at least for any kind of long-term living arrangement.

On the other hand, if we look at a person's deeper personality traits, rather than just at surface characteristics, then a different picture emerges. For instance, a person who is somewhat dependent and emotionally needy would no doubt be quite happy in a relationship with a highly nurturing, giving person.

There is evidence to support the idea of this kind of complementarity. Sociologist Robert Winch,[55] for example, studied the personality characteristics of engaged and married couples, and he found that there was a tendency for opposites to attract—that is, for people to choose people whose deeper needs and basic characteristics complemented (rather than coincided with) their own needs and characteristics. Other research has shown that a man and a woman who have opposite sex-role attitudes are more likely to be attracted to each other than if they have similar sex-role attitudes.[56, 57] For instance, a man who has a strong need to dominate is likely to be attracted to women who have a need to be submissive and dominated. The same holds true for such polar opposites as masculinity–feminity, and assertiveness–passivity. In my clinical work, I have seen example after example of what sometimes happens in love relationships when one of the partners—usually the woman—stops being opposite to the man in terms of passivity or submissiveness and becomes more assertive or dominant. Some men get frightened and quit the relationship; others applaud her spirited attitude and find her a more exciting person. Suffice it to say, if either partner in a relationship is intolerant of changes in the other, if there is a shift in the emotional balance of power, then the relationship may be in trouble.

You may be interested to know that, when it comes to love relationships, the roles of similarity and complementarity are both important—but at different stages. For example, research by Kerckhoff and Davis[58] has shown that similarity of values, attitudes, and social-status variables such as religion and socioeconomic position are most important during the *early* phases of a relationship. That is, similarity of these variables serves as a good predictor of whether or not a relationship is apt to continue. However, for couples who have been together for a long time (over 7 months, in this case), complementarity is the best predictor of whether the relationship will continue. In other words, similarities seem important in drawing couples together during the early phases of a relationship and complementary needs play an increasingly important part *after* the relationship becomes more established.

The findings growing out of E. Lowell Kelley's[59] longitudinal investigation of several hundred couples over a 20-year period shed some interesting light on the functions of similarity and complementarity in marriage relationships. One of the major findings of this study was that men and women who made successful marriages were similar enough in important ways to satisfy each other physically and mentally, but were also sufficiently different to be interesting and challenging to each other. Kelley further observed that one of the factors that make marriages successful is the ability to find ways of balancing the need for "the security of being similar" with the need for "the novelty of being different." As you might imagine, these needs varied greatly from one couple to another. A notable characteristic of successful couples, however, was their ability to maintain *both* their similarities and differences throughout the life of the marriage. They accomplished this by flexibly adapting to changes in their partners, as opposed to rigidly clinging to old ways of thinking and doing things. For example, if the wife changed her ideas about a woman's role to a more liberated position, the husband might shift just enough to maintain the original difference in their views. If the husband changed his political stance over the years, the wife might move just enough in the same direction to keep the similarity between their attitudes about the same as it had always been.

Just as we tend to like people who are like us—usually—and are drawn to certain others who have opposite characteristics, it is also generally true to say the following.

We Like People Who Like Us

One of the most powerful considerations influencing whether we like someone or not is whether that person likes us. It seems a simple, verifiable social truism: we like people who like us. And why not? In terms of reinforcement theory, it is likely to be rewarding; in terms of exchange theory, we are likely to profit from the relationship; in terms of equity theory, we are likely to maximize our chances for a fair and equitable interpersonal bond. We know from personal experience that it is almost impossible not to have some kind of positive response or warm feeling to the news that someone likes us.

The inclination to reciprocate liking was cleverly demonstrated by Carl Backman and Paul Secord[60] in a study designed to find out how people behaved when they thought certain other people liked them. They had the participants in their study meet as a group of strangers, and then each member of the group was told that prior test information (actually rigged by the researchers) indicated that specific members of the group were likely to like them. The researchers informed them that they might eventually be divided into two-person groups and asked them to indicate three other members with whom they would most prefer to work. The entire group continued to meet for six sessions and "partner preference" rankings were taken again at the end of the third and sixth sessions. The results clearly indicated that after the first session, but not after later sessions, the subjects chose as their partners those who had been designated as likely to like them. However, this preference pattern broke down by the third group meeting. By then, group members were no more likely to choose expected "likers" than other persons in the group as a discussion partner. In a more controlled way, this research underscores what we have learned from experience; when we hear that someone likes us, we are inclined to return the feeling, at least initially. But, as the Backman and Secord study demonstrates, whether we *continue* to like someone who likes us depends on our actual interactions with that person. Knowing that a person likes us, or even loves us, may be enough to start a relationship, but it is seldom enough, it seems, to keep a relationship going.

We can get an even clearer idea of why being liked is so important by looking at what happens to people when they're *not* liked. Daniel Geller and his associates[61] did an interesting study along this line by arranging discussions among different groups, each made up of three women, two of whom were accomplices of the researchers. In half of the groups, the accomplices were instructed to essentially ignore the third woman by looking at her and responding to her only minimally, and in addition, by changing the topic whenever she said anything. In the other half of the groups, no such efforts were made. Under one condition, women were made to feel unliked and unwanted, and under the other, women were made to feel liked and recognized. Predictably, the ignored women who felt disliked hardly spoke at all in their groups and afterward described themselves in negative, unhappy terms—withdrawn, alone, anxious, bored, and uninteresting. There is, as you can see, considerable personal pain associated with not being liked, which is a powerful motivation for liking those who like us—we not only avoid pain, but we experience pleasure.

Reflections

Think a moment. What TV commercials can you think of that play on and even exploit the need to be liked, accepted, recognized, and approved? For example, ads that suggest that if you purchase and use a certain product, then people will like you better and approve of you more?

But Sometimes We Don't Like People Who Like Us—Some Cases in Point

There are basically two conditions in which we may find ourselves putting the brakes on when it comes to automatically liking someone who gives the appearance of liking us: (1) when we think the other person is trying to get something from us and (2) when the praise or feedback we receive is greatly different from our own self-estimation. If, for instance, we suspect that the person who professes to like us has some ulterior motives in mind, we may feel appropriately wary of his or her positive regard. For example, the salesperson who fawns all over us is probably more interested in his or her sales records than in us as persons, and we know it. The person who praises indiscriminately or who doles out unconditional positive regard to everyone may be more interested in being liked than in being honest, and we know it.

A word of caution here. Sometimes we may *not* know it. You may recall from an earlier discussion in this chapter that people with low self-esteem are more inclined to uncritically accept the good will of others because it is missing in themselves. Hence, it may make less difference to a low-self-esteem individual whether or not the positive regard he or she gets from others to motivated by ulterior reasons. (A starving person is not likely to be particularly concerned about the motivations of his or her provider.)

With regard to the second point mentioned above, we may be somewhat suspicious of persons whose praise exceeds our own self-perceptions. For example, if we view ourselves as being somewhat below average on a scale of physical attractiveness, being called beautiful or handsome will probably be heard as insincere flattery, whether it is intended as such or not. If we see ourselves as being of quite average intelligence and someone labels us as brilliant, we may feel a strong urge to pull away rather than to get closer—for at least two reasons: (1) we may fear one's judgment when he or she finds out we *aren't* so brilliant, and/or (2) we may fear having to live up to unreal expectations. In any case, if we suspect the other person wants something from us or if his or her feedback is vastly different from our own self-perceptions, then we may attribute all sorts of ulterior motives to his or her behavior: we may conclude that he or she is sarcastic, dishonest, manipulative, patronizing, or even stupid—which could reduce our liking for him or her.

Research literature[62, 63] suggests that we are more likely to be attracted to those who like us and "have nothing to gain" than to those who like us, but who may profit in some way from liking us. (From the point of view of reinforcement theory, being liked by those who have something to gain is not rewarding to us, and from an equity theory angle, it is not particularly fair.) Dickoff[64] conducted an interesting study that demonstrated the dynamics at work here by having women students listen to evaluations of themselves delivered by an accomplice of his who had watched each woman being interviewed through a one-way mirror. The evaluations were rigged so that some women were evaluated positively, some were evaluated negatively, and still others received essentially neutral evaluations. Under one condition of the study, the subjects were told that the evaluator was trying to be as accurate and honest as possible. Under another condition, the subjects were led to believe that the evaluator was going to ask them to participate in one of her own studies after the current experiment was over—in other words, the idea of an ulterior motive was planted. The results quite clearly showed that the feedback the subjects received strongly influenced their attraction to the evaluator. As you may suspect, the subjects liked those evaluators who praised them better than those who gave them negative feedback, but there was a sharp drop in how much they liked the positive evaluator with the ulterior motive. In fact, when the possibility of an ulterior motive was present, attraction went down as praise went up.

In sum, we generally like people who like us, but we're far less apt to do so if we feel that they like us for ulterior reasons. For instance, although we might ordinarily be attracted to people who continually agree with our views, and to those who use our first name in the course of a conversation, research indicates that we feel far less positive about people who do these things when we know that they have something to gain from the relationship.[65, 66]

At this point, you may be wondering, "How can I ever be sure that the person I'm complimenting or praising or being friendly to won't think I'm doing it for some ulterior reason?" That's something you'll never know for sure. Some people are chronically suspicious and may doubt any good-faith effort on our part to give them something positive. Most of us, however, like to be liked and are discriminating enough to tell the difference between a sincere compliment and manipulative flattery. If you are interested in minimizing the possibility of being viewed as a person with ulterior motives yourself, there is a basic principle to extract from all of this that may be helpful: Don't be positive and complimentary only when you want something from another person. Rather, let your positive feedback become a natural part of your ongoing interactions, which includes as much a willingness to share constructive criticism, gently given, as it does a willingness to share honest compliments, sincerely expressed.

There is something else that can attract us to others, and it is directly related to the idea of openness and honesty that we've just been discussing.

We Like People Who Disclose Themselves to Us—With a Few Exceptions

There is something particularly rewarding about conversing with people who seem willing and able to reveal something of themselves to us.

Reflections

Before reading further, consider a few questions. What kind of people do you find yourself attracted to—those who continually focus on small talk and issues pretty much outside of themselves or those who share something of their own inner feelings? What is your own style in this regard? How do you feel about people who seem ready to divulge their inner workings and private lives before you've gotten to know them very well? How would you rate yourself on your ability and willingness to disclose your inner self to others? How do you think that your disclosure —or lack of it—affects whether or not people are attracted to you?

An interesting cycle of mutual trust and reciprocal liking is set in motion when I tell you something of myself. This usually makes it easier for you to tell me something of yourself, which helps me to be more open with you, and you with me, and so on throughout our relationship. A cycle of this sort typically increases the attraction between two people, because it is a sign that each trusts the other; that is, each trusts the other not to misuse or abuse the information so that the other person is hurt in some way. In the absence of trust, there is little in the way of self-disclosure. On the other hand, in the absence of self-disclosure, there can be little in the way of trust. When either one of these two key elements is missing between two people—or among a group of people, for that matter—it is not likely that much more than a superficial relationship will develop.

Ralph Waldo Emerson once observed: "A friend is a person with whom I may be sincere. Before him, I may think aloud." There is, no doubt, considerable truth in that statement. But there is more to it than is immediately apparent. That is, our friends are our friends not only because we can be sincere and think aloud to them, but also because they can be sincere and think aloud *to us*. In other words, our good friend is not only willing to listen to our tales of joy and woe, but is also willing to bend our ear from time to time. Psychological research[67, 68, 69] has shown time and again that this sort of reciprocity and mutuality of disclosure is necessary for a strong and enduring attraction to develop between two people. As suggested by Irwin Altman and Dalmas Taylor,[70] reciprocity builds trust, and the mutuality of disclosure continues until a level of intimacy is reached that satisfies a particular relationship. For example, we may be inclined to reveal more about our private lives to a loved one than to a casual friend. The conclusion from both research and theory is that self-disclosure, reciprocally given and mutually received, is necessary for a high level of attraction. This may help explain why some people who would like more friends, but don't have many, find themselves in that spot. It's not that they're *unwilling to listen to others,* but they may be *unwilling to say much about themselves,* which could have the effect of making their relationships seem more like one-way streets than two-way exchanges.

Although it is generally true that we are attracted to people who are able to disclose themselves to us, there are moments when disclosures can have precisely the opposite effect. One of those moments has to do with the *timing* of material disclosed. An individual, for example, who jumps in with deep self-revelations early in a relationship is apt to be viewed as immature, insecure, and even something of a phony. Research[71, 72] indicates that the *timing* of a person's self-disclosure can greatly affect how he or she is accepted by another person. When we hear people make highly self-revealing remarks to us early in a conversation, we may suspect that this has less to do with their motivation for developing a relationship and more to do, perhaps, with their insecurities and need for attention. On the other hand, if someone makes a self-disclosing comment after getting to know us, we are more likely to take the remark personally and infer that it has possible implications for developing a relationship.

Another factor that may make us wary of a person's disclosures is the amount of self-revelation. People who disclose *too much* are apt to be as much of a bore as those who disclose too little. For example, Doug Daher and Paul Banikiotes[73] have shown in their research that people are most attracted to those who come reasonably close to matching them in *how much* they disclose and who are similar as to *what* they disclose.

Reflections

Are you a self-disclosing person or do you see yourself as more of a self-containing sort? Perhaps you could collect a little research data in the next week or so by deliberately revealing more of your inner self to people in your day-to-day interactions. How will those interactions be affected? How will people feel about you? How will *you* feel about you? It might be interesting to find out. If you would like to know more about the psychology of self-disclosure, you will find Sidney Jourard's, *The Transparent Self,* (revised) (Van Nostrand, 1971) helpful and informative reading.

Synopsis and Overview

There are many working parts involved in the machinery of interpersonal attraction. Some of the important ones that stand out as factors influencing whom we're attracted to and whom we like include the following:

1. We like competent people who are good at what they do, but we are particularly drawn to them when they don't seem to be so perfect as to be more god-like than human-like. Apparently, when competent people blunder, we understand this fact in them just as we do in ourselves, which makes them seem not so much unlike us after all. So, if you're inclined to project (and perhaps

protect) the image of the perfect person who's got it all together, you may not only find yourself with fewer problems, but with fewer friends as well.

2. We are attracted to physically attractive people. This is a process that is apparent even among nursery school youngsters, who tend to like their better-looking peers more than their less attractive peers. People who present a "pleasing appearance," however you define this—perhaps by virtue of sheer physical beauty and/or by the kind of clothes they wear and how they wear them—are considered to be more happy, more able, and more socially skilled than less attractive persons. There is, however, truth in the old adage about beauty being only skin deep. In the final analysis, it is what is inside a person, and not on the outside, that makes the greatest difference.

3. We are attracted to people who are similar to us in terms of basic attitudes and values. Being around people who are similar to us is more rewarding, it involves fewer hassles, and it reduces the possibilities of having to change basic attitudes and behaviors, something that most people tend to resist strongly. On the other hand, we are not likely to be attracted to stupid or obnoxious persons who may otherwise be similar to us, because we don't want to be associated with their negative characteristics.

4. There is a modicum of truth to the idea that opposites are attracted to each other. However, a successful long-term attraction of opposites is more likely to happen when there is a merger of deeper complementary traits, rather than opposite surface behaviors. For example, a slob and a compulsive housecleaner may not make it as roommates or marriage partners. On the other hand, a bossy person and a submissive individual may get along just fine.

5. If we hear from person A that person B likes us, our almost automatic response is to like person B in return. We like people who like us. But whether we *continue* to like them depends on what happens once a relationship is started.

6. We are not inclined to like people who like us, if we feel they are trying to manipulate us or get something from us, or if we feel that the feedback we're getting from them is too different from our own self-estimates. We want to be liked for who we are and not for what we may be able to do for another person.

7. We like people who disclose themselves to us. We feel we can do the same with them, and it is an important way to develop a feeling of trust—a state of feeling that is absolutely necessary in deeper relationships. Timing is an important aspect of the disclosure process. Revealing too much of our deeper self too early in a relationship is more apt to be seen as a display of exhibitionistic self-centeredness than as a sincere sharing of inner feelings with a trusted friend. Self-disclosure is as much a *consequence* of trust as it is a *cause* of it. Easing into it, rather than jumping into it, is probably the wisest course to follow.

This has been a look at some of the major factors about others that can influence whom we're attracted to, and some of the reasons why. The next step is to look at what happens after we're attracted to another person—or not attracted, as the case may be—in order to understand how this may affect specific behaviors.

WAYS OUR BEHAVIOR CAN BE AFFECTED BY PEOPLE WE LIKE

Once we feel attracted to another person, there are changes not only in how we feel about that person, but also in how we behave toward him or her. Our shifts in behavior are not always dramatic and obvious, but frequently subtle and subliminal. Consider some examples of the sorts of things we are inclined to do naturally and unconsciously when we feel attracted to others:

1. The more we like a person, the more often we will look directly at that person as we interact with him or her.[74, 75] Conversely, the more another person looks directly at us, the more apt we are to conclude that that person feels positively toward us.[76,77] It may not surprise you to know that a woman is more likely than a man to experience direct eye contact as pleasant and intimate.[78] Men also like direct eye contact but can get uncomfortable with it more easily than women.

2. When we are with people we like, we are inclined to feel and look more relaxed, to communicate better, and even to laugh more frequently.[79] This idea of feeling good and communicating with greater ease when we're with people we like has important educational implications when it is paired with research that points to the fact that when students are in an atmosphere of mutuality and friendship, their learning is enhanced.[80, 81]

3. The more we like a person, the closer we will sit or stand next to that person.[82, 83] In addition, Albert Mehrabian's research[84, 85, 86] indicates that there are subtle body language cues that we use quite unconsciously, and which reflect our basic feelings toward others. For example, Mehrabian's findings suggest that when we like the person to whom we are talking, we unwittingly tilt the direction of our head, the position of our arms, the lean of our torso, and the orientation of our shoulders toward that person. In other words, we unconsciously move toward a person we like in a variety of subtle ways, as if to say, without words, "I want to be closer to you." An interesting footnote worth adding here, from the work of Paul Ekman and Wallace Friesen,[87] is that, while people are generally unaware of their own body language, they feel that the body cues transmitted by others are intentional and consciously motivated. It would be an education, indeed, to see ourselves as others see us.

Reflections

You may learn a great deal by observing the body language expressed between persons who like each other as opposed to those who don't particularly care for each other. Pay particular attention to this in the next several days. What do you note in yourself in this regard, when you are with people you like or don't like? What differences do you see in same-sex and opposite-sex nonverbal interactions between others and between yourself and others?

You can see that liking or not liking a person affects not only how we *think* about him or her, but also—many times unconsciously—how we *behave* toward that individual. Earlier in this chapter we developed the idea that physical attractiveness is a factor that plays a part—an important part, it turns out—in influencing whom we're attracted to. How does physical attractiveness influence how we *behave* toward the "beautiful people" in our lives?

WAYS THAT PHYSICAL ATTRACTIVENESS CAN INFLUENCE OUR BEHAVIOR

Physical attractiveness is a double-edged personal attribute. As suggested in a review of research by Glenn Wilson and David Nias,[88] attractive people are perceived as kinder, stronger, more interesting, more poised, more sociable, and sexier than unattractive people. On the other hand, those very qualities are the ones that Marshall Dermer and Darrel Thiel[89] say lead many people to conclude that attractive people are vain, egotistical, snobbish, and more likely to experience marital disasters and have extramarital affairs. Although we may attribute certain haughty attitudes to attractive people, the evidence still points to the idea that we like to be associated with people who exceed our own level of self-perceived attractiveness.[90] Physical beauty is apparently not something we are inclined to be neutral about. It affects our behavior, for better or worse, in rather specific ways. Consider some examples.

A Man May Strive Harder to Prove Himself to a Beautiful Woman Who Evaluates Him Negatively

Embedded in our social folklore is the idea that a beautiful woman can pretty much wrap a man around her little finger. The results that Harold Sigall and Elliot Aronson[91] found in a cleverly designed research effort showed that there may be some truth to this.

Psychologists Sigall and Aronson had a group of college men interviewed by a woman who was made to appear physically attractive in one phase of the study and physically unattractive in the second phase. They worked with a naturally beautiful woman; in the unattractive phase, they gave her a somewhat oily complexion, dressed her in sloppy clothes, and had her wear a frizzy, blond wig. Posing as a graduate student in clinical psychology, first as a beautiful woman and then as a "not-so-beautiful" woman, she conducted the interviews with groups of college men. Under each of these conditions, half of the men received highly favorable evaluations and the other half highly unfavorable evaluations. How did the men respond? When the woman was homely, the men were somewhat indifferent to whether they received good or poor evaluations and, in both cases, they liked her a fair amount. However, when she was beautiful, they liked her a great deal when they got favorable evaluations, but when they got unfavorable evaluations, they disliked her more than under the other conditions. But there was also another very interesting finding. Although the men who were evaluated negatively by the beautiful woman said they didn't like her, they nonetheless expressed considerable interest in talking to her again in a future experiment! Apparently, the negative feedback from the attractive woman was so important (or perhaps so threatening) that they wanted the opportunity to try to change her mind.

Reflections

What other reasons can you think of that a man should want to return to a beautiful woman who evaluates him negatively? Is ego involved? Do you suppose women evaluated negatively by an attractive man would respond in the same way?

Offender Attractiveness Can Influence Our Judgment of the Crime

Although justice is supposed to be blind, there is evidence to suggest that beauty may affect the final verdict. And it may affect the verdict even when children as young as seven years of age are involved. Karen Dion[92] discovered this when she gave two hundred women written descriptions of alleged misbehaviors commited either by a seven-year-old boy or girl, along with a photograph clipped to the corner of the description. When the report included a photograph of an attractive child, the women were inclined to excuse the misdeed or see it as an isolated accident. But when the same report came with a photograph of an unattractive child, the raters were inclined to assume that the naughtiness was a typical incident and a reflection of generally bad behavior. While the attractive child was still seen as charming or cute, in spite of misbehaving, an unattractive child, with the same misbehavior attributed to him or her, received comments such as: "I think she would be quite bratty and troublesome to teachers . . . would probably try to pick fights . . . all in all, a real problem." Whereas the misbehavior of attractive children was viewed as being caused more by the situation and circumstances, the misconduct of unattractive children was more apt to be attributed to flaws in their personalities.

There is also evidence to suggest that we're more merciful to attractive adults, who may stand accused of more serious matters. Clarence Darrow once said, "Juries seldom convict a person they like or acquit one they dislike . . . facts regarding the crime are relatively unimportant." There may be some truth to this. For example, Michael Efran[93] asked subjects to decide the fate of a defendant in a college cheating case and found that the physically attractive people who allegedly cheated were liked better, judged less guilty, and received less severe punishments than defendants who were unattractive.

When the attractiveness variable is taken into account, justice may even be affected in the courts. As a test of this, Harold Sigall and Nancy Ostrove[94] asked 120 male and female college students to read the account of a crime committed by a woman, whose picture was attached, and then suggest an appropriate punishment for the offender. One group of students read a report in which the guilty woman was depicted in a photograph as beautiful; another group saw the same account, but with a picture attached where the guilty woman was made to look homely; still another group of students dealt out sentences without knowing what the defendant looked like.

An analysis of the suggested punishment revealed that at least the lack of beauty didn't *increase* the length of sentence; that is, the homely offender fared no worse than her anonymous counterpart. The attractive woman, however, did get special treatment. When the crime was a $2200 burglary, she got off easy, but when the crime involved inducing a middle-aged bachelor to invest $2200 in a nonexistent organization, beauty hurt her case. In this instance, the attractive woman received a slightly stiffer sentence than either the homely woman or the anonymous defendant. In other words, if attractive women use their looks to help them commit a crime, their beauty will hurt them in court. In other cases, their attractiveness may help shorten their prison stay. Physical attractiveness *can* work in an offender's favor—which is, of course, why lawyers like the defendants they represent to look their best in court—but it can also work to the detriment of the accused if that person is viewed as having used his or her beauty in devious ways for illicit gains. (If you're thinking about a criminal career, you may be well advised first of all to check yourself out in the mirror so you can see what the jury will see in the event things don't go well for you.)

Not only do attractive people get breaks in the courtroom, but in the schoolroom as well.

Teachers Tend to Favor Good-Looking Students

An attractive student, it seems, has a better chance of being the teacher's pet than other students. Not only do we generally like attractive people more, but if we're teachers, we may also evaluate students' behavior based on their attractiveness. Margaret Clifford and Elaine Walster[95] found evidence for this when they gave 400 fifth-grade teachers the same report card to evaluate. Sometimes the card was accompanied by a photograph of an attractive youngster; other times it carried the photograph of a plain child. The results clearly indicated that when the child was good-looking, the teachers were more apt to guess that he or she had a higher I.Q., had parents who were interested in his or her education, and got along better with his or her peers than did less attractive children.

These results are generally consistent with Richard and Jacqueline Lerner's[96] research conclusions, which showed that, for a group of 104 fourth- and sixth-graders, good looks, good grades, and high ratings from both teachers and classmates tended to go together. A correlational study of this sort cannot tell us what is cause and what is effect, but it does underscore the idea that attractiveness and good grades were related.

David Landy and Harold Sigall[97] looked at the cause-and-effect issue by examining the relationship between a woman's attractiveness and the way others rated her work. They prepared two essays, one well-written, the other poorly-written and simplistic in its ideas. They made thirty copies of each essay and attached pictures, supposedly of the author, to twenty of each: ten pictures were of an attractive woman, ten pictures of an unattractive woman. Ten essays in each group had no picture. These were then graded by sixty male college students. The results? Attractive writers swept the ratings across the board, and they far surpassed the unattractive writers when the poor essay was judged. In other words, the same essay tended to get higher marks when it was accompanied by a photograph of an attractive woman than when the presumed author was plain.

SOME SUGGESTIONS FOR ENCOURAGING MUTUAL LIKING

Embedded in our discussion of the determinants and the effects of interpersonal attraction is the underlying theme that suggests that it is desirable and healthy to like and to be liked, undesirable and unhealthy to dislike and to be disliked. Research[98] is rather clear in helping us to understand that liked persons are generally evaluated more positively than disliked persons, and, further, that liked persons have a more positive effect on both the work performance and attitudes of others than do disliked persons. Each of us has no doubt learned from our personal experiences that likable people are pleasant to be with; they help us feel good about ourselves, each other, and life in general. Think of any essentially negative, unlikable person you know, and you will have a quick idea of the emotional difference between being with someone you like and someone you don't like. The question, then, is what can we do to encourage mutual liking in order to enhance positive connections between ourselves and others? Some suggestions:

1. We can begin with the conscious awareness that very likely there is more to *every* person we know than meets the eye. If we begin with this premise, we may be more motivated to get to know people more than superficially. Attraction research[99, 100] suggests that the more we know a person, the more difficult it is to dislike that person. Knowing increases understanding and empathy, which usually increase acceptance and liking.

2. We can allow others to know us more deeply, particularly those to whom we want to be closer. Self-disclosure enhances trust, which is the foundation of mutual liking. We can praise others, but we would be wise to exercise caution and not overdo it. Research in this area points out that, although people like to be praised and tend to like the praiser, they also dislike the feeling of being manipulated if the praise is too lavish, or if it seems unwarranted.[101]

3. Doing favors for others is generally a good way to generate positive feelings, but it also keeps a relationship lopsided *if we're always the ones doing the giving.* There is research[102] to show that asking someone to do *us* a favor is a more certain way to use favors to increase mutual liking. It's a way of saying, "I trust you enough to do this for me." We like to be trusted. And more particularly, we like people who trust us.

Some people we like and other people we love, which brings us to an important consideration.

WHEN INTERPERSONAL ATTRACTION GOES BEYOND LIKING: THE NATURE OF LOVE

For most people, "liking" someone or "loving" someone signify quite different emotional states and personal sentiments. When we talk about liking someone, we're usually referring to the affection we feel for casual acquaintances and good friends. When we love someone, however, we usually feel more emotionally involved with that person and have a greater investment in the relationship. Probably the only real difference between liking someone and loving someone is the depth of our feelings and the degree of our attachment to another person. The deeper and more profound the feeling, the more likely it is that what we are experiencing is this thing we call love.

There are many different expressions of love and, as lucidly discussed in psychoanalyst Erich Fromm's classic book, *The Art of Loving,*[103] these range from parental love, to brotherly love, to romantic love, to self-love, to love of God. Each of these expressions is different and, indeed, there are probably as many different individual expressions as there are different kinds of people. Each love relationship is different and each has its own rules of behavior. The kind of love we will focus on is romantic love, since it is most closely associated with the interpersonal attraction processes with which we're concerned in this chapter. What is it? What causes it? What determines who we love? Does love change?

Perhaps the place to begin is with a very basic question.

What Is Romantic Love?

Of all the emotions we are capable of feeling, romantic love is probably the most complex. It has different meanings for different people, and its emotional content varies from person to person. For one person, it is the feeling of intense excitement associated with being physically and emotionally close to someone; for another person, it is the feeling of quiet security associated with being in a stable, predictable relationship. It depends on the person and *what that person wants from the relationship.* Knowing what your partner wants from the relationship will give you a good idea of what he or she is willing to give to it.

Reflections

You may want to think about this for a moment. Why do you suppose the meaning of a romantic love relationship varies with what a person wants from that relationship? How will knowing what your partner wants from the relationship help you understand what he or she will give to it? How does what *you* want from a love relationship influence what you give to it?

Romantic love can be expressed in two quite different forms: passionate love and companionate love. Elaine Walster and G. William Walster (wife and husband, by the way) have concluded from their research that passionate love " . . . is a wildly emotional state, a confusion of feelings: tenderness and sexuality, elation and pain, anxiety and relief, altruism and anxiety. Companionate love, on the other hand, is a lower-key emotion. It's friendly affection and a deep attachment to someone."[104]

As you might suspect, passionate love, characterized by its ups and downs, its sexual vitality, its competitive edge, its jealous eye, and its strong emotional overtones, does not last long. There are at least three good reasons for this: (1) Its high level of emotional intensity is, although exciting, an exhausting activity, (2) the novelty of it is, to some extent, lost in time, because of repeated exposure, and (3) perhaps most important, both our bodies and minds change, and these changes may affect our once passionate feelings.

Most couples in romantic relationships go through stages of liking each other, loving each other, and then being more or less passionately involved with each other during the early phases of their love relationship. If the basis for their attraction to each other is primarily a physical one, the relationship inevitably cools and grows boring as the delights that once fueled its passion dim, flicker, change, or disappear altogether. Teen-agers and young adults seem especially vulnerable to the error of confusing sexual knowledge of their partners for personal knowledge. If one believes that physical intimacy is an ultimate and final way of knowing the other person, you may see how this could have the effect of blocking further efforts to know and experience one's partner in a greater variety of ways. Thus, for some, when sexual interests wane, the relationship may cool and eventually die, if no other interests have been developed to help give the relationship other sources of energy, purpose, and emotional content.

Of course, not all passionate love relationships terminate because sexual attraction dims, with nothing to replace it. Charles T. Hill, Zick Rubin, and Letitia A. Peplau[105] studied 231 college couples for 2 years and found a wide range of reasons why 103 of those couples broke up during that 2-year period: differences in intelligence and interests; conflicts about dependence and independence; differences about how much romance was enough romance; and, in some cases, meeting someone new and presumedly more appealing. You may be interested—and surprised—to learn that research indicates that men tend to fall in love more quickly and out of love more slowly than women. However, when the passionate

©1971 United Feature Syndicate, Inc.

No one ever said that love is easy to understand.

phase of the relationship is most dominant, women are likely to experience the peaks and valleys of love more intensely than men. Furthermore, women are usually the ones who determine when a relationship should be terminated, whereas men seem more willing to stick it out to the bitter end. When the dust finally settles, it is the men who tend to feel more depressed, more lonely, and less happy after a breakup, which may help explain why three times as many men as women commit suicide after a disastrous love affair.[106, 107]

Reflections

Why do you suppose men tend to fall in love more quickly and out of love more slowly than women? Why do you suppose they suffer more than women after a relationship ends? Women, apparently, pick up the pieces better. How would you explain this?

Passionate relationships don't always end when the flame cools. They can grow into the next phase of romantic love known as companionate love, which psychologist Theodore Reik has described as "A new kind of companionship . . .[in which] the lover has changed into a friend . . .[and in which] there is . . . the peacefulness of tender attachment."[108] This doesn't mean that companionate love is without its more passionate moments. Research[109, 110, 111] shows that passionate love does not disappear with time; it simply decreases and changes over the years. What seems to happen is that the primary basis for attraction shifts from sexual intimacy and passionate togetherness to a deeper emotional commitment and companionate sharing.

All in all, the research findings and clinical observations related to romantic love suggest that it can last a lifetime, but that the nature of love may be changed by time. Passion, intense communication, and high levels of self-disclosure are most important during the early phases of a love relationship, while companionate love, with its sense of tenderness, loyalty, commitment, and deeper sharing develops more slowly over time.

Whereas passionate love tends to lose some of its zest with time, companionate love does not. The person who listened to us, who bolstered our self-esteem when it was shaky, who loved us when we didn't love ourselves, who shared some of our basic attitudes and interests, and who helped us achieve some of the goals we thought were important continues to be appreciated—and loved—long after the honeymoon is over and the bells have stopped ringing.

Which brings us to a logical question: What determines to whom we are attracted in a love relationship?

FACTORS THAT INFLUENCE OUR CHOICES FOR LOVE RELATIONSHIPS

Probably the most important factors affecting to whom we're attracted for dates and mates are our expectations for that person. Most of us are inclined to view our expectations for a partner as reasonable, attainable, and even a bit modest. "I ask for very little," we say. "All I want is to love someone and have someone love me."

Ah, were our hopes *really* that modest. Because the moment we start getting into the specifics, the "little" we claim to be seeking has a good many more fringe attachments than may be apparent at first glance. We want a nice-looking person, a successful person—or one who is promisingly so, a sensitive person, a person who devotes a lot of time to us, a person with intelligence and a sense of humor, and, perhaps most of all, a person who is tolerant, accepting—forgiving even— of our more obvious flaws and shortcomings. Although seldom aware of it, perfection is what we really want.

Reflections

You may be thinking, "That's not true. I'm really an accepting, flexible individual in search of a good partner, not a perfect one." Maybe. Let me suggest a small "field" research project you can carry out in the next several days. As you go through your daily activities, make it a point to observe closely *everyone* you encounter—at work, in class, in stores, on the bus, and so forth. Take some mental notes. Keep a running tally of the number of men or women you would be willing to date. How fussy are you? Try it and find out.

There Are Certain Cultural Dictates

Every culture transmits its own particular criteria as to whom its members should consider for dates and mates. And most of us, without really thinking about it, stick reasonably close to those cultural dictates when it comes to considering romantic possibilities. For example, most of us want partners of the opposite sex who are approximately our own age. In addition, we prefer them to be of our own race, educational level, socioeconomic class, and religion. If you're a woman, you probably prefer a man taller than you, and if you're a man, you generally feel more comfortable with a woman a bit shorter than you. You can see how these preliminary considerations cut out a surprising number of candidates.

We Have an Eye for People Who Are Similar to Us

Actually, it is a good thing that we do look for a person with whom we have as much in common as possible. It enhances the possibilities for having mutual interests to talk about and for sharing various activities, which help to nurture the roots of companionate love and assist in keeping the embers of passionate love warm and ready. Social science research helps us see that we tend to look for partners who approximate our own social and educational values,[112] and who are more like us than unlike us in basic personality needs.[113] Indeed, the more successful we are in achieving these ends, the more likely it is that the relationship will last a longer time.

Equity in Relationships Is Important

Of course, not all couples are neatly matched in all areas. There are some remarkable mismatches—we can probably all think of some. Ellen Berscheid and her colleagues[114] found in their research that if couples were markedly mismatched in one dimension—say, physical appearance, there would probably have to be a compensating mismatch in other areas in order for the relationship to last. For example, the men and women who were more physically attractive than their partners felt that their partners' assets—being unusually loving, or giving, or in some cases, rich—balance things out. On the other hand, if men and women saw themselves as less good-looking than their partners, they were inclined to view themselves as the ones with the compensating assets. It is this ability to compensate—to make up the difference—that enables mismatched couples to feel that each partner is both getting and giving a fair deal—a crucial prerequisite for sustaining a love relationship. This is an important factor because, as discovered by Elaine Walster and her colleagues[115] in interviews with over 600 dating, married, and living-together couples, those couples who were most content, happy, and sexually satisfied were in reasonably equitable relationships. The discontent that can grow from unequal relationships can go both ways. For example, men and women who felt they were getting *less* than they deserved were, as you might suspect, a lot less content and happy. But so, too, were those who felt they were getting far *more* than they deserved. Those who got less than they deserved felt angry about it, while those who got more than they deserved felt guilty about it. (It would appear that if you're *too* good to your partner, you're really not doing him or her any great favor.)

Self-Esteem Makes a Difference

Self-esteem is another factor that can influence our choices for love relationships. You may recall from our earlier discussion in this chapter about self-esteem that interpersonal attraction can vary with how people feel about themselves, as well as how they feel about each other. We saw an example of how this works in Sara Kiesler and Roberta Baral's[116] research. They found that men with high self-esteem were more romantic toward attractive women, while men with low self-esteem were more romantic toward unattractive women. Apparently, people react more romantically toward the kind of person they think, for better or worse, they deserve.

Reflections

How does this square with your own life experiences? Have you ever caught yourself yearning for someone you felt you just didn't deserve? What relationships do you see between your feelings of self-esteem and the romantic choices you have made in your life?

Not only does our self-esteem affect how we feel about others, but these feelings about ourselves—whether we have basically a positive attitude or dark misgivings —inevitably color our perceptions of how others feel about us. For example, high-self-esteem people are quick to recognize when others are interested in them, which helps them to decide whether or not to reciprocate. Low-self-esteem people, on the other hand, are so alert to negative input and criticism that they tend to miss subtle, but positive, signals of interest.[117] When our self-esteem is low we are more sensitive to rejection; since we don't feel too good about ourselves, we're inclined to think others won't feel too good about us either. And this can warp our judgment about how others *really* feel about us.

An example: I had a friend in graduate school who had grave doubts about himself. He worried that he was too short, that he wasn't good-looking enough, that he didn't say the right things to his dates, and so on. If he went out with a woman whose hair wasn't combed (or so it appeared to him), he interpreted this to mean that she didn't care enough about him to look nice; if a date wanted to go home from a party at 1:30 A.M., he perceived this as a sign that she was bored with him; if a woman told him she had a nice time, he wondered how she could possibly mean that. For every positive thing that happened, he was ready—willing, even—to see a darker, more negative side. He missed not only subtle signs of interest, but obvious ones as well. Ultimately, he ended up marrying a woman who was quite different from him in terms of socioeconomic background, educational level, and intellectual ability. The marriage ended five years later, not an inevitable event, but one that became increasingly probable as the years went on and the momentum of his natural abilities and background propelled him to new and higher levels of success and self-esteem.

Reflections

Before reading further, consider several questions. If you're a woman, do you think a man would find you more desirable, or less so, if you played hard to get? If you're a man, what kind of woman attracts you—one who is relatively easy to get or one who is more difficult to get? How does it usually work? Read on.

There Is Something Appealing About a Hard-to-Get Woman

Embedded in our cultural folklore is the idea that being "hard to get"—or reasonably so—is a way of increasing one's appeal. This is supposed to be particularly true for women. But is it really? Elaine Walster and her colleagues[118] started their research assuming that it was true and by asking men not *if* they were attracted to the hard-to-get woman, but *why* they were. Most men said what the researchers expected they would say: An easy-to-get woman spells trouble—she may be desperate, she may be the kind who gets too serious too soon, she may make too many demands, and so on. The elusive woman, on the other hand, was viewed by most men as more desirable, because she would probably be more personable, pretty, and sexy—a tough-to-beat package of appealing characteristics. In addition, there was mention of the obvious social rewards associated with being with this sort of woman. All in all, most men were intrigued by the challenge presented by a distant woman.

Some men, however, said that the elusive woman was not necessarily the most desirable. They observed that some women are not merely *hard* to get, they are impossible to get—they are cold and dislike men. These views weren't taken too seriously by the researchers.

The researchers then conducted five experiments they thought would verify the idea that hard-to-get women are more highly prized than easy-to-get women. Not so. All five revealed that men liked both types equally well. Being hard to get doesn't automatically make a woman desirable.

Puzzled by the findings, Walster and her colleagues interviewed the men again, but this time they began with a different question: "Tell us about the advantages *and* disadvantages of hard-to-get and easy-to-get women." Much more information came of this approach. They learned that *both* types have their desirable and frightening qualities. Although the elusive woman was viewed as a popular, prestigious date, she was also seen as a source of possible problems. For example, the men saw here as more likely to stand them up, embarrass them in front of friends, or be somewhat cold and unfriendly. An easy-to-get woman, though she was viewed as possibly hard to get rid of or too clinging, was also seen as the sort who could boost one's ego and make a date relaxing and enjoyable. In other words, each kind of woman had certain assets and liabilities that helped explain why men liked both types equally well.

With this in mind, the researchers conducted a sixth experiment and discovered that what made the biggest difference in a man's romantic inclinations toward a woman was not how hard or easy she was for *him* to get but how hard or easy she was for *other men* to get. A major finding was that if an elusive woman was easy for one man to get but difficult for others, she would be highly appealing to the man who won her charms. What seems to happen is that dating such a woman brings a man both pleasure and prestige, and, since she is available to him, his dates with her are relaxing and enjoyable. Thus, she possesses the assets of both types of women, while avoiding their liabilities. The findings suggest that a woman will be most successful in attracting a man if she is friendly, warm, but highly selective in her expressions of affection. Although there is no research to substantiate it, I can think of no good reason why the dynamics here would not be somewhat similar in terms of a man attracting a woman. Perhaps what this all boils down to is what we have suspected all along: we like to feel special, and if we know that the person we love has chosen us over others who may be equally available, it helps to enhance that special feeling.

Reflections

Did you ever have the experience of having to oppose your parents when it came to your choice for a love relationship? If so, how did their opposition affect you? Did you give up the relationship? Or did you hang on more tenaciously?

Impact of Parental Opposition

It sometimes happens that one of the most significant influences on a person's choice for a love relationship—particularly among adolescents—is parental opposition. Richard Driscoll and his colleagues[119] found, for example, that the intensity of this sort of relationship may increase *because* of the interference from parents to stop it. What seems to happen in some cases is that the strong feelings a couple may have about opposing parental interference get emotionally translated into strong feelings for each other. Sometimes parents fail to realize that trying to force young lovers apart is the very thing that keeps them together. Driscoll found in his research with 122 couples what legions of parents discover from their own personal experiences—namely, as soon as they resign themselves to the relationship and interfere less, the lovers' interest in each other begins to wane. (After all, it is usually those forbidden things that are most tempting.) Parental opposition adds a bit of zest—take it away and there may not be as much to the relationship as the lovers may have thought.

These, then, are some of the factors—cultural expectations, degree of similarity, equity, our self-esteem, selectivity of our partners, and even parental opposition—that may influence our choices for love relationships and the extent of our personal investment in them.

Let's turn now to what seems an appropriate conclusion to this chapter.

SOME SUGGESTIONS FOR MAINTAINING HEALTHY LOVE RELATIONSHIPS

Love, no matter how intensely it is studied or how deeply it is investigated, will no doubt always retain a certain mysterious quality. It is, for sure, a complex and sometimes unpredictable emotional state that affects different people in different ways. People fall in love, out of love, and sometimes they take years to get over it. It can trigger both peaks of ecstasy and depths of despair. Its presence sends people to altars, while its absence frequently sends them scurrying to lawyers. When we wonder "what she sees in him," we fail to realize that what she sees (and what no one else may see in him) is the secret essense of love. Love is always, to some extent, an overevaluation—a distortion, if you will—of the other person. Whatever else it may be, it is exciting and rewarding, which may help explain why, when it is absent, life seems dull and routine.

The question, then, is what can we do to enhance the possibilities of maintaining healthy love relationships. Some suggestions:

1. Perhaps we should begin with the important distinction Erich Fromm offers us in his insightful book, *The Art of Loving,* in which, among other things, he discusses the differences between immature and mature love. As Fromm explains it, immature love says, "I love you because I need you." Mature love says, "I need you because I love you."[120] This is an important distinction. If we love another person primarily because we need that person, then we are usually more concerned with *taking something from the relationship than we are with giving something to it.*

Lesson: We need to give as much as we get.

2. We can recognize (and perhaps more deeply appreciate) the idea that love relationships go through modifications with time and, as that happens, the basis for attraction will also change.

Lesson: We can accept the fact that love, like people, changes and further, we can practice this acceptance by allowing our love to have the flexibility it takes to continue to love the person our loved one is *becoming* rather than rigidly loving the person they once were or, worse, the person we want them to be. (Of course, change is by no means always positive, and for good reasons we may choose *not* to love the person that he or she is becoming.)

3. The attraction that two people in a love relationship feel for each other is influenced, in part at least, by the needs of each partner for both closeness and autonomy. As pointed out in an insightful analysis by Michael Miller,[121] in every intimate relationship there is a need to be independent and self-reliant, but at the same time there is a need to be deeply attached to someone else. The origins of these needs can go far back in life. When a child is very young, the need for attachment first emerges as a fear of separation from one's parents, since the child is dependent on them emotionally and physically. At the same time, however, the desire for autonomy grows from the child's need to feel competent and self-reliant. There is, then, in most love relationships a delicate balance between the need for sharing and the need for privacy, between wanting to be alone and wanting to be together. You may see how these needs both spring from and express a basic childhood anxiety: *fear of abandonment and fear of engulfment.* Children want to feel free and independent, yet close to someone and looked after. So do adults.

Lesson: A love relationship has a better chance of working when its boundaries are flexible and negotiable enough to allow each partner to experience both the freedom of autonomy and the security of closeness.

4. There is some truth, it appears, to the old saying, "You always hurt the one you love." This can be explained by the gain-loss theory of interpersonal attraction, which suggests that once we have grown certain of the rewarding behavior of a person, that person becomes less potent as a source of reward than a stranger.[122] To put it in the context of this discussion, once we have learned to expect love, favors, and unconditional support from a loved one, such behavior no longer represents as much of a psychological "gain" for us as it once did. In other words, the closer the loved one and the greater his or her past history of invariant encouragement and reward, the more devastating it is when these things are withheld or withdrawn. In effect, we appear to have the power to hurt the one we love, but very little power to reward that person. The reason for this may be that we are already operating at near-ceiling level as to what that individual can expect from us in terms of positive feedback. If, for example, a man always compliments his wife's hair style or cooking, no matter how she looks or how the food tastes, those compliments will eventually mean little because they're stuck on one level.

Lesson: A way to reduce the danger of getting stuck at a plateau where gains are minimal is to work on keeping the relationship honest and open. In a closed relationship, people tend to keep their critical feelings and minor annoyances to themselves. This frequently results in a pleasant, no-rocking-the-boat facade; the bonding has all the outward appearances of being solid and unshakeable, but is, in fact, easily toppled by a sudden shift in emotional sentiment. A way of avoiding this possibility is to develop a give-and-take "authentic" relationship in which partners are willing and able to share their true feelings and impressions. Two people are more likely to have a more satisfying relationship over a longer span of time when they are able to express whatever negative feelings they have than if they are completely "nice" to each other at all times. In this way, there is a continuous give and take of positive *and* negative sentiment, so that the deadening plateau of getting only one kind of feedback and, hence, experiencing no further "gains," is reduced. If you tell me I'm awful when I really am, I'm more apt to feel I've "gained" something if you tell me I'm terrific when I really deserve it.

5. Over the years I have come to develop a deep respect and appreciation for what interpersonal attraction research and my own clinical experiences with persons working through relationship difficulties have taught me: There is no single, or simple, or "best" way to be happy (fulfilled, at peace, actualized, or whatever you care to call it) in a love relationship. There are many best ways for achieving this state, and these ways depend on the people involved—who they are, what they value, what they want from the relationship, and how they decide to work it out.

Lesson: Life does not involve one choice or one way, but a continuing series of choices selected from a variety of options for ways of living. For the first time, men and women realize that they have the option to create a relationship uniquely suited to their individual tastes and desires. In addition, people are freer than they've ever been to continuously redesign their lives as they grow and change. Partners can create an egalitarian relationship or a traditional one; they can live in a house or in a commune; they can have children or remain childless. The choices are all there. No one can predict with accuracy how a love relationship —whatever form it takes—will evolve. The reason for this is that love alone, in its simplicity, is not enough to carry the burden of the relationship. Usually, couples have to go through a stage of "being lost in each other" before they are able to know for sure what they have *discovered* in each other. It is at this point that we begin to understand that love requires the addition of other elements— patience, understanding, tact, forgiveness, the willingness to be hurt or disappointed from time to time—in order to play its proper role. Love begins as a simple feeling, but as time goes on, it grows into a complex emotional blending of two personalities who need to resolve their differences, coordinate their similarities, and discover ways for each person to retain and further develop the uniqueness of his or her individuality. Ultimately, all that two people can do is choose the kind of life they want and then do what they can through negotiation and renegotiation to make it last.

PUTTING IT ALL TOGETHER: WHY ARE PEOPLE ATTRACTED TO EACH OTHER?

People are attracted to each other because people need each other. We live in a social world, and the more complex and technological and impersonal it becomes, the more we may feel a need to connect with and relate to others. The evidence we've looked at in this chapter, for example, does not suggest that we go around looking for reasons to *dislike* others (although, let us admit that there are some neurotic souls who do), but, rather, that we search for reasons to *like* others. What we yearn for are *closer,* not more distant, relationships.

There is good reason for this. When people are with people, they are happier. Psychologist Jonathan Freedman[123] surveyed over 100,000 people about their level of happiness and the factors that contributed to it and found that the strongest predictors of happiness were social factors—friends, marriage, love relationships, and children. There are, however, vast individual differences among people when it comes to how *much* social contact they want or how *many* friends they need to feel happy with themselves and their lot in life. For one person, having a few close friends and many casual acquaintances is sufficient; for another person, having many close friends and fewer casual contacts is necessary. Some like to have people around all the time, while others prefer social interaction on a less intense basis.

In the long run, it does not seem to be the sheer *quantity* of a person's contact with others that makes a crucial difference, but, rather, the *quality* of the contact that he or she has with others. Again, this seems to be something that is quite individualized. For some, the quality of an interpersonal contact is measured in terms of the depth of feelings and self-revelations that are shared; for others, it is measured more in terms of the ideas or personal experiences that are exchanged; for still others, the quality of an interpersonal contact is based less on verbal content and more on activities that are shared together. For many others, of course, there is a nice blend of all three possibilties.

People are attracted to each other so they can feel important, wanted, supported, encouraged, accepted, and loved. We don't get these feelings from just anybody, which is why we have an eye out for the kinds of people who are most apt to help us feel this way. A politician woos the voters who will most likely vote for him; a man pursues the woman of his dreams (and more and more, she pursues the man of her dreams) who is most apt to return those amorous intentions; salespeople go after customers to whom they are most apt to sell things; we choose friends who are most likely to share our interests and values; to the extent it is possible, we choose to work in a place where we like others and others like us.

Whom we are attracted to is the result of a quite selective process. It is moderated by how we see ourselves and how we see others. It is motivated by a deep and largely conscious need to belong to and relate to the social world in which we live.

IN PERSPECTIVE

The psychology of interpersonal attraction is a complex mix of self- and self-other perceptions that, together, help us determine whom we like and whom we don't, whom we will get involved with and whom we won't. Interacting with others is such an ongoing and daily activity that, for most of us, choosing whom we're attracted to and whom we're not attracted to are largely subliminal processes. Usually, however, we have an awareness of two aspects of our existence, although not necessarily at the same time: (1) an awareness of how we feel about ourselves and (2) an awareness of how we feel about others. These are overlapping awarenesses and each influences the other to some extent.

As we have seen in this chapter, our feelings about ourselves—self-esteem—can dramatically affect whom we're attracted to and whom we like. When our self-esteem is high, we are less vulnerable to negative feedback and more attracted to persons of equal or superior qualities. When our self-esteem is low, we are generally reluctant to take the initiative in relationships and are more sensitive to the possibility of rejection. Although a low-self-esteem person may feel attracted to someone, he or she is less inclined to do much about it.

Our feelings about others have a great deal to do with whom we're attracted to and whom we're not attracted to. We like people who are competent, but we don't like them as well if they come across as superhuman models of perfection. We like it when they goof now and then—it makes them more like us.

We particularly like people who are physically attractive. Although, on a conscious level, we seem inclined to discount the importance of beauty, on a less conscious level we not only treat beautiful people—young and old—more kindly, but attribute to them more positive traits and show them more mercy. Attractive students have a better chance of getting higher grades, and attractive defendents have a better chance of receiving lighter sentences.

Generally, we like people who are similar to us, but opposites do attract when their basic characteristics complement each other. For example, people who are somewhat passive may be attracted to those who are more assertive.

Although we tend to like people who like us, we're less inclined to feel that way if we feel that they're trying to get something from us or if their regard for us is greatly different from our own self-estimate. (This is another example of how our own self-feelings interact with our feelings about others and influence whom we're attracted to.)

We like people who disclose themselves to us. We feel trusted and worthwhile —important prerequisites in building relationships between people. On the other hand, we tend to be somewhat suspicious of people who disclose themselves too much, too soon. We suspect that these early self-revelations may have more to do with insecurities and needs for attention than with a sincere interest in building a relationship.

Romantic love is a special version of interpersonal attraction between people, and it comes with an assortment of motivations and in various expressions. The passionate phase of romantic love, although exciting, emotional, and sexual, does not last long. It remains an important undercurrent in a love relationship, but it is not enough to sustain that kind of relationship over a long period of time. The sustaining energy comes from companionate love, which, although it is lower key, is a more stabilized deep attachment to, and commitment to, a particular person.

To a large extent, people are attracted to people they end up loving for pretty much the same reasons they are drawn to people they end up liking. What differs is the intensity of feeling and the degree of emotional commitment.

Understanding how and why people are attracted to each other can help us see how our responses and feelings toward others may be unconsciously motivated by our perceptions of their competency, their looks, their similarity to us, or their self-disclosing tendencies. Teachers, for example, might be more fair to all students, if they are aware of their natural inclination to give the attractive students more breaks. With greater teacher awareness, maybe some of the ugly ducklings would begin getting some breaks.

Although we tend to like people who like us and dislike those who don't like us, we sometimes forget that it may be something in us and not something in the other person that starts the negative interaction. It is useful to know this and to be aware of it. It may help to see that interpersonal attraction is a two-way street and that the problem of negative attraction is not necessarily something "out there" in the other person, but "in here" in ourselves—and that something is eminently fixable.

In Chapter 1 we examined some of the major factors determining how people see each other. In this chapter we have tried to better understand how and why people are attracted to each other. In Chapter 3, we will examine how this all relates to how people influence each other.

REFERENCES

1. D. Carnegie, *How to Win Friends and Influence People,* New York: Simon & Schuster, 1937.

2. D. Byrne and G. L. Clore, "A Reinforcement Model of Evaluative Responses," *Personality: An Interpersonal Journal* 1 (1970): 103–128.

3. A. J. Lott and B. E. Lott, "The Role of Reward in the Formation of Positive Interpersonal Attitudes," in T. L. Huston (Ed.), *Foundations of Interpersonal Attractions,* New York: Academic Press, 1974.

4. G. Homans, *Social Behavior: Elementary Forms,* New York: Harcourt Brace, and World, 1961.

5. J. W. Thibaut & H. H. Kelley, *The Social Psychology of Groups,* New York: Wiley, 1959.

6. G. C. Homans, *Social Behavior: Elementary Forms,* New York: Harcourt Brace, 1961, p. 62.

7. E. Walster, G. W. Walster, and E. Berscheid, *Equity: Theory and Research,* Boston: Allyn & Bacon, 1978, p. vii.

8. W. Stroebe, "Self-Esteem and Interpersonal Attraction," in S. Duck (Ed.), *Theory and Practice in Interpersonal Attraction,* New York: Academic Press, 1977.

9. B. Spinoza, "The Ethics," in *Spinoza's Ethics* and *'De Intellectus Emendatione,'* translated by A. Boyle, New York: Dutton, 1910.

10.   E. Aronson, "Some Antecedents of Interpersonal Attraction," in W. J. Arnold and D. Levine (Eds.), *Nebraska Symposium on Motivation,* Lincoln, Nebr.: University of Nebraska Press, 1969.

11.   E. Walster, "The Effect of Self-Esteem on Romantic Liking," *Journal of Experimental Social Psychology* 1 (1965): 184–187.

12.   L. Jacobs, E. Berscheid, and E. Walster, "Self-Esteem and Attraction," *Journal of Personality and Social Psychology* 17 (1971): 84–91.

13.   S. B. Kiesler & R. L. Baral, "The Search for a Romantic Partner: The Effects of Self-Esteem and Physical Attractiveness on Romantic Behavior," in K. J. Gergen and D. Marlowe (Eds.), *Personality and Social Behavior,* Reading, Mass.: Addison-Wesley, 1970.

14.   W. Stroebe, "Self-Esteem and Interpersonal Attraction," in S. Duck (Ed.), *Theory and Practice in Interpersonal Attraction,* New York: Academic Press, 1977.

15.   D. E. Hamachek, *Encounters with the Self,* 2nd ed., New York: Holt, Rinehart & Winston, 1978, pp. 69–107.

16.   M. Deutsch and L. Solomon, "Reactions to Evaluations by Others as Influenced by Self-Evaluations," *Sociometry* 22 (1959): 93–112.

17.   R. Bales, "Task Roles and Social Roles in Problem Solving Groups," in E. E. Maccoby, T. M. Newcomb, and E. L. Hartley (Eds.), *Readings in Social Psychology,* 3d ed., Holt, Rinehart & Winston, 1958, pp. 437–447.

18.   E. Aronson, B. Willerman, and J. Floyd, "The Effect of a Pratfall on Increasing Interpersonal Attractiveness," *Psychonomic Science* 4 (1966): 227–228.

19.   R. Helmreich, E. Aronson, and J. Lefan, "To Err is Humanizing—Sometimes: Effects of Self-Esteem, Competence, and a Pratfall on Interpersonal Attraction," *Journal of Personality and Social Psychology* 16 (1970): 259–264.

20.   K. Deaux, "To Err is Humanizing: But Sex Makes a Difference," *Representative Research in Social Psychology* 3 (1972): 20–28.

21.   E. Berscheid and E. Walster, "Physical Attractiveness," in L. Berkowitz (Ed.), *Advances in Experimental Social Psychology,* Vol. VII, New York: Academic Press, 1974.

22.   E. Walster, E. Aronson, D. Abrahams, and L. Rottman, "Importance of Physical Attractiveness in Dating Behavior," *Journal of Personality and Social Psychology.* 4 (1966): 508–516.

23.   R. W. Brislin and S. A. Lewis, "Dating and Physical Attractiveness: Replication," *Psychological Reports* 22 (1968): 976.

24.   J. P. Curran and S. Lippold, "The Effects of Physical Attraction and Attitude Similarity on Attraction in Dating Dyads," *Journal of Personality* 43 (1975): 528–539.

25.   R. E. Kleck and C. Rubenstein, "Physical Attractiveness, Perceived Attitude Similarity, and Interpersonal Attraction in an Opposite-Sex Encounter," *Journal of Personality and Social Psychology* 31 (1975): 107–114.

26.   K. Dion, E. Berscheid, and E. Walster, "What is Beautiful is Good," *Journal of Personality and Social Psychology* 24 (1972): 285–290.

27.   K. Dion and E. Berscheid, "Physical Attractiveness and Sociometric Choice in Nursery School Children," (mimeographed research report) 1971.

28.   J. Staffieri, "A Study of Social Stereotype of Body Image in Children," *Journal of Personality and Social Psychology* 7 (1967): 101–104.

29. R. M. Lemer and E. Gillert, "Body Build Identification, Preference, and Aversion in Children," *Developmental Psychology* 1 (1969): 456–463.

30. G. R. Adams and T. L. Huston, "Social Perception of Middle-Aged Persons Varying in Physical Attractiveness," *Developmental Psychology* 11 (1975): 657–658.

31. M. Snyder, E. Berscheid, and E. D. Tanke, "Social Perception and Interpersonal Behavior: On the Self-Fulfilling Nature of Social Stereotypes," *Journal of Personality & Social Psychology* 35 (1977): 656–666.

32. E. Berscheid and E. Walster, "Physical Attractiveness," in L. Berkowitz (Ed.), Advances in Experimental Social Psychology, Vol. VII, New York: Academic Press, 1974.

33. G. Wilson & D. Nias, *The Mystery of Love: The Hows and Whys of Sexual Attractions,* New York: Quadrangle/The New York Times Book Co., 1976.

34. S. B. Beck, P. M. McLean, and C. I. Ward-Hull, "Variables Related to Women's Somatic Preferences of the Male and Female Body," *Journal of Personality and Social Psychology* 34 (1976) 1200–1210.

35. P. J. Laurakas, *Female Preferences for Male Physiques,* Paper presented at the meeting of the Midwestern Psychological Association, Chicago, May 1975.

36. J. S. Wiggins, N. Wiggins, and J. C. Conger, "Correlates of Heterosexual Somatic Preference," *Journal of Personality and Social Psychology* 10 (1968): 82–90.

37. E. Berscheid and E. Walster, "Beauty and the Best," *Psychology Today,* March 1972, p. 74.

38. D. Byrne, *The Attraction Paradigm,* New York: Academic Press, 1971.

39. D. Byrne and D. Nelson, "Attraction as a Linear Function of Proportion of Positive Reinforcements," *Journal of Personality and Social Psychology* 1 (1965) 659–663.

40. G. L. Clore and B. Baldridge, "Interpersonal Attraction: The Role of Agreement and Topic Interest," *Journal of Personality and Social Psychology* 9 (1968): 340–346.

41. H. A. Bowman and G. B. Spanier, *Modern Marriage,* 8th ed., New York: McGraw Hill, 1978, pp. 222–249.

42. D. Byrne and W. Griffitt, "Developmental Investigation of the Law of Attraction," *Journal of Personality and Social Psychology* 4 (1966): 699–702.

43. W. Griffitt, J. Nelson & G. Littlepage, "Old Age and Response to Agreement–Disagreement," *Journal of Gerontology.* 27 (1972): 269–274.

44. D. Byrne, G. Clore, and P. Worchel, "The Effect of Economic Similarity–Dissimilarity on Interpersonal Attraction," *Journal of Personality and Social Psychology* 4 (1966): 220–224.

45. D. Senn, "Attraction as a Function of Similarity–Dissimilarity in Task Performance," *Journal of Personality & Social Psychology* 18 (1971): 120–123.

46. W. G. Bennis, K. D. Benne, and R. Chin (Eds.), *The Planning of Change,* New York: Holt, Rinehart and Winston, 1961.

47. B. L. Kell and W. J. Mueller, *Impact and Change: A Study of Counseling Relationships,* New York: Appleton-Century-Crofts, 1966.

48. D. E. Hamachek, *Encounters with the Self,* 2nd ed., New York: Holt, Rinehart and Winston, 1978, pp. 18–33.

49. D. Byrne and B. Blaylock, "Similarity and Assumed Similarity Between Husbands and Wives," *Journal of Abnormal and Social Psychology* 37 (1963): 636–640.

50.   N. Miller, D. Campbell, H. Twedt, and E. O'Connell, "Similarity, Contrast and Complementarity in Friendship Choice," *Journal of Personality and Social Psychology* 3 (1966): 3–12.

51.   D. R. Mettee and P. C. Wilkins, "When Similarity 'Hurts': Effects of Perceived Ability and a Humorous Blunder on Interpersonal Attractiveness," *Journal of Personality and Social Psychology* 22 (1972): 246–258.

52.   D. Novak and M. Lerner, "Rejection as a Consequence of Perceived Similarity," *Journal of Personality and Social Psychology* 9 (1968): 147–152.

53.   S. Taylor and D. Mette, "When Similarity Breeds Contempt," *Journal of Personality and Social Psychology* 20 (1971): 75–81.

54.   J . Cooper and E. E. Jones, "Opinion Divergence as a Strategy to Avoid Being Miscast," *Journal of Personality and Social Psychology* 13 (1969): 23–30.

55.   R. Winch, *Mate-Selection: A Study of Complementary Needs,* New York: Harper & Row, 1958.

56.   B. A. Seyfried and C. Hendrick, "When Do Opposites Attract? When They are Opposite in Sex and Sexrole Attitudes," *Journal of Personality and Social Psychology* 25 (1973): 15–20.

57.   B. A. Seyfried, "Complementarity in Interpersonal Attraction," in S. Duck (Ed.), *Theory and Practice in Interpersonal Attraction,* New York: Academic Press, 1977, pp. 165–186.

58.   A. Kerckhoff and K. E. Davis, "Value Consensus and Need Complementarity in Mate Selection," *American Sociological Review* 27 (1962): 295–303.

59.   E. L. Kelley, cited in J. V. McConnell, *Understanding Human Behavior,* 2nd ed., New York: Holt, Rinehart and Winston, 1977, pp. 625–626.

60.   C. W. Backman and P. F. Secord, "The Effect of Perceived Liking on Interpersonal Attraction," *Human Relations* 12 (1959): 379–384.

61.   D. M. Geller, L. Goldstein, M. Silver, and W. C. Sternberg, "On Being Ignored: The Effects of the Violation of Implicit Rules of Social Interaction," *Sociometry* 37 (1974): 541–556.

62.   E. E. Jones and C. Wortman, *Ingratiation: An Attributional Approach,* Morristown, N. J.: General Learning Press, 1973.

63.   C. A. Lowe and J. W. Goldstein, "Reciprocal Liking and Attribution of Ability: Mediating Effects of Perceived Intent and Personal Involvement," *Journal of Personality and Social Psychology* 16 (1970): 291–298.

64.   H. Dickoff, *Reactions to Evaluations by Another Person as a Function of Self-Evaluation and the Interaction Context,* Unpublished doctoral dissertation, Duke University, 1961.

65.   E. E. Jones, R. G. Jones, and K. J. Gergen, "Some Conditions Affecting the Evaluation of the Conformist," *Journal of Personality* 31 (1963): 270–288.

66.   C. L. Kleinke, R. A. Staneski, and P. Weaver, "Evaluation of a Person Who Uses Another Person's Name in Ingratiating and Noningratiating Situations," *Journal of Experimental Social Psychology* 8 (1972): 457–460.

67.   V. J. Derlega, M. Wilson, and A. L. Chaikin, "Friendship and Disclosure Reciprocity," *Journal of Personality and Social Psychology* 34 (1976): 578–582.

68. I. Altman, "Reciprocity of Interpersonal Exchange," *Journal for the Theory of Social Behavior* 3 (1973): 249–261.

69. S. Jourard, *Self-Disclosure: An Experimental Analysis of the Transparent Self,* New York: Wiley, 1971.

70. I. Altman and D. A. Taylor, *Social Penetration: The Development of Interpersonal Relationships,* New York, Holt, Rinehart and Winston, 1973.

71. C. B. Wortman, P. Adosman, E. Herman, and R. Greenberg, "Self-Disclosure: An Attributional Perspective," *Journal of Personality and Social Psychology* 33 (1976): 184–191.

72. R. Archer and J. Berg, "To Encourage Intimacy, Don't Force It," *Psychology Today,* November 1978, pp. 39–40.

73. D. M. Daher and P. G. Banikiotes, "Interpersonal Attraction and Rewarding Aspects of Disclosure Content and Level," *Journal of Personality and Social Psychology* 33 (1976): 492–496.

74. M. G. Efran, *Visual Interaction and Interpersonal Attraction,* Unpublished doctoral dissertation, Austin: University of Texas, 1969.

75. L. Scherwitz and R. Helmreich, "Interactive Effects of Eye Contact and Verbal Content of Interpersonal Attraction in Dyads," *Journal of Personality and Social Psychology* 23 (1973) 6–14.

76. M. Wiener and A. Mehrabian, *Language Within Language: Immediacy, A Channel in Verbal Communication,* New York: Appleton-Century-Crofts, 1968.

77. R. V. Exline and L. C. Winters, "Affective Relations and Mutual Glances," in S. S. Tompkins and C. E. Izard (Eds.), *Affect, Cognition, and Personality,* New York: Springer, 1965.

78. P. C. Ellsworth and L. Ross, "Intimacy in Response to Direct Gaze," *Journal of Experimental Social Psychology* 11 (1975): 592–613.

79. R. J. Wolosin, "Cognitive Similarity and Group Laughter," *Journal of Personality and Social Psychology* 32: (1975): 503–509.

80. A. J. Lott and B. E. Lott, "Group Cohesiveness and Individual Learning," *Journal of Educational Psychology* 57 (1966): 61–73.

81. D. Nelson and B. L. Meadow, *Attitude Similarity, Interpersonal Attraction, Actual Success, and the Evaluative Perception of that Success,* Paper presented at the meeting of the American Psychological Association, Washington, D.C., September 1971.

82. A. R. Allgeier and D. Byrne, "Attraction Toward the Opposite Sex as a Determinant of Physical Proximity," *Journal of Social Psychology* 90 (1973): 213–219.

83. D. Byrne, C. R. Ervin, and J. Lamberth, "Continuity Between the Experimental Study of Attraction and Real-Life Computer Dating," *Journal of Personality and Social Psychology* 16 (1970) 157–165.

84. A. Mehrabian, "Inference of Attitudes from Posture, Orientation, and Distance of Communicator," *Journal of Consulting and Clinical Psychology* 32 (1968): 296–318.

85. A. Mehrabian, "Relationship of Attitude to Seated Posture, Orientation, and Distance," *Journal of Personality and Social Psychology* 10 (1968): 26–30.

86. A. Mehrabian, "Orientation Behaviors and Non-Verbal Attitude Communication," *Journal of Communication* 17 (1967): 324–332.

87.   P. Ekman and W. Friesen, "Nonverbal Leakage and Clues to Deception," *Psychiatry* 32 (1969): 88–106.

88.   G. Wilson and D. Nias, "Beauty Can't Be Beat," *Psychology Today,* September 1976, pp. 96–99.

89.   M. Dermer and D. L. Thiel, "When Beauty May Fail," *Journal of Personality and Social Psychology* 31 (1975): 1168–1176.

90.   W. Stroebe, "Self-Esteem and Interpersonal Attraction," in S. Duck (Ed.), *Theory and Practice in Interpersonal Attraction,* New York: Academic Press, (1977) pp. 86–88.

91.   H. Sigall and E. Aronson, "Liking for an Evaluator as a Function of Her Physical Attractiveness and Nature of the Evaluations," *Journal of Experimental Social Psychology* 5 (1969): 93–100.

92.   K. Dion, "Physical Attractiveness and Evaluation of Children's Transgressions," *Journal of Personality and Social Psychology* 24 (1972): 207–213.

93.   M. Efran, "The Effect of Physical Appearance on the Judgment of Guilt, Interpersonal Attraction, and the Severity of Recommended Punishment in a Simulated Jury Task," *Journal of Experimental Research in Personality* 8 (1974): 45–54.

94.   H. Sigall and N. Ostrove, "Beautiful But Dangerous: Effects of Offender Attractiveness and the Nature of the Crime on Juridic Judgement," *Journal of Personality and Social Psychology* 31 (1975): 410–414.

95.   M. M. Clifford and E. Walster, "Effect of Physical Attractiveness on Teacher Expectations," *Sociology of Education* 46 (1973): 248–258.

96.   R. M. Lerner and J. V. Lerner, "Effects of Age, Sex, and Physical Attractiveness on Child–Peer Relations, Academic Performance, and Elementary School Adjustment," *Developmental Psychology* 13 (1977) 585–590.

97.   D. Landy and H. Sigall, "Beauty is Talent: Task Evaluation as a Function of the Performer's Physical Attractiveness," *Journal of Personality and Social Psychology* 29 (1974): 299–304.

98.   D. Bryne and W. Griffitt, "Interpersonal Attraction," *Annual Review of Psychology* 24 (1973): 317–336.

99.   I. Ajzen, "Effects of Information on Interpersonal Attraction: Similarity Versus Affective Value," *Journal of Personality and Social Psychology* 29 (1974): 374–380.

100.   G. L. Clore and K. Jeffery, "Emotional Role-Playing, Attitude Change, and Attraction Toward a Disabled Person," *Journal of Personality and Social Psychology* 23 (1972): 105–111.

101.   R. E. Farson, "Praise as a Motivational Tool: Negative Aspects, Positive Functions, and Suggestions for Using it in Healthy Ways," in D. E. Hamachek (Ed.), *Human Dynamics in Psychology and Education,* 3rd ed., Boston: Allyn & Bacon, 1977.

102.   J. Jecker and D. Landy, "Liking a Person as a Function of Doing Him a Favor," *Human Relations,* 22 (1969): 371–378.

103.   E. Fromm, *The Art of Loving,* New York: Bantam, 1963.

104.   E. Walster and G. W. Walster, *A New Look at Love,* Reading, Mass: Addison-Wesley, 1978, p. 2.

105.   C. T. Hill, Z. Rubin, and L. A. Peplau, *Divorce and Separation,* New York: Basic Books, 1978.

106.   C. T. Hill, Z. Rubin, and L. A. Peplau, *Divorce and Separation.* New York: Basic Books, 1978.

107.   E. J. Kanin, K. D. Davidson, and S. R. Scheck, "A Research Note on Male–Female Differentials in the Experience of Heterosexual Love," *The Journal of Sex Research* 6 (1970): 64–72.

108.   T. Reik, *A Psychologist Looks at Love,* New York: Holt, Rinehart and Winston, 1972, p. 150.

109.   R. S. Cimbalo, V. Faling, and P. Mousaw, "The Course of Love: A Cross-Sectional Design," *Psychological Reports* 38 (1976): 1292–1294.

110.   M. N. Reedy and J. E. Birren, "Loving Happily Ever After: Age Differences in Satisfying Love Relationships," Paper presented at the American Psychological Association meeting, Toronto, Canada, September 1978.

111.   R. Rollins and M. Feldman, "Marital Satisfaction Through the Life Span," *Journal of Marriage & the Family* 32 (1970): 20–27.

112.   B. I. Murstein, *Who Will Marry Whom,* New York: Springer, 1975.

113.   J. P. Meyer and S. Pepper, "Need Compatibility and Marital Adjustment in Young Married Couples," *Journal of Personality and Social Psychology* 35 (1977): 331–342.

114.   E. Berscheid, E. Walster and G. Bohrnstedt, "The Body Image Report," *Psychology Today,* Nov. 1973, 119–131.

115.   E. Walster, G. W. Walster, and J. Traupmann, "Equity and Premarital Sex," *Journal of Personality and Social Psychology* 37 (1978): 82–92.

116.   S. B. Kiesler and R. L. Baral, "The Search for a Romantic Partner: The Effects of Self-Esteem and Physical Attractiveness on Romantic Behavior," in K. J. Gergen and D. Marlowe (Eds.), *Personality and Social Behavior,* Reading, Mass.: Addison-Wesley, 1970.

117.   A. Cohen and I. Silverman, "Repression–Sensitization as a Dimension of Personality," in B. A. Maher, (Ed.), *Progress in Experimental Personality Research,* Vol. I, New York: Academic Press, 1964.

118.   E. Walster, G. W. Walster, J. Piliavin, and L. Schmidt, "Playing Hard-to-Get: Understanding an Elusive Phenomenon," *Journal of Personality and Social Psychology* 26 (1973): 113–121.

119.   R. Driscoll, K. E. Davis, and M. E. Lipetz, "Parental Interference and Romantic Love: The Romeo and Juliet Effect," *Journal of Personality and Social Psychology* 24 (1972): 1–10.

120.   E. Fromm, *The Art of Loving,* New York: Bantam, 1963, p. 34.

121.   M. V. Miller, "Intimate Terrorism," *Psychology Today,* April 1977, 79–82.

122.   E. Aronson and D. Linder, "Gain and Loss of Esteem as Determinants of Interpersonal Attractiveness," *Journal of Experimental Social Psychology* 1 (1965); 156–171.

123.   J. Freedman, *Happy People: What Happiness Is, Who Has It, and Why,* New York: Harcourt Brace Jovanovich, 1978.

Chapter 3

HOW WE INFLUENCE OTHERS—HOW OTHERS INFLUENCE US

OVERVIEW

PROLOGUE

What factors determined whom you voted for in the last election? Why have you chosen to dress as you do? If you want to go to movie A and your friend wants to go to movie B, how do you typically resolve the issue? What factors have most affected your thinking and feelings about religious matters? In general, when you want another person to see things your way—or at least to understand your position—what is your usual approach to achieving this end? These are, as you can see, questions that have to do with influence—how you influence others and how others influence you. Interpersonal influence is an on-going process which begins early in life and continues for as long as we live. Sometimes influence is overt, in the sense that it is deliberate and intentional—for example, when we try to persuade our friends to vote for a particular candidate. Or influence can be covert, in the sense that it is indirect and unintentional—when our friends vote for the same candidate we do, not because we've persuaded them to do so, but because they like us and identify with the way we think politically.

However you look at it, interpersonal influence is a fascinating process. Every idea, attitude, and feeling we have about ourselves and others, and about what we consider to be right and wrong and good and bad, in one way or another has been shaped, molded, "influenced" by our social interaction with others over time. How does this process work? Why are we influenced by some people, but not others? Why do we tend to resist those who try to force us to change? What is the relationship between our self-esteem and our susceptibility to persuasion? How do groups influence behavior? What happens when a group gets into a "groupthink" process? If you want to influence people either to buy your product or to accept your ideas, what are some good ways to do so? These and other related issues will be the focus of our attention in the pages ahead. Let's begin by asking an important question.

HOW VULNERABLE ARE WE TO INFLUENCE?

The answer is: we're probably more vulnerable than we think we are. Others are molded by public opinion, others are suckers for a clever ad, others can be manipulated by a smooth salesperson, but not *us*. This somewhat myopic self-perception is reflected in our frequently stated belief that *we* would not have acted the way so-and-so did in a given situation. You may recall from our discussion in Chapter 1 that this egocentric power orientation is called the *attribution error,*[1] which explains that our susceptibility to influence is proportional to the degree to which we *underestimate* the power of others to influence us and *overestimate* our own power to resist them and control our own actions. We are inclined to attribute more potency to our *dispositional* factors (personality, morals, personal values, character) than is warranted. At the same time, we fail to assess accurately the influence that *situational* forces (group pressures, outside author-ity, public opinion, group norms) can have on our own behavior. For example, it is difficult for most of us to think that we could have acted as Adolf Eichmann did in his supervision of the murder of thousands of innocent people during World War II, or as Lt. Calley and other members of Charlie Company did in the My Lai massacre, or as Patty Hearst did when she helped the Symbionese Liberation Army rob a bank after being kidnapped by them.

A major conclusion emerges from the research on attribution: Although we are highly susceptible to situational or external pressures, we remain blissfully un-aware of how much our own behavior can be influenced by these outside pressures and forces. The fact is, we are constantly being influenced, changed, persuaded, and manipulated in our daily interactions. Efforts to persuade us to buy this product, to vote for that candidate, to agree with this position, to accept that argument are continuous. In fact, many times we're influenced to buy a particular product without being consciously aware of why we're doing so in the first place —a quirk of ours that Madison Avenue psychologists know how to exploit fully.

Yes, we are vulnerable to being influenced. This is not, by the way, necessarily a negative virtue. It's a matter of avoiding extremes. You might look at it this way: Being vulnerable implies a certain openness to change. Carried to an extreme on the side of change, a person can be so open or vulnerable as to have neither convictions nor beliefs that can withstand the challenge of other points of view; we might call that person wishy-washy, even spineless. Carried to the other extreme—opposing change—a person can be so invulnerable to influence that he or she ends up with a certain hardening of the intellectual and emotional arteries; we might call that person rigid and inflexible. A certain amount of "influenceabil-ity," then, is both healthy and necessary. It allows us to change our minds, to see things in new ways, and to be flexibly adaptive when necessary. What we want to know now is how the influence process works so that: (1) we can be more aware of others using it—thus increasing our control of the input, and (2) we can be more aware *when* we're using it and know *how* to use it when we need to—thus increasing our control of the output. Whether we're selling shoes or ideas, this can be helpful, functional knowledge.

There are three basic communication components in the influence and persua-sion process. First, there is the *source:* Who is doing the influencing? Second, there is the *message:* What is being said? And finally, there is the *audience:* Who is the target of the influence? Let's begin with the first one.

THE SOURCE OF INFLUENCE: PERSONAL FACTORS THAT STAND OUT

Imagine that following scene: You walk into a department store with the idea that you will buy a new television set if you find the right one at the right price. As you approach the television area, a somewhat disheveled-looking salesman—loud jacket, open shirt, unpressed pants, unshaven—walks up and wonders if he can help. He tells you that this is his second day on the job, that he's still learning the ropes, but that he would like to sell you a television set. Imagine the scene differently: As you approach the television area, a neat salesman—navy blazer, white shirt, tie, clean-looking—walks up and wonders if he can help. He mentions that he's been working in the department for over 10 years and would be happy to sell you a television set. From which man would you be more likely to make a purchase?

It wouldn't be hard to decide in this case, would it? There are certain aspects about that second salesman that would enable us to trust his judgment and to have a certain amount of faith in him as a person. Let's take a closer look at some of those aspects.

Perceived Attractiveness Is Important

As we saw in Chapter 1, we are inclined to attribute more positive characteristics to physically attractive persons, and as we saw in Chapter 2, we are inclined to be more attracted to attractive people. It comes as no surprise, then, to find that attractive people may have an edge when it comes to influencing either our buying habits or our opinions.

Edward Young[2] found that how salesmen dress can make a big difference in their sales records. For example, he discovered that when salesmen in a Montgomery, Alabama, men's store wore suits, the average value of their sales was 43 percent higher than when they were in shirtsleeves and ties, and 60 percent higher than when they wore open-collar shirts. He got his data by observing seven male employees for 3 months, during which time they all wore each outfit on several occasions. Their sales were not affected by their age and experience, since every salesman increased his output when he wore a suit. Nor were the salesmen with high sales records working in parts of the store with high-priced items, since all salesmen covered all parts of the store.

Although these results are very suggestive, they do not prove that suits alone were the crucial factor. For example, since the men were free to dress as they chose, it may be that they dressed more casually when they weren't feeling well and sold poorly because they didn't feel well. Putting on suits may have enhanced their confidence, and hence, their performance.

Not only is it possible that wearing a suit may increase a salesperson's self-confidence, but it may also serve to escalate our confidence in him or her. We are more ready, more open, it seems, to be influenced by an attractive person because we attribute more positive qualities to that person. For instance, Shelly Chaiken[3] found that physically attractive men and women communicators had significantly more success persuading men and women target subjects to do what they wanted them to do than less attractive communicators. It may be that physically attractive, pleasant-appearing individuals really are more persuasive—

positive feedback helps them to feel more confident and assertive; or it may be that our own positive attitude about them renders us more persuadable. Probably a bit of both.

Physical attractiveness affects not only what we think of salespeople who want to sell us TV sets, but also what we think of psychologists, of all people, who may want to sell us their counsel. For example, Thomas Cash[4] and his co-workers found that, relative to physical unattractive counselors, attractive counselors are generally perceived more favorably by both sexes—especially with regard to intelligence, friendliness, assertiveness, warmth, and competence. In light of research results[5,6] indicating that a high degree of client attraction toward the therapist enhances the possibility of a favorable therapeutic experience and outcome, this is an important finding. It may not surprise you to learn that it works the other way, too. That is, not only do clients start with more favorable expectations if their counselors are more attractive, but counselors are also inclined to have more favorable expectations for their attractive clients. Ralph Barocas and Forrest Vance[7] discovered this when they looked at the clinical work-ups by eleven male and four female counselors of seventy-five male and eighty female students at a university counseling center. A major finding was that, regardless of the sex of the counselor or the client, the more attractive a client was to a counselor, the more likely it was that the counselor would state a favorable prognosis. This was even more likely if the client was a woman.

Most of us, it seems, are ready—not always consciously—to be influenced by people whom we find attractive. Thus, it is possible for movie stars and athletic heros to plug products about which they know virtually nothing, and to convince us that this wine or that cereal or this car is really the best on the market. Judson Mills and Elliot Aronson[8] did a simple laboratory experiment which showed that a beautiful woman—just because she was beautiful—could have a significant impact on an audience's opinions about a topic that had nothing to do with her beauty. In addition, her impact was greatest when she openly expressed a desire to influence the audience. Thus, we seem open to the influence of people we like. It is not, however, an indiscriminate openness. The more we're attracted to people for reasons other than their expertise, the less likely it is that they will be successful in changing our minds about important issues. For example, a football player may persuade us to use a certain shaving cream or a gorgeous movie star may get us to use a particular hand lotion, but neither one would be nearly as successful in changing our opinions about, say, abortion or the legalization of marijuana—which brings us to an important question.

Credibility: Is the Source Believable?

This component of the influence package has two parts—expertise and trustworthiness. These qualities become increasingly more important to us when we are assessing the credibility of people who are trying to influence us about matters more crucial than shaving cream or hand lotion.

This idea was nicely illustrated in a revealing study by Carl Hovland and Walter Weiss,[9] who presented large groups of people with an argument favoring the development of atomic-powered submarines. (The study was conducted in 1951 when such a possibility seemed remote.) One group of people was told that the argument came from a nationally known and respected atomic physicist (J. Robert Oppenheimer), while another group was told the argument came from *Pravda,* the Communist Party's official newspaper. First, both groups filled out rating scales that reflected their opinions on the topic. Then they read the argument. The results? When people read the "Oppenheimer" argument, they were much more apt to change their opinions in favor of atomic subs. Very few, however, changed their opinion to favor the atomic subs when they read the "Pravda" Argument, which, of course, was identical to Oppenheimer's.

In the Hovland and Weiss study, the name of the author appeared at the end of the article. Sociologist T. R. Husek[10] wondered if knowing the author of a persuasive communication before or after its delivery would make a difference in whether people changed their attitudes. To check this, he played a 20-minute talk to a large group of high school students, promoting more favorable attitudes toward mental illness. During a third of the presentations, the speaker was introduced at the outset as a former mental patient; during another third, this fact was mentioned at the end; and during the remaining third, the speaker's identity was not revealed.

Credibility can sometimes be stretched too far.

Reflections

Of the three groups in Musek's study mentioned above, which group do you think changed their attitudes toward mental illness the least? Why? Consider the following claims: The American Cancer Society says, If you want to breathe, not cough, and live, not die—don't smoke. The life you save may be your own. The American Tobacco Industry says, The relationship between lung cancer and smoking has not been proven. Light up and enjoy. Which position do you believe? Which is most trustworthy? How is your own attitude toward smoking linked to whom you do or do not see as credible?

Musek found that when the speaker was identified at the outset as a former mental patient, there were fewer positive attitude changes than in either of the other two situations. This finding is consistent with the idea developed in Chapter 1—namely, that our first impressions about people tend to influence our subsequent impressions. On the other hand, it is possible that withholding information about the source of the communication may make it more possible for the quality and reasonableness of the talk itself to influence, whereas giving this information at the outset may promote inattention and/or a tendency to be closeminded about the ideas presented. This is an important point, because as pointed out by William McGuire,[11] the keys to influencing a person's attitude are *attention, comprehension,* and *yielding.* When one's attention is lost, so are the other two. (This helps explain why television programs, political announcements, and TV ads tend to be brash, bold, loud, and overly dramatic in their opening moments—anything to grab one's attention.)

A *working principle:* We are apt to be most effective in changing others' attitudes when we are viewed as having some expertise in the area we're talking about. Our credibility enhanced. But a word of caution. Credibility, like beauty, is in the eye of the beholder. William F. Buckley, Jr., for example, may be a high-credibility source for conservative Republicans, but he is viewed somewhat more suspiciously by liberal Democrats.

Credibility is enhanced when we are viewed as trustworthy. If a persuasive argument comes from a source that, for one reason or other, we hold suspect—like *Pravda* or the former mental patient—then we are less likely to believe that source. Which brings us to an important consideration.

Ways to Increase Trustworthiness

One clear and effective way of doing this is to take a position contrary to one's own self-interests. If a person has nothing to gain—and perhaps even something to lose—by convincing us of something, the chances are good that we'll listen intently to what he or she has to say. Consider an example: Suppose that a convicted smuggler and peddler of heroin was attempting to convince us that the

American judicial system was unfair and prejudicial. Would we be influenced? Probably not. Most of us would consider him or her less than credible or trustworthy. We would see that he or she had everything to gain from such an argument and nothing to lose; his or her own self-interest would seem blatantly evident. But let's suppose for a moment that this same convicted smuggler was arguing for a tougher stance against crime—that sentences ought to be stiffer and longer, not softer and shorter. Would he or she influence us? Very likely. In fact, this was confirmed in an interesting experiment done by Elaine Walster, Eliot Aronson, and Darcy Abrahams.[12] They had a group of subjects read a newspaper clipping of an interview with convict Joe "The Shoulder." One group of subjects read a clipping in which Joe "The Shoulder" argued for more lenient courts and less severe sentences. Another group read a clipping in which he argued for stricter courts and longer sentences. There was also a parallel set of conditions in which different groups read the same statements, which were attributed to a respected public official. As you might suspect, when Joe "The Shoulder" argued for lenient courts, he was totally ineffective. In fact, readers exposed to that argument from him changed their opinions to *opposite* his. However, when he argued for stricter courts, he was extremely effective—as effective as the respected official delivering the same argument. You can see that a communicator can be socially unattractive and even immoral, but still influence us—if it is clear that he or she has nothing to gain by doing so.

Our judgment of a person's trustworthiness is apt to improve when we are certain that he or she is *not trying* to influence us. Again, it's a question of what we think the communicator is after. Let's say you're in the market for a used car and a car salesperson tells you that a certain car is a very fine car, with dependable wheels you can count on. Will you buy? Maybe. Maybe not. If he or she is an expert on cars and has been in the business for a long time, you may be influenced to buy the car. But then you realize that he or she has a commission to gain, lowering his or her trustworthiness. Let's suppose, however, that you overhear the salesperson telling someone who is not looking for a car that this car is particularly good, in excellent shape. Now what do you suppose you will think about the car? Precisely because he is *not trying* to influence you, you may, in fact, be more easily influenced. In other words, as long as we know that a person is not trying to influence us, we don't have to worry about ulterior motives.

Elaine Walster and Leon Festinger[13] found this to be true in a study in which a conversation was staged between two female graduate students, one of whom expressed her direct opinion on an issue. The situation was arranged so that an observer was allowed to overhear the conversation. In one instance, it was clear to the observer that the graduate students *knew* of her presence in the next room. In this situation, the observer knew that whatever was said could be stated with the intent of influencing her opinion. In a second instance, the situation was arranged so that the observer believed that the graduate students were unaware that she was in the next room. And it was with this condition—where observers knew that the graduate students weren't trying to influence them—that the observers' opinions changed significantly more toward the opinions expressed by the graduate students.

Reflections

When does a compliment mean the most: When someone compliments you directly? Or when you overhear a flattering remark about yourself said to someone else? Why do you feel as you do? When are you most apt to question a direct compliment? How is your answer related to the discussion about trustworthiness we've been having?

Perceived attractiveness, credibility, trustworthiness—these are important elements in a communicator's ability to influence others. There is one other element worth noting.

Perceived Similarity Is Important

People can be similar to each other in many ways, but as H. W. Simons and his co-workers[14] have pointed out, the similarities can be either relevant or irrelevant. For example, both you and an encyclopedia salesperson may be fans of the New York Yankees and drive Honda cars, but these similarities are largely irrelevant to your need for encyclopedias. However, if you have two children who are not doing well in school and you find that the salesperson has two children who were not doing well until they got a set of encyclopedias, then this similarity is highly relevant. When we talk about a relevant similarity, we're talking about one that is logically related to the message that one person is communicating to another. The research[15,16] in this area indicates that when people see a similarity between themselves and the person who is in a position to persuade or influence them, they are more apt to identify with that individual and shift their attitudes in the direction of his or her influence. We tend to see people who are similar to us as more able to truly understand our situation; hence, we listen to them carefully. This helps us understand why a former drug addict can sometimes be more influential in getting someone off drugs than a person who's never had a drug problem, why a black police chief may be more effective with black police officers who may be working a beat in a section of the city that is mostly black, why vote-seeking politicians emphasize their youthful days on the farm when they address a rural audience, or why there may be a certain skepticism about an unmarried marriage counselor's marriage counseling.

Well, you get the idea. If you want to influence others, it helps to underscore the things you have in common with them. We are inclined to listen to people who are similar to us because to the extent we know something about ourselves, we know something about them, too—something that gives a boost to the trust factor.

Concluding Overview

The source of influence makes a difference, in terms of whether or not we are swayed, in at least five major ways:

1. Our opinions on trivial issues are influenced by individuals whom we perceive as physically or socially attractive, but we are less apt to be swayed by them when deeper, more important issues are involved.
2. Our attitudes are influenced by persons whom we perceive as expert and trustworthy.
3. People can increase their trustworthiness and, hence, their effectiveness when they are honest enough to say things that may be contrary to their own self-interests.
4. People can also enhance their trustworthiness and their effectiveness when they do not seem to be trying to influence our opinion.
5. Our opinions are influenced by people whom we believe to be similar to ourselves; our identification with them decreases their unknown qualities and increases their trustworthiness.

THE MESSAGE: WHAT YOU SAY AND HOW YOU SAY IT MATTERS

Suppose you are trying to convince an audience that the use of nuclear power for energy-producing purposes is a bad idea. How should you try to persuade the greatest number of people to vote against a nuclear plant proposal in the next election? Should you use a one-sided argument or a two-sided one? If you use a two-sided approach, is it best to present the side you favor first or last? Would you convince most people by arousing their fears or by appealing to their reason? Should you draw a final conclusion for them or let them arrive at their own? How will you handle any discrepancy that may exist between your position and the audience's original opinion? Important questions. Let's take them one at a time and see if we can come up with a strategy that might enhance your argument.

A One-Sided or a Two-Sided Approach: Which Is Best?

This is a tough choice because many factors are involved. If, for example, you mention arguments favoring nuclear power, you might be considered objective and fair-minded, thus enhancing your effectiveness. On the other hand, mentioning pronuclear arguments may suggest to your listeners that the issue is a controversial one, causing them to hesitate and to postpone making a decision about the subject. As you can see, there is no simple relationship between one- or two-sided arguments and your effectiveness. Whether you use one or the other depends.

Reflections

Turn the process around for a moment. Imagine yourself in the audience. You're listening to a speaker deliver an intensely one-sided argument opposing nuclear power plants—they're not safe, they're too expensive, something could go wrong, and so forth. She concludes by suggesting that you write a letter to your state senator protesting plans for nuclear plant development. How do you suppose you would react to this? What's your usual response to one-sided arguments? Why do you suppose you react the way you do?

It depends, to some extent, on the initial attitude of your audience. Social psychological research[17] has shown that one-sided communications are usually more effective with those who initially agree with the point of view that's being offered. However, if members of the audience are leaning in the opposite direction, then a two-sided presentation is more effective. We see examples of this all the time in politics. When talking primarily to their faithful followers, politicians may deliver a one-sided, hell-raising oration favoring their own policies and candidacy. However, when addressing an audience with mixed loyalties, they tend to behave somewhat more diplomatically, giving the opposition's view reasonable "air time" before proceeding to destroy it.

It also depends on the intelligence of the audience. The more intelligent the members of an audience are—at least in terms of knowing something about the issues being discussed—the more likely it is that they will be persuaded, if first you give the opposing arguments and then you systematically refute them.[18] This is understandable; people versed in the issues are more likely to know some of the counterarguments, and if you fail to acknowledge these positions, the intelligent listeners may think you are either unfair or incapable of refutation, neither of which is the sort of quality that is likely to motivate an audience to identify with your position. In addition, there is research[19] to indicate that when people realize that there is a second side to an issue that is not mentioned, they may be resistant because they interpret your one-sidedness as pressure on them to change. A one-sided communication will normally be seen as exerting greater pressure to adopt a particular position than a two-sided communication. This is important to know, because a general truism about human behavior is that *a person is least likely to change when he or she feels pressured to change.*

Take this idea a step further. Imagine that you have an opportunity to debate publicly the pros and cons of nuclear power with a person who is strongly in favor of it. Before the debate, your opponent asks, "Do you want to speak first or last?" You have to make an important decision and you find yourself asking the following question.

What Is the Most Effective Order of Presentation?

This is another tough question. On the one hand, going first may enhance your chance of creating a lasting first impression because there is nothing in the audience's mind to interfere with your point of view; this is the *primacy effect*. On the other hand, it is equally plausible that speaking last may be a wiser choice because when people leave they may be apt to remember better the last argument; this is the *recency effect*.

At first glance, it may seem to you that it makes no difference in which order you speak. Actually, it does. The crucial variable here is *time,* and it is important in two ways: (1) the amount of time between your presentation and your opponent's presentation and (2) the amount of time between the end of the last presentation and the moment when your listeners have to make up their minds one way or the other. There are two critical points to keep in mind: (1) When there is very little time between two communications, the first communication interferes with the learning of the second communication, and the first speaker will have the advantage—an example of the primacy effect. (2) When an audience must make up its mind immediately following the second communication, the second speaker will have the advantage because there is greater retention of the presentation just heard—an example of the recency effect.

These effects were verified in a novel experiment by Norman Miller and Donald Campbell,[20] who arranged a simulated jury trial by giving a group of subjects a condensed version of an actual court case involving negligence. As you know, the prosecution and the defense have a chance to give summations to a jury. The prosecution always goes first. What varies, however, are the frequency and duration of the recesses during the proceedings. In one instance, the prosecution's summation was followed immediately by the defense's summation. After one week, the "jury" was asked to decide the case. The prosecution's side won more often—that is, the primacy effect prevailed. In another instance, there was a week's recess *between* the summations of the prosecution and the defense, and the jury was asked to decide immediately following the defense's wrap-up. In this case, the jury was more favorable to the defense—an example of the recency effect. There was no advantage in the order of presentation for two other conditions, which were: (1) when the prosecution's summation was immediately followed by the defense's statement, which was followed promptly by the jury's decision and (2) when a long delay followed both the prosecution's and the defense's summations.

How would you apply this information to your decision about when to speak? If you are going to present your arguments back to back, but the vote on the nuclear plant is several days away, you will probably be more effective if you speak first. The primacy of your communication will tend to interfere with the audience's ability to assimilate your opponent's views, and with the vote not too far off, they will not be likely to forget that much of your message. However, if the audience has to vote immediately following the second speech, and there is a prolonged break between the two speeches, you will probably be more effective speaking last. Inasmuch as there is a lengthy period between speeches, the first speech will not interfere that much with the audiences assimilating what you, as the last speaker, have to say. Also, because the audience must vote right after the second speech, you're likely to have the recency principle working for you.

Your next task is to think about what you want to emphasize in your speech; as you do, you confront another important question.

What Works Best—Fear-Arousing or Logical Appeals?

If your intent is to influence people to vote against nuclear power plant proposals, what is the best way to do so? Is it more effective to arouse just a little fear by presenting the cold facts about the failures of "fail safe" nuclear plants around the country, or should you try to scare the pants off people by citing catastrophic examples and casualty statistics, and perhaps even by showing a few gory pictures, to support your argument that the dangers of possible radiation are serious and irreversible?

Reflections

We've all seen the seat belt ads. Some appeal to our sense of concern for others (buckle up for the one you love); others show us the tragic consequences if we don't use our seat belts (a man lies bleeding on the curb, thrown from his seat). Which type of ad is likely to influence you to buckle up? Why? What is its effect on you?

If you find yourself buckling up after seeing a particularly gory ad showing the possible consequences of *not* using your seat belt, then you are like most other people. The overwhelming weight of the research evidence comparing the effects of logical or pleasant appeals and fear-arousing ones suggests that people who are frightened by communications are more likely to take positive preventative action. For example, Howard Leventhal and his colleagues[21] found that more people were more motivated to stop smoking in a high-fear condition—they saw a vivid, gory color scene of a lung cancer operation—than were people in a moderate-fear condition, who saw charted relationships between cigarette smoking and lung cancer. The same relationship between fear and attitude change has been noted in studies on the advisability of getting tetanus injections,[22] following safe driving recommendations,[23] and even upgrading dental hygiene practices.[24] In these cases, the people most likely to be influenced in the direction of positive change were those who were made fearful of what would happen if they *didn't* change.

But just a minute. Before you rush out to put together your scariest presentation, consider the evidence of some early research done by Irving Janis and Seymour Feshbach,[25] who found that when people are highly fearful, they are *least* likely to change. They explored the relationship between fear and the tooth-brushing practices of a group of people. There were these conditions: *low-fear*—subjects were told how teeth and gums can become diseased when not brushed properly; *moderate-fear*—the pain and disease were made slightly more vivid, and the same recommendations were made; *high-fear*—subjects were told that improperly brushed teeth can lead to gum infections that might "spread to your eyes, or your heart, or your joints, and cause paralysis, kidney damage, or total blindness," and on top of this, they saw slides of rotten teeth and ugly gum infections. Surprisingly, when the subjects reported their attitudes and dental practices in the week following the study, more people in the *low-fear* and *moderate-fear* conditions made positive changes than those in the high-fear condition.

The question is, why? What seems to happen to some people—not all—is that when *too much* fear is aroused, they are overwhelmed, and feel that no matter what they do, they can't possibly avoid all of the possible consequences. Too much fear has a paralyzing effect. (Remember those dreams where you've been so frightened that you couldn't move?)

There are two pieces of advice that you might consider as you prepare your nuclear power plant speech. One, don't go overboard with fear tactics. People are motivated to reduce a manageable fear, but they're not motivated to do much of anything when they're frightened to death. And, two, give your audience specific instructions about what they can do to help fight the construction of nuclear power plants. Leventhal,[26] for example, found that although a high-fear communication produced great *intentions* to stop smoking, it produced little in the way of an actual reduction in smoking unless it carried *specific suggestions about how to do so.* (Drink plenty of water when you have the urge to smoke; chew gum; buy a magazine instead of cigarettes.) So if you want to influence both attitudes *and* behavior, the combination of fear-arousal and specific suggestions will likely produce the best results. The helpful information you give to your audience following your speech might include when and where to vote, the proposition number, the names of city, state, and federal officials to write to, and perhaps some advice about what to do if they're ever exposed to radiation.

As you think about your speech, there is another issue to consider.

Drawing Conclusions: A Good Idea or Not?

What do you think—will you be more apt to influence people to see your point of view if you spell out explicit conclusions or will you win over more people by presenting a rational argument and letting them draw their own conclusions? Carl Hovland and Wallace Mandell[27] tested this out by giving two groups different written communications advocating the devaluation of the U.S. dollar. The only difference between the communications was that one came to the clear conclusion that the dollar should be devalued, while the other simply presented the evidence and encouraged the audience to arrive at their own conclusions. The findings?

More than twice the number of subjects changed to support devaluation when the conclusion was specifically drawn as when the conclusion was left to them. You may be interested to know that the audience's intelligence made no difference whatsoever. You don't have to worry about insulting people's intelligence if you go ahead and draw conclusions for them. (You're likely to do that only if you draw *poor* conclusions.)

On the other hand, Darwyn Linder and Stephen Worchel[28] found in their research that when people are *motivated,* they will not only work harder to reach a conclusion, but they will also be more influenced by communications that allow them to draw their own conclusions.

What have we learned about drawing conclusions? Two important ideas: (1) If, in your speech, you draw clear conclusions about the dangers of nuclear power, you are likely to be more persuasive than if you leave those conclusions to be drawn by your audience; (2) however, if your audience is highly motivated, you may be more effective by moderating your conclusion-drawing and letting them think about it a bit.

Everyone who hopes to influence other people has to cope with the next question at one time or another.

The Discrepancy Issue: What Happens When the Message and the Audience Are Far Apart?

If you're talking to an audience that strongly disagrees with your point of view, are you likely to be more effective presenting your position in its most extreme form, or will you be more successful if you present your opinion in such a way that it does not differ greatly from the audience's position?

Reflections

Suppose that you believe that vigorous, daily exercise is an excellent way to achieve physical health and psychological well-being. You're going to talk to a group of people who believe that exercise is for the birds and possibly damaging to the heart. Do you think you will influence them to a greater extent by arguing in favor of the benefits of a daily 30-minute run or by suggesting a brisk 10-minute daily walk?

The related evidence is mixed. On one hand, there has been research[29,30] indicating that the greater the difference between the opinions of the audience and the opinions of the communicator, the greater the attitude change. If we take this at face value, we might expect to be most convincing with the anti-exercise group by arguing for a 30-minute daily run.

There is, however, a danger in this approach. It is that such an argument may fall outside the range of the anti-exercise group's *latitude of acceptance,* which means that if our communication is radically different from their point of view, they will *not* be much influenced by what we have to say. Carl Hovland, O. J. Harvey, and Muzafer Sherif [31] discovered this possibility in an experiment in which they found a *curvilinear* relation between discrepancy and opinion change. This means that as the small discrepancy between the speaker's message and the audience's attitudes increased somewhat, so did the degree of opinion change; however, as the discrepancy grew much larger, opinion change was minimal. When the discrepancy was very large, there was practically no opinion change at all. In other words, the further our point of view is from what other people already believe, the more likely it is that we will run into their *latitude of rejection* —an area including those ideas or opinions they would not consider adopting.

Hovland and his co-workers found this out when they divided a great many Oklahoma residents into three groups, each group representing a different attitude toward prohibition. (This was when Oklahoma was still a dry state with prohibition statutes.) One group felt strongly that the state should stay dry, another group felt strongly that it should go wet, and a third group took a more moderate position. They were then divided into groups in which all three opinions were represented. Each group was exposed to a different communication, so that in each group, there were some who found the message close to their own position, some who found it moderately discrepant from their point of view, and some who found it extremely discrepant from their position. For example, one of the communications was a "wet" message, which advocated that there be no restrictions on the sale of liquor; another communication was a "dry" message, which advocated no liquor at all; a third communication was a more moderate suggestion that advocated some drinking, but with certain controls and safeguards. The results quite clearly showed that the greatest opinion changes occurred when there was a *moderate* discrepancy between the actual communication and the attitudes of individual members of the groups. Extreme wets and drys were not inclined to change their opinions when exposed to views that were extremely discrepant from their own. In fact, they were not even apt to change when exposed to the moderate communication, for this message fell into their latitude of rejection. For example, the extreme wets judged the moderate position to be more prodry than it really was, and the drys judged it to be more pro-wet than it really was. The moderates, on the other hand, distorted the statement to make it more nearly coincide with their own opinion. (You can see why it is possible for three people to see or hear the same event and to arrive at three different conclusions about what actually happened.)

There is as you see, evidence on both sides. There is research to show that the greater the discrepancy between what we say to others and what they believe, the greater the attitude change. But sometimes when there is a great discrepancy, there may be little in the way of opinion change. How can we account for this?

A few pages back we saw how the credibility of the source of a communication affects whether or not people are influenced by it; the more credible the source, the more people are likely to change their opinions. This is an important point, because it helps explain why there may be a great deal of opinion change in one instance where there is a wide discrepancy between what the message conveys and what the audience believes, but not in another instance. Look at it this way: When there is a large discrepancy between what we believe and what we're told by another person, there is usually a certain amount of discomfort. There are at least two basic ways to reduce this unease: (1) We can change our opinion, or (2) we can derogate the communicator—convince ourselves that he or she is dumb, incompetent, or a Commie—and thus invalidate his or her point of view. Let's return for a moment to our antiexercise group. Suppose they heard a high school track coach speak on the positive merits of a 30-minute run each day. Do you suppose many of them would be convinced? Probably not. But let's suppose they heard 63-year-old Dr. George Sheehan, cardiologist, author of numerous books on running, holder of over fifty world records in the mile and the 1500-meter race, and frequent competitor in 26-mile marathons, talk about the value of that 30-minute daily run. Do you suppose that they would listen more carefully, that some might more seriously consider exercise, and that some might actually get out and start exercising? Probably. People might successfully rationalize that the track coach didn't know what he was talking about, but they would have trouble using the same excuse not to consider Sheehan's message. In other words, we are inclined to consider an extremely discrepant communication that is outside the latitude of our acceptance when the communicator is highly credible.

To see if this speculation held up under more controlled conditions, Elliot Aronson, Judith Turner, and J. Merill Carlsmith[32] set up an experiment in which they systematically varied the degrees of discrepancy and credibility of the communicator. First they asked a group of college women to rate several stanzas of relatively obscure poetry. Then they had each woman read an essay that supposedly was a criticism of modern poetry and which specifically mentioned a stanza she had rated poorly. For some subjects, this particular stanza was described in glowing terms by the essayist, thus creating a large discrepancy between what the subjects thought and what the essay said, while for another group of students, the essayist was only mildly favorable in describing the stanza, thus setting up a moderate discrepancy condition. For a third group, the essayist was mildly negative in treating the stanza, thus placing women in this condition in a mild-discrepancy situation. This though, was the important part. The essayist was identified to one-half of the women in the experiment as T. S. Eliot, a highly credible communicator; to the rest of the women, the essayist was identified as Agnes Sterns, from a local teachers college. After reading the essays, the women ranked the stanzas once again. The findings were interesting. When T.S. Eliot was the alleged essayist, the women who were most influenced were those whose evaluations of the stanza were most different from his; when Agnes Sterns was identified as the essayist, what she said produced a little opinion change when it was slightly discrepant from the view of the students, a great deal of change when it was moderately discrepant, and only a slight opinion change when it was extremely discrepant.

An overview of the discrepancy issue looks like this: When the opinions of people are greatly discrepant from that of the communicator, they will be far more likely to be persuaded if the communicator is a person of high credibility rather than an individual of low credibility. On the other hand, when the communicator's credibility is low, that person will produce maximum opinion change when discrepancies are moderate. A word of advice: Unless you're someone like Dr. George Sheehan, don't hope for great success if you advocate a 30-minute daily run to an antiexercise group (even if you believe in it); you'll probably be more successful by being *more* moderate and less discrepant, suggesting instead a brisk daily 10-minute walk around the block.

Concluding Overview

The message, in terms of what you say and how you say it, is a vital aspect of the communication package. Ideas to keep in mind as you think about ways to organize and present your views to others in hope of maximizing the influential effects of your message can be stated as follows:

1. A one-sided approach is usually effective with those who already agree with you, but a more balanced, two-sided approach (stressing your point of view, of course) has a greater likelihood of reaching those who may be leaning the other way. Generally, presenting both sides of an issue, while making your own preferences clear, is a good strategy, because it reduces the possibility that people will feel pressured, and hence be resistant to your influence.
2. When it come to deciding which side gets presented first, time is the crucial variable. When people have a lot of time to make up their minds and they are exposed to side A first and then side B in rapid succession, they will tend to be influenced more by what they hear first. If they have to make up their minds soon after being exposed to both positions, they will tend to be influenced more by the side they hear last.
3. A message that is moderately fear-arousing, combined with specific instructions about what to do, has a greater chance of influencing people to change their behavior than a message that is too fear-arousing (it immobilizes some) or too logical (it may not be motivating enough).
4. It is generally better to draw conclusions in your message, but not so much so that you discourage further thinking. This is particularly true when your audience is highly motivated; they will be more inclined to want to draw their own conclusions.
5. When your message and your audience are far apart, your chances of influencing them at least to consider your point of view are good if you have high credibility. Generally, the greater the discrepancy between your message and the audience's beliefs, the more resistance you can expect to encounter. You can reduce the resistance by (1) underscoring your credibility (make the audience aware of relevant experience and background details), and/or (2) by reducing the discrepancy in your message.

So far, we have seen that *who* is doing the influencing, along with *what* the influence message is and *how* it is presented are important variables in predicting how successful the attempt will be. There is still another variable we need to consider.

THE NATURE OF THE AUDIENCE: WHOM YOU ARE TALKING TO MAKES A DIFFERENCE

Your personal experiences have no doubt taught you an important psychological truism: Some people are highly resistant to virtually all forms of influence, others are swayed easily even by weak appeals, and most people fall somewhere between these two extremes. Informal observation suggest that a highly persuasive message delivered by a highly credible person will fail to change the attitudes of all the people who hear it. But it sometimes happens that a very low credibility person with a very weak appeal will succeed in changing the attitudes of *some* of the listeners. How can we explain this? What are the factors that may help us understand the variability of an individual's or an audience's response to influence? There are at least five factors—self-esteem, intelligence, mood, the listener's prior experience, and the listener's reactions when personal freedom is threatened. Let's consider each of these.

Self-Esteem: Its Effect on Persuasibility

You may recall from our discussion in Chapter 1 that self-esteem is that aspect of our personality that reflects how we *feel* about ourselves. As in most other aspects of human behavior, self-esteem is an important factor to consider here, because it is the personality variable that is most consistently related to persuasibility.[33,34] Research literature, for example, is quite clear in pointing out that high-self-esteem people are more apt to be in a position of *doing* the influencing,[35] while lower-self-esteem people are more apt to be the ones who are *being* influenced.[36,37] There is good reason for this; people with low self-esteem are more concerned about personal adequacy, think more negatively about themselves, are generally less confident, and usually are not as happy as people with high self-esteem. Hence, an individual who feels inadequate as a person is more inclined to be influenced by a persuasive message that is an individual who has higher self-regard. Not being sure of one's own ideas makes one more susceptible to the ideas of others.

Reflections

How about your own self-esteem? Do you find yourself wondering how right or worthwhile you ideas are? Do you give in to others easily, and do you find it difficult to stand up and argue for what you believe in? Do you have a gnawing sense that others either won't listen or might even laugh at what you have to say? If you find yourself answering "yes" to these questions, do you see how you might allow yourself to be too easily influenced?

A general truism about human behavior is that people like to be right. And why not? Being right gives us good feelings—a sense of competency, importance, self-regard, and self-confidence. When people with high self-esteem are exposed to a point of view at variance with their own opinion, they have to make up their mind about whether they stand a better chance of being right if they stand pat or change their opinion. High-self-esteem people may even experience great conflict when they are in basic disagreement with a highly credible communicator. However, for persons with low self-esteem, conflict is minimal; since they don't think very highly of themselves, they are inclined to believe that they stand a better chance of being right if they go along with the point of view of the communicator.

Returning for a moment to our earlier discussion of whether fear-arousing or logical appeals are more apt to change people's attitudes, there is evidence to suggest that if a fear approach changes anyone's opinion, it will morely likely be the opinion of a high-self-esteem person. For example, Howard Leventhal[38] found that where low-self-esteem people seem overwhelmed and somewhat immobilized by fear-arousing communications—particularly when they have to take immediate action, high-self-esteem people are inclined to mobilize themselves to do what needs to be done. The reason for this difference seems to have something to do with the idea that low-self-esteem people have trouble coping with the world. High-fear circumstances and communications overwhelm them until they don't know what to do. The insurance salesperson, for example, who uses scare tactics ("You could die tomorrow" or "You may get hit by a car and end up disabled for life") to try to pressure buyers into singing *now,* may lose a significant number of potential clients just because they are made to feel too fearful, which results in their inability to make a decision. Or a teacher who uses pop quizzes to motivate students to study may challenge those with high self-esteem to mobilize their thinking and do their best, but the pop quiz strategy may also serve to freeze the thinking of low-self-esteem students, who may easily feel overwhelmed by the sudden pressure to perform. What Leventhal's research teaches us is that if we use high fear-arousing or high anxiety-producing tactics to change people, we run the risk of emotionally paralyzing a fair number of low-self-esteem people, thereby keeping them in a no-change position. Better to use low- or moderate-fear tactics, which influence both high- and low-self-esteem people. For instance, rather than administer a pop quiz now, a teacher will likely get the same level of motivation and study from students by announcing that *next* week there will be a quiz.

There is an important question we need to consider in order to understand more about how successful we might be in influencing an audience.

Does Intelligence Affect the Persuasibility of an Audience?

The answer is yes, but this is a complex relationship. You may recall that earlier we noted that the influence process includes at least two steps: *comprehension* of the message and *yielding* to the message. Intelligent people, as you may suspect, are usually better able to understand any given message and therefore are in a position to be persuaded by it. On the other hand, they may be more aware of other points of view and so may be more resistant to change. Similarly, less intelligent people may be more influenceable because they are less aware of other points of view, but their lesser ability to comprehend may make a particular message somewhat ineffective. William McGuire[39] speculated that these offsetting processes for people on different intelligence levels may result in the appearance of no difference in final attitude change, which subsequent research[40] has shown to be the case.

What are the resulting implications for influencing heterogeneous audiences— say, classroom groups, or political groups, or business groups? You should keep your message relatively simple, so everyone can understand, offer some conclusions or solutions, and acknowledge other points of view. The more intelligent people will appreciate you, the less intelligent people will understand you, and you will enhance your chances of encouraging the greatest number of people at least to consider what you have to say.

Another question we need to consider that has important ramifications for the receptivity of an audience is. . . .

How Does Mood Affect Influenceability?

Certain things make us feel good, and opinions can be shaped and attitudes can be formed by a simple association with good feelings. We are more apt to be receptive to a communication if we are well-fed, relaxed, and reasonably happy. For example, Irving Janis and his colleagues[41] found that people who are given something tasty to eat while reading a persuasive communication are more influenced by what they read than people who read the same thing but who are given nothing to eat. We see many examples to this relationship between good food and receptivity to persuasion in everyday life: the politician who plies his audience with a fine meal before delivering an appeal for campaign donations; the man who takes a woman to a fine restaurant at the beginning of what he hopes will be memorable evening; the salesperson who takes a client to lunch, after which he or she displays the latest line of products.

Positive feelings and receptive moods can be created not only by a savory taste experience, but by pleasant visual and auditory experiences as well. This is why products advertised on televison and in magazines are frequently associated with pleasant scenery, people having an enjoyable time, and so on. Madison Avenue psychologists are not nearly so interested in teaching us about their products as they are in having us associate the products with pleasant sounds and sights. For example, one of the ways that Richard Nixon was packaged and sold to the American public in 1968 took the form of short spot commercials, each of which included pleasant background music. The psychology behind all of this is simple and effective: When we feel good—positive, happy, at peace, whatever you care to call it—we are more apt to be nondefensive, open to change, and open to other points of view. There is research[42] to indicate, for instance, that people who hear a persuasive message accompanied by pleasant music—folk music in this case— are more influenced by the message than people who are given the same communication, but *without* background music. Ralph Norman[43] found that an attractive young man was more effective than an unattractive middle-aged man in persuading a group of women that people should get less sleep at night than they usually do. Whereas the unattractive man was sometimes effective if he used a sufficient number of persuasive arguments, the attractive man was effective *regardless* of the number of arguments he used; the women felt good with, and about, him.

Openness to influence and good feelings—however they are derived—go together, and we would be well advised to combine them when we want to encourage a receptive mood. A colleague of mine makes very practical use of this idea; he always plays a quiet FM music station as his students come into class. An elementary school teacher of my acquaintance does the same thing as her students start the morning and the afternoon. Both claim that doing so has a certain soothing effect, which helps make their students more quiet and receptive.

The person or persons we want to influence may or may not have prior information about the topic we want to discuss with them, which leads us to ask the following question.

How Does Prior Knowledge Affect Influenceability?

You are already familiar with the concept that a medical inoculation of a weakened form of some virus can stimulate the body's immune system so that a person can later resist a more massive viral attack. Somewhat analogously, the same thing seems to happen on a cognitive level when people are "inoculated" with information that helps them resist full-blown efforts to persuade them to see a new or different point of view.

Let's return to our antiexercise group for a moment—the group that, you are trying to influence to do more daily walking or running exercises. Assume that the people you are talking to are going to hear a presentation next week that will attempt to link foot complications, leg problems, and angina symptoms to the sort of stress that walking or running exercises sometimes produce. What can you do to help make your audience more resistant to this antiexercise message?

Reflections

You might want to think about this for a moment. If you wanted your audience (children, students, clients, or whomever) to resist another point of view, what would be some good ways to achieve this end? Would you withhold information so people wouldn't be exposed to it or tempted by it? This is a favorite tactic of many parents when they deal with information about sex and drugs—they just don't say much about these topics. Does it work?

There are at least three things you can do to reduce the receptivity and persuasibility of your audience to the antiexercise communication: (1) you can give them weakened forms of the counterarguments they are likely to hear, along with refutations of the counterarguments (2) you can give them a stronger version of your own arguments, and (3) you can tell them to expect that someone will try to talk them out of the idea of exercising. Let's briefly consider each of these possibilities.

By giving them weakened forms of the counterarguments they are likely to hear, along with refutations of the counterarguments, you can, in effect, inoculate your audience against the full-blown counterpropaganda. For example, you can point out that people *do* sometimes have foot problems, that there *can* be muscular aches in the legs, and that angina symptoms *may* be present for some. But you can go on to point out that these are not particularly effective arguments against walking and running, because these problems are largely preventable with good, well-padded tennis shoes, with a thorough warm-up before starting, and by going short distances before trying a longer pull. By anticipating with them the antiexercise argument they are likely to hear, you can provide your audience with a kind of "cognitive inoculation." What is likely to happen is that your listeners will begin producing their own "anti ideas" (in the way that weak viruses produce additional antibodies), which will enable them to be somewhat more resistant to anti-exercise arguments. It is not uncommon to see parents unwittingly apply this inoculation principle in their child-rearing practices—forewarning their teenage daughters about the wily arguments that boys have been known to use to entice young women into more tempting ventures, or anticipating with their children the sort of arguments that others may use to get them to try drugs of various kinds. There is more than a little truth in the old adage that to be forewarned is to be forearmed.

William McGuire and Dimitri Papageorgis[44] verified this inoculation principle under more rigorous experimental conditions by having a group of people state their opinions, which were then subjected to a *mild* attack. The attack was refuted, and then these people were subjected to a *powerful* argument against their initial opinions. Was there much change in their opinions? Some, but not nearly as much as in a control group, whose opinions were not first subjected to the mild attack. In effect, those whose points of view were mildly attacked by counterarguments were inoculated agianst opinion change and were relatively immune. Earlier the point was made that a two-sided refutational presentation is usually the most effective means of influencing an audience with your point of view. As you see here, it has the additional advantage of increasing the audience's resistance to subsequent counterpropaganda.

The implications of the inoculation effect are powerful and far-reaching. If you really want to persuade your audience that your point of view is worth their consideration and adoption, then the way *not* to do this is to offer a single, unchallenged argument. For example, teaching more courses only in American history and exposing students only to the concepts of patriotism and Americanism will likely not be enough to help them develop a resistance to anti-American propaganda. The best way to achieve this result is to expose them to the concept of communism and its doctrines. Edgar Schein[45] found, for example, that many of the captured American soldiers during the Korean conflict in the 1950s who were most susceptible to Chinese brainwashing were relatively uninformed about communistic philosophy and ideology. Along this same line, psychological studies[46,47] have pointed out time and again that many of the young people who join religious cults are those who either haven't been given any systematic education about religious points of view or whose existing ideas about religion have never been seriously challenged. Whether captured by a Chinese communist or by a religious cult, it would appear that those who are likely to be among the most susceptible to their influence are those whose religious and/or political ideologies and beliefs have been narrowly developed and largely unquestioned by either themselves or someone else. *Principle:* If you want to increase your chances of people—whether they are your students, constituents, parishioners, clients— being influenced by your point of view and hanging on to it in the face of opposition counterarguments, then tell them not only what you believe, but what the other side believes, too. Then challenge them to think about what they believe and why they do so by mildly confronting their attitudes and beliefs.

Reflections

Consider, for a moment, the now-famous (and rather successful) advertising campaign launched by the Avis Car Rental Company when, in reference to the Hertz Car Rental Company, Avis proudly proclaimed, "We're number two, but we try harder." How would you explain the psychology of that approach in terms of what we've just be talking about? What are some other examples in advertising, religion, or politics that reflect the ideas discussed above?

A second thing you can do to reduce the receptivity of your audience to counterarguments is to give people additional evidence to support your point of view. Applying this idea to the group you're going to talk to about walking and running exercises, it would strengthen your position to give specific data about how leg, foot, and heart muscles get stronger when subjected to the systematic and controlled stress of daily use. Cite statistics and hard evidence showing the relationship between daily exercise and emotional–physical health. In other words, give your audience concrete information—the kind that will allow them to evaluate critically other points of view. If you tell me that exercise is good for me, I may believe you, but unless you tell me *why* it's good for me, I may be a sitting duck for someone who comes along with a persuasive pitch about why I am subjecting myself to needless stress when I could be reading a good book.

A third thing you can do to make your audience less persuasible is to forewarn them that an attempt will be made to persuade them. For example, if, at the conclusion of your exercise presentation, you mention that next week someone is going to try to convince them of the folly of exercise, your listeners will have time to prepare themselves *against* that happening. Television commercials, for example, might be more effective if they weren't preceded by the announcement, "And now, a message from our sponser...." A forewarning of that sort seems to say, "Be on your toes, someone's going to try to persuade you." This phenomenon was demonstrated by Jonathan Freedman and David Sears,[48] who told a group of teenagers that someone would be talking to them on the topic, "Why Teenagers Should Not Be Allowed to Drive." Ten minutes later they heard such a talk. Another group of teenagers—the control group—who *weren't* warned, heard the same talk. When the two groups were tested to find out how many had been convinced by the anti-driving talk, it was discovered that many more in the control group were persuaded by the speaker. Forewarning can be a useful way to get people to strengthen their defenses against counterarguments, but only, as research[49,50] has shown, if the arguments are against something in which they have an ego-involvement. For example, if there are people in the group you are talking to about the value of exercise who don't care one way or the other about its alleged value, forewarning them that someone will be talking to them about the hazards of exercise is not likely to make them more resistant. In fact, they may be even more receptive to the other point of view *because* of their lack of ego-involvement. *Principle:* When people are ego-involved in a particular attitude or belief, warning them that you or someone else may try to talk them out of such an attitude or belief gives them a chance to construct their defenses against your persuasion. So, if you hope to influence others with your point of view, it probably would not be helpful to your cause to make a big announcement of your intentions; rather, go quietly about your business without a lot of fanfare. But if you would like to encourage others to hang on to their beliefs, then forewarning them that someone's going to try to change their minds will help them resist the persuasion.

You may sense from our discussion that people are not terribly influenceable when they feel that someone is about to tamper with their personal freedom. Which beings us to an important final point about the nature of the audience.

Threats to Personal Freedom: Their Effect of Persuasibility

I suspect that if we each made a list of ten things in life we value very highly, personal freedom—"being our own person"—would rank high on that list. On an international scale, wars are waged because people are willing to fight, and even die, for personal freedom. On a more individual, daily living scale, we see examples of the need for a sense of freedom all around us: youths who want greater freedom from their parents, spouses who desire more freedom within their relationships, workers who want greater freedom in expressing their views and needs, students who desire more freedom in determining what is relevent, and on and on.

Freedom to express what we want and how we feel is important, and when someone threatens that freedom, we usually react. In fact, people's need to preserve their individual freedom is so universal that a psychological theory has evolved to help us understand this phenomenon. Jack Brehm[51] has developed the idea of what he calls, appropriately, *psychological reactance,* which is a motivational attitude that is triggered when a person's freedom is somehow endangered. It is a reflection of our emotional readiness to resist persuasive or coercive efforts that threaten to reduce or take away freedom of choice. There are examples of reactance behavior all around us, and each example reflects what a particular person or group regards as a threat to personal freedom: smokers feel their right to smoke is threatened by nonsmokers; nonsmokers feel that their right to clean (at least cleaner) air is violated by smokers; proabortionists feel that their right to terminate an unwanted pregnancy is threatened by antiabortionists; antiabortionists feel that a fetus's right to life is denied; some white people feel that desegregation laws eliminate their freedom to choose where their children go to school; some black people feel that segregation conditions limit their freedom to get a good schooling. And so it goes. There are endless examples of how and when people are apt to resist persuasive efforts when their personal freedom is involved.

The theory of psychological reactance is based on the reasonable assumption that each individual has certain *free behaviors.* A free behavior is simply an act which we feel we can engage in at a particular time, and which we know we have the capacity and ability to perform. Choosing to go to a movie this evening would be an example of one of our free behaviors. Voting for the candidate of our choice would be another of our free behaviors. If someone tried to talk us out of going to the movie, we would probably offer less resistance than if someone said we couldn't vote for the candidate we preferred. The more important the free behavior that is threatened, the more intense the reactance is likely to be, and consequently, the more a person will resist the efforts of others to minimize or eliminate his or her sense of freedom or free behaviors.

Reflections

How do you suppose you would react if you were told you *had* to go to a particular church (or that you couldn't), or that you *had* to choose a particular menu offering, or that you could *not* read a particular magazine, or that you *had* to donate $100 to the community agency fund? Why do you think you'd react that way?

As a general rule, the more people feel that their freedom is threatened, the more intensely they will try to safeguard it. There are two basic ways of doing this: (1) by resisting the pressure to adopt a particular position, and (2) by adopting a position clearly at variance with the one recommended.

Pushing people to the point where they feel that their personal freedom is being infringed upon is an almost guaranteed way to reduce the amount of influence you will have on them. Good teachers, managers, administrators, parents, and spouses who have successful interpersonal relationships have an intuitive understanding of the deep truth in this principle.

When people feel they're being pushed too far or pressured too intensely, they may not only resist the argument they're being confronted with, but they may also feel an increased attraction to the opposing point of view. Each of us can probably testify from personal experience that when someone tells us we *can't* do something, we frequently want to do it even more. There is some interesting research verifying this. For example, M. B. Mazis[52] found that when residents of Miami, Florida were told that they could not use laundry soaps containing phosphates because of an ordinance banning their sale, they rated phosphate soaps much highter in terms of overall effectiveness than did the residents of nearby Tampa, where there was no such ordinance. College students, as you may know, typically rate their dormitory meals about as low on the cuisine scale as food can be rated. (This brings back memories.) But what do you suppose would happen if a group of students were told that they couldn't eat at the dormitory cafeteria for two weeks because there had been a fire in the facility? Reactance theory predicts that eliminating their freedom to eat there would improve their assessment of the food. The reasoning is as follows: If the students cannot assert their freedom and do what they want, they will reestablish the sense of freedom by other means. They will do this is by feeling more positively about what they've been denied, which is exactly what happened in a study[53] investigating a situation of just this sort. Do you remember those times when your parents may have opposed your dating a certain person or your romantic involvement with a particular individual? What effect did their opposition have on your feelings for the other person? Richard Driscoll and his co-workers[54] found, in their study of forty-nine dating couples, that parental interference in love relationships tends to intensify the feeling of romantic love between members of such couples.

When people feel too much pressure not to do something, they may not only be more attracted to whatever it is they're not supposed to do, but they may end up doing the exact opposite of what was intended. Stephen Worchel and Jack Brehm[55] demonstrated this phenomenon by having two groups listen to similar arguments advocating equal treatment for the Communist party in the United States. The information in the two messages was identical, except that one group was told "you cannot believe otherwise" and "you have no choice but to believe this." Of this group, 50 percent accepted the speaker's position, 10 percent showed no change in opinion, but *40 percent* changed their position in the *opposite* direction. In contrast, in a control group of people who heard the same speech without and freedom-threatening comments, 67 percent accepted the argument, 18 percent did not change their opinion, and only 15 percent moved in the opposite direction. In earlier research, Jack Brehm and John Sensening[56] found that a group of high school students reacted the same way when they felt their freedom was threatened—they rejected the influence and did the opposite of what was expected. This has been dubbed the *boomerang effect*. Thus, if we are too hard-nosed in the way we go about trying to persuade people that they *should not* do something, we may unwittingly convince them that there is something very attractive about whatever it is we want to dissuade them from doing. This may be one reason why book censors and movie censors are so unsuccessful at persuading people not to read this book or not to go to that movie. There is something both enticing and exciting about forbidden fruit. When we go ahead and do something that we've been told not to do, we reaffirm a very important feeling—the feeling that we have the freedom to choose. For most people, this is a vital human need, one that has it roots as far back as the toddler years when "No, I do it my way" was a favorite, and sometimes first, expression of budding autonomy. Dictators—whether political despots, chairpersons, bosses, teachers, or parents—do not understand or appreciate this human characteristic, which may help explain why history is littered with so many of their failures.

Coercing people to the point where they feel that their freedom is being violated is one way to trigger reactance behavior. But what happens when someone tries to persuade us more subtly with gifts or favors?

Reflections

Imagine yourself in the following situation: You're a high school teacher, and two days before you assign year-end grades, one of your students (in the C+ to B range) leaves you an expensive gift, saying in a note that he wants to thank you for making his education so meaningful. How do you feel about receiving that gift? Does it influence the grade you give? Why or why not?

If you thought that you might feel uneasy, uncomfortable, and even suspicious —to the point where you gave the student a C+ rather than a possible benefit-of-the-doubt B, then you experienced the same kind of reactance behavior that can occur when someone tries directly to pressure you. You may not have felt free to give the B grade because, in light of the gift, that may have been the grade you felt you *had* to assign. The way to feel free was to assign to C+, a choice that was not compromised by the gift.

Reactance behavior, then, can also be prompted by people who try too hard, who flatter too much, who "kill" others with their kindness. When the need to behave freely is important—as in the case of teachers who must grade, employers who must evaluate, and others who must weigh and assess performance, reactance behavior is easily triggered by those who use excessive flattery and compliments. It, for example, you write a paper and hand it in to your instructor hoping that he or she will not be biased (at least *against* you) when evaluating it, then avoid doing anything that may make him or her feel obligated to you before he or she is finished with the evaluation. Reactance behavior is easily aroused when either the magnitude or timing of favors or compliments is suspect.

Jack Brehm and Ann Cole[57] verified this human tendency under more controlled conditions when they gave a group of subjects an opportunity to help an experimenter's confederate—one who had or had not given them a free soft drink. The experiment was set up in such a way to make the feeling of nonobligation to each other either of high or low importance. When feeling nonobligated to each other was of low importance, the confederate was helped by 95 percent of the subjects who had been given a soft drink, as opposed to only 60 percent of those who had received nothing. However, when remaining nonobligated was a high-importance condition, only 12 percent of the subjects helped the confederate who gave them a soft drink, while 45 percent helped the confederate who had not done so. Thus, a clear reactance effect: When the need to feel free (nonobligated) is important, people are less inclined to return a favor with a favor.

Reflections

We all know people who find it difficult to accept favors or gifts from others. (Are you one of these people?) In light of what we've been discussing, what is a possible explanation for the problem some have in accepting help from others? How would you explain this in terms of reactance behavior?

In most cases, *for most people,* a sense of personal freedom is important. If you want to influence people to change their ways or at least to consider your point of view, you can be sure that methods depending on coercion, demands, or overzealous flattery probably will not be very effective. For example, if you're a nonsmoker and you are bothered by someone nearby who is in the process of lighting up, a polite freedom-encouraging request ("Would you mind if I asked you not to smoke?) will very likely get you more positive results than if you come out with a blunt demand ("I wish you wouldn't smoke!"). And if you're a smoker, you may feel more inclined to comply with the first request.

Concluding Overview

Influencing a single individual or a group of people is a complex and not always predictable process. Some people are easily persuaded to change their behavior or attitudes; they fall quickly into line (sometimes *for* someone's line). Other people resist practically all attempts to influence them; they stand unbending in one spot. Most of us, however, are somewhere in the middle, resisting sometimes, giving in other times, depending on who is trying to influence us and what the message is. Many factors contribute to an audience's response to influence:

1. Self-esteem affects how people respond to influence attempts. High-self-esteem people are more apt to be mobilized and responsive to fear-arousing, emotional approaches, while low-self-esteem people tend to become more frightened and immobilized by approaches of this kind. *Lesson:* We are likely to be more successful in influencing greater numbers of people by using moderate approaches and by offering specific advice for others to follow or consider.
2. Intelligence affects what people can follow and comprehend. *Lesson:* We would be advised to keep our message simple so *everyone* can understand, to acknowledge other points of view (an intelligent audience likes that), and to offer some possible solutions or plans of action.
3. People's moods affect their receptivity to persuasive attempts. *Lesson:* A positive mood and receptivity to different points of view and new ideas go together, which suggests that whatever we can do to make people feel good (relaxed, at peace, happy) prior to our influence attempt will help them be more open to it.
4. People who have prior knowledge of someone else's viewpoint are more apt to be "inoculated" against accepting it indiscriminately. *Lesson:* There are at least three things we can do to help people be more discriminating when it comes to considering other points of view: (1) make them aware of some of the counterarguments, (2) give them supporting evidence for our point of view, and (3) forewarn them that someone may attempt to influence them in the other direction.
5. People who feel that their personal freedom to make up their own minds is threatened will tend to: (1) resist the influence that threatens that freedom, and (2) find something attractive about the opposite point of view. *Lesson:* Don't tamper with people's freedom. An authoritarian dictator may be successful, but largely with those who *choose* to follow in the first place.

When it comes to influencing others, you have seen that the source makes a difference, the message matters, and the nature of the audience has to be taken into account. When you influence a person to your point of view, you have probably used a particular kind of approach or "power" to achieve that end. What kind of power sources are available to us? A good question for us to consider.

SOCIAL POWER BASES USED TO INFLUENCE OTHERS

The term *social power* refers to the particular resource or resources that one person uses to influence another. Different people tend to prefer different power bases, and it may be interesting for you to think about the power bases you are inclined to use when you are trying to persuade others to accept your point of view.

John French and Bertram Raven[58] identified five common power bases—*reward, coercive, legitimate, referent,* and *expert*—that people tend to choose from when trying to influence others. The idea of *informational* power[59] was added later as a sixth power base. Subsequent research[60,61] points to the fact that we derive our influence power from more than one base and that the kind we use depends on both the situation and our preferences.

For purposes of discussion and illustration let's assume that we would like to convince a group of teenagers, all of whom are heavy cigarette smokers, to change their attitudes toward smoking and their smoking behavior. The question confronting us is: What methods should we use to influence them away from the smoking habit? Let's take our six power bases one at a time and see what we can come up with.

Reward Power (Give People Something Good If They Do as You Ask)

We could offer them some kind of positive reinforcement or reward for changing their smoking habits—a certain amount of money, special prizes, or even praise and special recognition. Rewarding people for doing what we want them to do has a long and impressive history of being an effective way to influence behavior. There are, however, certain aspects about the use of rewards that we need to keep in mind: (1) The size of the reward should be somewhat proportionate to the size of the accomplishment or the receiver may feel uneasy or manipulated, either one of which may trigger the sort of psychological reactance behavior we talked about earlier; (2) the reward ought to be something that the receiver values and is ready to work for—our group of teenagers may be motivated more by the promise of winning tickets to a rock concert than by free admissions to the local museums; (3) some people respond best to pure ego rewards—"you've done a good job" or "I'm really pleased with your effort," others respond best to tangible payoffs, and still others respond best to a combination of these two reinforcements.[62]

Coercive Power (A Threat to Punish If There's Resistance)

Dictatorial governments, authoritarian personalities, and bullies rely heavily on this particular power base as a primary means of influence. It can work, but it has two big drawbacks. In the first place, most people don't like being pushed around, and if forced to do something they don't want to do, they tend to resist. A second drawback, of course, is that if muscle is our primary means of influence, we have to keep a close eye on those we hope to change. Thus, coercive power is only as effective as the surveillance system available to enforce it. Threatening our group of teenagers with the promise that something awful will happen to them if they don't change their smoking habits may bring about some changes in surface behavior, but the deeper attitudes about wanting to smoke will likely remain the same. Research[63] has shown, time and again, that reward power is much more effective in effecting positive change than coercive power.

Legitimate Power (The Role You're in May Influence People)

The power we're talking about here comes from being in a particular role or position. Legitimate power is a certain vested authority limited to a particular domain. For example, your instructor may have legitimate power to influence how you behave in the classroom, but he or she does not have legitimate power to determine how you behave at someone's party. Dean Pruitt[64] has observed that legitimate power is based on the norm of "oughtness," in the sense that we are socialized from childhood on to follow the orders of people in certain positions.

The possessor of legitimate power is not obliged to explain why people "ought" to behave in a certain way. This person is influential not because he or she says the right things but because he or she has the "right" to influence. Parents, teachers, bosses, generals, ministers, and the like are all examples of roles that may give people a certain legitimate power over particular individuals. An anti-smoking, nonsmoking father, for instance, may remind his cigarette-puffing 16-year-old daughter that, since he is her father, he has a responsibility to guide her behavior, and that she should feel obliged to join the unhooked generation as he asking her to do. This is an example of legitimate power. Unless you have a particular role that "legitimizes" your attempt to influence the group of teens away from their smoking behavior, your chances of changing their minds are rather poor.

Referent Power (The Kind of Person You Are May Influence Others)

This can be a particularly powerful influence base, because when people want to be like the person who is influencing them, they are self-motivated to emulate the model's behaviors. Martin Luther King, Jr. is an example of a person who had this kind of power. (You can also see that he had legitimate power, which made him even more effective.) He was admired and revered by millions because of his foresight, courage, and charismatic personality. Hence, many people wanted to be like him and acted as he did *because* they liked him.

Referent power can be positive or negative. That is, people may be influenced to behave like the person they admire and to whom they are attracted (positive power), and they may act in a way that is contrary to that of the person they dislike (negative power). One of the things we could do with the teenagers we're trying to convince is expose them to certain nonsmoking adults they may admire (athletic heroes and entertainers would be good choices) in hope of providing them with models they might imitate, thus using the positive aspects of referent power.

Expert Power (Your Experience and Know-How May Be Persuasive)

We may be able to influence our group of teenagers away from smoking on the basis of our own experience and our personal knowledge of the physiological effects of tar and nicotine. This gives us some expertise. This kind of power can be quite influential in getting people to consider what we have to say and persuading them to our point of view. Like legitimate power, expert power is usually limited to a specific area. Our family doctor may be able to influence us on health-related issues, but we would not necessarily follow his advice as to what car to buy. Martin Luther King, Jr. had expert power. It was based on his vast experience with civil rights issues and buttressed by his Ph.D., his various honorary degrees, the Nobel Peace Prize he received. Part of the secret of influencing others is convincing them in the first place that you know what you're talking about. Perhaps what it boils down to is being able and demonstrating one's ability enough times to validate it. At this point, you might be wondering, "Well, what about those people who only act like they know what they're talking about, and whose game plans sound believable, even workable?" To answer this quite reasonable question, I'm reminded of an observation made by former President Harry S. Truman: "Everyone has the right to express what he thinks. That, of course, lets the crackpots in. But if you cannot tell a crackpot when you see one, then you ought to be taken in."

Informational Power (What You Know Can Be Influential)

The five bases of influence power we've talked about so far depend to a large extent on specific individuals; that is, each base of power lies within a particular person. On the other hand, there are many examples of people who are able to influence the behavior of others not because of any particular personal characteristics, but because of the information they possess. For example, a witness to a crime has the power to influence a jury, a newscaster may have certain facts that can influence a listening audience, and a professor has access to knowledge that may be persuasive to a group of students. In each case, however, once the person dispenses the information, his or her power is reduced. For example, once the newscaster has delivered the news, he or she no longer has the power to influence the audience. In this sense, the power lies in what the person knows and not in the person him- or herself. If we want to use this sort of influence base with our group of teenagers, we might want to expose them to a person who has made an in-depth study of the effects of smoking on body chemistry. You can see that influence bases using expert power and informational power are somewhat similar. The major difference is that expert influence usually draws on some kind of personal experience, while purely informational influence usually draws on other sources.

These, then, are six basic sources of social power. Each works in a particular way and each has specific effects. Which leads us to ask. . . .

Which Power Bases Are Most Successful as Influence Sources?

Most of us have access to one or more of the six power bases under certain conditions. The more authority we have or the higher our position, the more influence bases there will be at our disposal. If you happen to be the President of the United States or a teacher or a parent or a department chairperson or someone's boss, you very likely have access to all six. The question is, which power base should you use?

Certainly one of the most direct ways to influence people to do what you want is by exercising some kind of coercive power such as force or threats. But this method has a long history of failure. There are at least four reasons: (1) it requires a high degree of surveillance to see that things are being done the way they're "supposed to be," which in turn leads to a high level of distrust and conflict;[65] (2) it frequently leads to people's disliking the person in authority and attributing negative characteristics to that person[66,67] (some of which may be richly deserved); (3) coercive influence encourages, at best, surface changes in behavior designed to pacify the leader (who may be variously referred to as a bully, tyrant, dictator, despot, or demagogue), while deeper core attitudes remain unchanged (of all the power bases, coercive power has the greatest likelihood of triggering the reactance type of behavior we discussed earlier); and (4) coercive influence makes it more difficult for a person to broaden his or her influence base to include other power bases, because there may be too many people who either don't trust or don't like this person enough to grant him or her referent or expert power. It may be worth noting that people who rely primarily on coercive power to get things done show more about their weaknesses than they do about their alleged strength. Research[68,69] is clear in pointing out that coercive power is most apt to be used by people who have generally low self-esteem and low self-confidence. All in all, coercive power, whether used in raising children, teaching school, or running a country has not proved to be either an effective or a positive means of influencing people and effecting change.

Reward power, as a means of influence, is generally more effective than coercive power primarily because it is more likely to lead to a positive personal relationship between the recepient and the rewarder.[70] This is a plus, because when the people we're trying to influence like us, they are more likely to be persuaded by our point of view (or at least be more open to it), and to grant us a broader base of social influence. A certain amount of watchdogging is necessary when reward power is used, but less so than when using coercive power. The basic principle behind this idea is that people will usually be more motivated to do what you want them to do when they can work toward something positive and rewarding (a compliment, an advancement, a higher grade, more money), and they will be less motivated to do as you hope when motivated primarily by a fear of punishment or a threat of failure.

Reflections

Consider your feelings about the following situations: Professor A promises you a better grade if you complete your assignments, while professor B threatens you with a failing grade if you do not complete your work. Supervisor A promises to write you a letter of recommendation for promotion if you do good work, while supervisor B threatens to withhold such a recommendation if you don't do good work. Which professor and which supervisor would you be most motivated to work for? To be influenced by? To like? Why? How can you explain your behavior in terms of positive or negative motivation?

The four other bases of social power—expertness, reference, legitimacy, and information—are generally preferable as sources of influence because surveillance is not necessary. In each case, the impact of the influencing person is evident. For example, some of the youths in the group we are trying to influence away from smoking might say that they stopped smoking because: (a) we know what we're talking about (expertness), or (b) we don't smoke (reference), or (c) we're older and know more than they do about it (legitimacy), or (d) we really seem to have some impressive knowledge about smoking that they weren't aware of (information).

Each of these four power bases has certain advantages and uses. Legitimate power is probably most effective when the person using it must remain separated from the people he wants to influence. Thus, an unseen general can command thousands of soldiers and a distant religious leader can influence millions of followers by virtue of the legitimacy of their roles. Expert power, too, is clearly vested in the individual, but has the added advantage that internalization of attitudes may follow its use. That is, people can be influenced by an expert not only because they're impressed by his or her credentials, but also because they believe that he or she has the correct information.

Of all the influence bases, referent power is probably the most effective in the long run. It does not require surveillance, it tends to bring the influencer and the recipient closer together (when there is a positive identification), and it's also likely to lead to deeper attitudinal changes rather than simply to changes in behavior. For example, if members of the group of teenagers are motivated to stop smoking in part because of their identification with those of us who are non-smokers, not only does their behavior change with respect to smoking (they stop), but they may also change their core attitudes about the value of cigarettes. The influence "punch" of referent power is one of the major reasons for the successes of such organizations as the Big Brother/Big Sister program and such behavior-change groups as Weight Watchers, Alcoholics Anonymous, Recovery, Inc., and Al-Anon, to name a few. In all of these cases, people find models they want to emulate because of who the people are and not because of what they know.

Up to this point, we have seen that we can, indeed, be influenced, that the source, the message, and the audience make a big difference on how one applies influence and on how effective it will be, and that there are at least six bases of social power for deriving a source or sources of influence. An important question to raise at this point is: Are there certain personal–social conditions that tend to make us more generally suggestible, or influenceable, or compliant to the wishes or demands of others? The answer is yes, there are at least four of them: (1) when someone has their "foot in the door," (2) when we feel guilty or embarrassed, (3) when we see ourselves in a subordinate position, and (4) when we feel a certain amount of group pressure to behave in a certain way. Let's consider how each of these conditions operates in the influence process.

WE'RE MORE COMPLIANT ONCE SOMEONE HAS A FOOT IN THE DOOR

Whether we're selling cosmetics, encyclopedias, or ideas, the first thing we have to do is get people to open—at least a little—their doors, pocket books, and in some instances, their minds. We will not convince people about anything, if they keep us outside of their "zone of influence." The problem is to crack that zone. Good salespeople intuitively known that one must get one's foot in the door. Are there some ways to do this? Yes, and they seem to work rather well. Consider some examples.

There is a basic principle that underscores foot-in-the-door techniques, and it is: If you want people to do something major for you, then first get them to comply with a very small and simple request. For example, suppose a man representing a consumer group called you and wanted to know if he could bring a six-man crew into your home in order to classify the various consumer products you had stored away in your kitchen, bedrooms, bathroom, and basement. Do you think you would comply with the request? If you wouldn't, you are like most other people. In a clever experiment by Jonathan Freedman and Scott Fraser,[71] only 22 percent of a group of women who were asked this said they would go along with it. But another group of women was far more willing. In fact, 53 percent of them agreed to permit this six-man survey team into their homes for a two-hour consumer inventory count. Why? Because they had been contacted three days earlier, at which time they had agreed to respond to a few simple questions about the kind of soap they used. When the second call came, these women had already been primed for the larger request.

Suppose you're facing the task of having to paint several large rooms in your home and you would like to ask someone to give you a hand. You know the job will be fairly lengthy and messy, and you realize that the person you have in mind could easily come up with some reasonable excuses for not helping out. What should you do? One possibility is to ask him to do something rather minor—say, paint one of the doors, a job so easy and quick to do that he probably couldn't turn it down. This action serves to get him involved and once involved, the likelihood of his complying with a larger request increases. This principle was nicely demonstrated in another part of the Freedman–Scott experiment, when they tried to persuade a group of homeowners to put up huge, ugly "Drive Carefully" signs in their front yards. They didn't have much luck—only 17 percent agreed to do this. However, a different group of homeowners was first "softened up" a bit by an experimenter who got his foot in the door by asking them to sign a safe-driving petition. Virtually all of those who were asked to sign the petition did so. A few weeks later, a different person asked the petition-signing homeowners if they would be willing to put up the same huge, ugly "Drive Carefully" sign. The results? More than 55 percent of the petition-signers allowed the sign to go up on their property! The basic principle of asking for something small for starters and then going for something bigger has been verified by other research.[72,73]

There is, however, evidence[74] to suggest that the initial request has to be large enough to encourage the person being asked to think of him or herself as a doer, a person who at least has the potential for doing more. For example, if a car salesperson convinces you to buy a set of whitewall tires, as opposed a set of plain black ones, you probably don't feel obligated or involved enough to buy a new car to go with them (although you may like to). However, if you have already agreed to purchase one of the dealer's used Chevettes, it may not take a great deal more to get you to consider buying a new Chevette instead.

Reflections

What practical applications do you see for the foot-in-the-door approach as a way of influencing or persuading others? How might teachers use this principle? Can you think of examples of how salespeople use it? (It's called "selling up" in sales work.) How does it work? Can you think of instances in your own life when someone has had his or her foot in your door, so to speak?

(You may be interested to know that one of the ways that a successful panhandler gets his or her foot in the door is by first asking a passerby some innocuous question having to do with time or direction, getting a response to that question, and *then* asking for a contribution to the cause.)

To understand why the foot-in-the-door approach works, we should look at it in terms of self-perception theory, an idea developed by Daryl Bem[75] that suggests our future behavior in a given area is determined by how we see ourselves. Thus, if you have first complied with someone's request to do something, you may come to see yourself as someone who does that sort of thing; for example, you may see yourself as a person who takes action on matters you believe in—such as "Drive Carefully" campaigns, or as a person who cooperates with good causes—such as consumer advocacy groups that want to inventory the products you buy, or as a person who is a decent human being—say, someone who gives the time of day and even a little change to a needy panhandler. In other words, we tend to behave in a way that is consistent with how we have come to see ourselves.

Two Variations on the Foot-in-in-the-Door Technique

We have all been asked by someone at one time or another for a nickel for a parking meter or for the correct time. And we have all complied. But why? Because so little effort was involved that it was easy to say yes? Or because the requests were so simple that it was difficult to refuse?

To the extent that compliance with very small requests stems from either of these reasons, an additional foot-in-the-door technique for influencing others is suggested: When asking someone for a favor, make it clear that you would appreciate even a very small favor, but leave the door open to any larger possibility. Keep in mind that most of us find it difficult to refuse small requests and that once we carry out a small one, the next, larger request may not seem so large at all.

Robert Cialdini and David Schroeder[76] demonstrated how this works in an experiment in which people were approached in their homes by individuals supposedly working for the American Cancer Society and asked to make donations. In one condition of the study, the solicitors made a straightforward request for money, while in a second condition the phrase, "even a penny will help," was added as a final note. The assumption was that once people felt that even a penny would be of some benefit, they would find it difficult to refuse to give at least *some* money. The results? While only 29 percent of the subjects receiving the standard request donated some money, almost half again as many—50 percent—of those appealed to with the "even a penny will help" approach contributed. And the average size of the donations was about the same in the two groups. *Lesson:* We can sharply increase our ability to influence others to give their time or money by making it somewhat difficult for them to come up with convincing reasons for saying no in the first place.

Another possible means of influencing the behavior of others has been appropriately dubbed the "door-in-the-face technique" by Robert Cialdini and his colleagues.[77] It's based on the principle that if we hope to influence someone to do something that is too far out of line with what we can reasonably expect from that person, we can expect to be refused. However, if we immediately follow an out-of-line request with a more modest request, we greatly increase our chances of compliance with the second request. For example, Cialdini found that when he stopped university students on the sidewalk and asked them to chaperone a group of delinquents on a 2-hour trip to the zoo, only 17 percent agreed to do so. He then stopped another group of students and first asked them to work at a detention center for two hours a week for two years as unpaid counselors. No one agreed to do this. However, when he then asked individuals in this second group if they would be willing to comply with the zoo-trip request, 50 percent agreed to do so!

Reflections

A stranger asks you for a ride home, but he is going five miles out of your way. You refuse. He then asks you for 20 cents to call a taxi. What do you do? Once, my wife brought up the possibility of buying a very expensive vacuum sweeper with many gadgets. I resisted. She wondered about the possibility of a new (and more reasonable) Hoover model. How do you suppose I responded?* Union negotiators start by demanding a $5/hour increase. Management refuses. Eventually, the union team asks for a $1.25/hour increase. What are the chances of management settling for this?

Why does the door-in-the-face technique work the way it does? Its psychology works something like that of equity theory, which we discussed in Chapter 2. That is, if someone makes an extreme request and we refuse, and then he or she makes a much more modest request, we are more apt to feel that we, too, should make a concession and meet the other person halfway. In other words, we'll do our part to make the relationship even out or equitable.

There are two important conditions that this approach has to meet in order for it to have a chance of working. One, the two requests have to be made by the same person; the reason for this seems to be that the person making the large request must be perceived as backing down or conceding by settling for the small request. And, two, as Arnie Cann[78] and his associates have shown in their research, the second request should follow the first request within a short period of time in order to enhance the possibility of compliance. When, for example, they tried the door-in-the-face approach with a week to ten days passing between the two requests, compliance did not increase. The need to appear equitable and fair and to meet halfway a person who starts out with a large request and ends up with a much smaller one seems to fade quickly with time. *Lesson:* Most people like to be fair in their relationships, and if they see you give in a bit on your original request (which may or may not be inflated), they are more apt to comply with a scaled-down second request, particularly if you, and not someone else, make the second request.

If you've ever had the sense that you're more agreeable and compliant when you feel guilty about something, you're probably right. Most of us are more susceptible to influence under that emotional "rain cloud," which brings us to our next point.

---

*With enthusiasm. We now have a new Hoover.

CAUTION: A GUILTY CONSCIENCE MAKES US MORE PERSUADABLE THAN USUAL

There is probably no more weighty feeling in the whole world than a guilty conscience. It is an inner feeling that can grow out of violating a personal standard and/or someone else's expectations, and it can leave us with a gnawing sense of having done something awful. And the more awful we feel about doing something harmful or bad to another person, the more anxious we are to make it up in some way—usually by being extra good or compliant. Guilt usually reduces our self-confidence, which is why we may feel less inclined and less able to resist efforts to influence us one way or another. Consider some interesting research examples of how this works.

Psychologists J. Merrill Carlsmith and Alan Gross[79] took a group of subjects and assigned each person to a "learner" for the purpose of participating in a so-called "learning task." In all cases, the subjects were to pull a switch each time the learner (a confederate of the experimenter) made a mistake in the learning task. For some subjects, pulling the switch merely sounded a buzzer, but other subjects were led to believe that pulling a switch delivered an electric shock to the learner. When the learning task was over, the learner casually mentioned that he was looking for volunteers to telephone people and ask them to sign petitions against freeway construction in a redwood grove. The assumption was that the group of subjects who were led to believe that they had shocked the learner would feel some guilt about what they had done and volunteer in greater numbers than subjects from the buzzer group. The results? Only 25 percent of the subjects in the buzzer group volunteered, but 75 percent in the shock condition volunteered!

Subsequent research has confirmed this guilt hypothesis. For example, it has been found that individuals induced into such guilt-arousing behaviors as lying to an experimenter and thereby ruining a study,[80] knocking over carefully arranged piles of index cards,[81] or wrecking what seems to be an expensive piece of equipment,[82] are far more willing to comply with various requests from others than are people not involved in such events.

Usually, "making it up" to the person we have in some way wronged helps relieve the guilt and reestablish an equitable relationship. But what happens when, for whatever reason, we are prevented from compensating the person we feel we've injured or wronged? Are we still as susceptible to influence because of a guilty conscience? In a clever experiment by R. B. Darlington and C. E. Macker,[83] college students worked individually with a partner in an effort to complete successfully three tasks so the partner could get extra credit toward his final grade in a psychology course. Actually, the tasks were impossible to solve, which meant the partner received no extra credit. In the control condition of the study, students worked with a partner who was indifferent to the extra credit, since he was "only auditing the course anyway." However, in the experimental condition, students worked with a partner (the experimenter's confederate, by the way) who was beset with problems—he was working twenty hours a week, his wife was pregnant, his psychology grade was borderline, and to make matters more urgent, his graduation might depend on the extra credit he could receive by completing the tasks. Can you imagine *not* feeling guilty at having failed to help this poor soul complete the three tasks? (Remember, the student helper didn't know that the tasks were impossible to complete.) In both conditions of the study, when time was up and the partner long gone, the student helper was left alone in a room, waiting, presumedly, for the experimenter. While waiting, an accomplice came in, explained that she was soliciting donations for the university blood bank, for the experimenter and, after a short conversation with the subject, asked whether he or she would donate blood to the blood bank. Only 43 percent of the control group subjects, who worked with the indifferent partner, were willing to do this, but *100 percent* of those who worked with the beleaguered partner volunteered! *Lesson:* Guilt is a pervasive feeling that tends to reduce our confidence and natural assertiveness and makes us more prone to being influenced by others' whims and wishes. If we are aware of this feeling when it exists in us, we can take whatever steps are necessary to avoid circumstances and people who may otherwise exploit our vulnerability. Doing something about the guilt— talking it out and working through it—is the best way to regain lost confidence.

Of all the people in our lives who have a chance to influence us, those in authority positions may have the greatest opportunity to do so. Which is why the next section begins with a heading that sounds more like a warning signal than an impartial title.

DOUBLE CAUTION: WE TEND TO BE EASILY INFLUENCED WHEN IN SUBORDINATE POSITIONS

On a test designed to measure a person's identification with basic authoritarian principles, there is an item worded the following way: "Obedience and respect for authority are the most important virtues children should learn." (Do you agree or disagree?) As it turns out, a great many people agree with that statement. Students are expected to obey their teachers. Children are expected to do as their parents say. Men and women in the armed forces are expected to follow orders. We are all expected to obey the law. A lesson we have all learned starting at a very early age (some of us more or less than others) is that when someone in authority tells us to do something, we'd better do it.

Reflections

How do you typically respond to authority? How did you respond to your parents' authority as you grew up? Was it your style to resist? Or did you usually do as you were told? Are you the kind who gets into a fair amount of trouble for being disobedient? Or do you feel that if a parent, teacher, or boss tells you to do something, then you better do it? How influential in your life are people with authority? Do you have trouble saying no when told or asked to do something by someone in authority?

Are the tragic lessons of history—the Wirzes at Andersonville, the Eichmanns at Nuremburg, the Calleys at My Lai, the Liddys in Watergate—isolated examples of blind obedience to authority, or is there something about human behavior in general that we need to be alert to when it comes to authority–subordinate relationships? In order to understand how this influence process works, let's turn our attention for a moment to what research has taught us about the dynamics of obedience behavior.

Obedience Behavior: Expressions and Consequences

Social psychologist Stanley Milgram spent some ten years developing and performing a series of experiments designed to test a person's obedience to authority under a variety of conditions. The basic design of Milgram's experiments was as follows: Two people were brought together in a psychological laboratory to take part in an alleged study of "memory and learning." One of them was the "teacher" and the other a "learner." The learner was seated in an arm chair, his arms strapped "to prevent excessive movement." An electrode was attached to his wrist. He was then instructed to learn a list of paired words, and he was advised that whenever he made an error he would receive electric shocks of increasing intensity.

The teacher, a person (selected at random) who did indeed believe that the experiment was a study of memory and learning, was taken to another room and seated before an impressive-looking "shock generator." Stretched out before him was an ominous line of 30 switches, ranging from 15 volts to 450 volts, in 15-volt increments. There was also labels ranging from *Slight Shock* to *Danger–Severe Shock*. The teacher was instructed by the experimenter to administer the "learning test" to his learner and to shock him each time he made an error. The teacher was advised to start at the lowest shock level (15 volts) and to increase the voltage 15 volts each time an error was made.

Actually, the learner received no shock at all. The shock generator was simply an impressive put-on. The learner's responses, all pre-taped verbal reactions, were synchronized with certain voltage inputs. On the surface, it may seem to you that the experience was so artificial and contrived that it was easy for the teacher to disobey the experimenter. However, this was not the case. As observed by Milgram:

> Observers of the experiment agree that its gripping quality is somewhat obscured in print. For the subject, the situation is not a game; conflict is intense and obvious. On the one hand, the manifest suffering of the learner presses him to quit. On the other, the experimenter, a legitimate authority to whom the subject feels some commitment, enjoins him to continue. Each time the subject hesitates to administer a shock, the experimenter orders him to continue. To extricate himself from the situation, the subject must make a clear break with authority. The aim of this investigation was to find when and how people would defy authority in the face of a clear moral imperative.[84]

All in all, the studies have involved over 1,000 people representing all socioeconomic and educational levels. It has been replicated in different parts of the world, including Australia, Germany, South Africa, and Italy, with subjects who have included skilled and unskilled workers, white-collar workers, homemakers, and representatives of the various professions. As viewed by Milgram, the most fundamental lesson of these studies is that "ordinary people, simply doing their jobs, and without any particular hostility on their part, can become agents in a terrible, destructive process. . . . Relatively few people have the resources to resist authority,"[85] In fact, research has shown that those *least* likely to resist the experimenter tended to have higher scores on a measure of authoritarian personality characteristics than those who defied him.[86]

Milgram ruled out the sadism hypothesis after giving forty subjects an opportunity to select the shock levels themselves and finding that only two of the forty administered shock at the danger level. Nearly all the rest went no further than the level at which the learner first indicated discomfort. Hurting others—or supposedly doing so in this case—is not the result of demonic inner needs but rather the result of what seems to be a strong compulsion to obey once people view themselves in positions subordinate to authority.

The question is: How could people persist in hurting another person even when they were against doing what they were doing, and even, as was the case for many, while they were protesting what they were doing? There were apparently two rather common adjustments in thinking that reduced a person's conflict in favor of obedience. One way was to justify the behavior by criticizing the learner: "He was so stupid and stubborn he deserved to be shocked." The most common adjustment, however, was for obedient subjects *to see themselves as in no position to contradict experiment directives and, thus, as not responsible for their own actions.* "I wouldn't have done it by myself. I was just doing as I was told," was a common reply.

Although there were many teachers who defied authority and refused to go on during the experiment, the fact remains that about 60 percent of the subjects were fully obedient to the orders of the experimenters. Some of the replications of Milgram's experiments, both in the American culture and elsewhere, have resulted in obedience levels as high as 85 percent.[87]

This idea about doing what one is told to do was illustrated clearly and tragically in an interview that CBS reporter Mike Wallace conducted with one of the participants in the My Lai incident that occurred during the Vietnam conflict, in which more than fifty innocent men, women, and children were massacred in a ditch. A portion of that conversation was as follows:

Q. How many people did you round up?
A. Well, there was about forty, fifty people that we gathered in the center of the village. And we placed them in there, and it was like a little island, right there in the center of the village, I'd say. . . . And. . . .
Q. What kind of people—men, women, children?

A. Men, women, children.

Q. Babies?

A. Babies. And we huddled them up. We made them squat down and Lieutenant Calley came over and said, "You know what to do with them, don't you?" And I said yes. So I took it for granted that he just wanted us to watch them. And he left, and came back about ten or fifteen minutes later and said, "How come you ain't killed them yet?" And I told him that I didn't think you wanted us to kill them, that you just wanted us to guard them. He said, "No, I want them dead." So. . . .

Q. And you killed how many? At that time?

A. Well, I fired them automatic, so you can't—You just spray the area on them and so you can't know how many you killed 'cause they were going fast. So I might have killed ten or fifteen of them.

Q. Men, women, and children?

A. Men, women, and children.

Q. And babies?

A. And babies. . . .

Q. Why did you do it?

A. Why did I do it? Because I felt like I was ordered to do it. . . .[88]

Evidence of extreme obedience to destructive authority has also been found in other research. For example, in a national survey conducted by Herbert Kelman and Lee Lawrence designed to measure attitudes toward the My Lai massacre and Lieutenant William Calley, it was found that 67 percent of the total sample of 989 respondents thought that most people would act like Calley.[89] About 50

©1964 United Feature Syndicate, Inc.

Automatic obedience, it seems, is not characteristic of all people.

percent of the sample said that they too would follow orders to shoot men, women, and children.

We are not concerned here with people who are able to say no to an order they consider destructive and then stand on their convinctions, but with individuals who acts as if they have no choice but to obey, regardless of either the nature of the order or the consequences of their actions. We might wonder how people are able to justify their obedience even when the consequences are destructive. Do such people give up their moral sense? Apparently not. As noted by Milgram:

> Although a person acting under authority performs actions that seem to violate standards of conscience, it would not be true to say that he loses his moral sense. Instead, it acquires a radically different focus. He does not respond with a moral sentiment to the actions he performs. Rather, his moral concern now shifts to a consideration of how well he is living up to the expectations that the authority has of him.[90]

The most disturbing phenomenon is that so many of us seem to behave as if we have been robbed of our free will once a directive is issued from a sufficiently powerful authority source. Which leads us to ask:

Why Are Some People Obedient to the Point of Being Destructive?

How can decent, normal, average, "ordinary" people be so easily persuaded to give up their right to resist, to say no? Indeed, why is it that a person may not even think in terms of having a right to resist? What are the psychological antecedents that make it possible for so many people to absolve themselves of personal responsibility for their behavior by claiming they are "just doing my duty" or "just following orders"?

Let us consider a rather simple premise: Obedience behavior is learned. This may seem a self-evident truth to you, but then again it may not. Milgram, for example, sees a person's capacity to "abandon his humanity" and to be obedient to the point of being destructive to his fellow humans as "a fatal flaw nature has designed into us, and which, in the long run, gives our species only a modest chance of survival."[91] This seems to me a fatalistic view of human behavior and surely one that offers little hope for change. If a person is obedient—rationally or irrationally—could it be because that person has *learned* to be so?

How Obedience Behavior May Be Learned

Although there may be other possibilities, I would like to offer three different perspectives for understanding this process of learning obedience behavior.

One possible explanation may be inferred from Erik Erikson's[92] theory of psychosocial development. In brief, it postulates that as an individual grows from infancy through adulthood he or she passes through a series of ordered "growth stages," each of which has its own particular crisis that must be resolved before moving to the next psychosocial stage. The first stage an infant goes through, according to Erikson, is "trust versus mistrust." Successful resolution theoretically results in a generalized feeling of trusting bigger, stronger, and presumably wiser people to tend to one's basic needs. Ironically enough, it may be precisely because some people have resolved the conflict *in favor of trusting* their environment that they may end up being less suspicious or critical of people they may view as wiser, if not bigger and stronger. Could it be that some people are inclined to be obedient to authority because they have learned to *trust* it?

A second possibility is that some people learn to be obedient to authority because they have learned to *fear* it. Obedience out of fear is essentially a defensive posture and reflects behavior concerned primarily with survival of the self. A classic, although tragic, example is the case of Franz Stangle, the Nazi commandant who supervised the murder of 1.2 million innocent human beings in two Nazi concentration camps. Before he became a commandant, he was, in many ways, a rather typical man—ordinary parents, devoted to his family and church, loyal to his apprentice weaver's job. But, as detailed by Gitta Sereny[93] in a penetrating biographical analysis, he was also a man seeking to resolve his insecurities and sense of helplessness by aligning himself with an authority he feared. In psychoanalytic psychology, this is commonly referred to as "identification with the aggressor." In other words, if I'm on your side and do your bidding, you won't hurt me. Child-rearing literature[94] is replete with examples of how punitive and/or inconsistent parenting may produce children who turn into overly fearful, compliant adults.

Third, people may learn to be obedient because parents, teachers, and other significant adults *expect* obedience of them. For example, in their monumental study of various patterns of child-rearing, Robert Sears, Eleanor Maccoby, and Harry Levin[95] found that, although there were differences among the mothers as to the levels of disobedience they would tolerate, the fact remained that 98 percent of the 379 mothers interviewed *expected* their children to be obedient. In our culture, obedience, proper manners, and respect for authority, (remember the old adage, "Children should be seen and not heard") are valued child behaviors. One need go no further than a social-learning point of view to explain that children learn to feel accepted (loved, rewarded) when they live up to expectations, and they learn to feel rejected (disapproved, punished) when they do not live up to those expectations.

Learning obedience is by no means a simple process. The three antecedent conditions we've looked at cannot be used as singular explanations for understanding individual instances of compliance. What very likely happens is that different individuals are motivated, to different degrees, to be obedient because of a complex socialization mix of learning to live up to expectations and learning to trust and/or fear authority.

Lesson: There is an important difference between what we call *rational* and *irrational* obedience. Rational obedience doesn't deny the essence of each person's selfhood, that is, his or her ability, or capacity, or willingness—whatever you care to call it—to choose. Rational obedience implies, "I hear you and I will think about it and, depending upon what I perceive to be the consequences of following your directive, I may or may not do as you say." Irrational obedience, on the other hand, implies, "I hear you, and I will do as you say because you say so." Could it be that some people are irrationally obedient to the point of being influenced to do things they might not ordinarily do because it never consciously occurs to them that they have a choice in the matter? (I've discussed this idea further elsewhere,[96] along with suggestions for ways to encourage rational obedience.)

Not only are we inclined to be more easily influenced by persons in authority positions, but we're also inclined to be swayed by how the people around us are behaving. Which brings us to an important concept related to interpersonal influence.

MAKE NO MISTAKE ABOUT IT—GROUP PRESSURE HAS A STRONG INFLUENCE ON BEHAVIOR

Ordinarily, when we see something with our own eyes, we're inclined to believe it. After all, seeing is believing, is it not? Usually, but apparently not always— or at least this is what might have concluded if you had been a participant in an experiment conducted by social psychologist Solomon Asch[97] some years ago.

Asch brought groups of college students together—eight at a time—and told them that they were taking part in research concerned with visual judgment. He then placed two cards in front of them. One card had a single line on it, known as the *standard line,* and the second card had three lines, one of which was the same length as the standard line. The three lines on the second card were different enough in length that it was obvious which one was the same size as the standard line. Asch held up the standard line and three comparison lines and asked each subject to specify which line on the second card was similar to the standard line. As a way of trying to see how group pressure influences individual behavior, each experimental group was set up so that seven of the eight subjects in each group who were confederates of the experimenter, gave unanimous incorrect answers in twelve of the eighteen trials.

Imagine yourself in a similar situation. Seven people (all in cahoots with the experimenter, but you don't know that) have just chosen line B as the one similar to the standard line, but your own sense tell you that line A is the same as the standard line (and it really is, but you don't know that with absolute certainty). How do you react?

Reflections

What's your usual style when what you want to do is different from what others want to do? Do you usually give in? Or do you assert yourself and stand your ground? What have you done recently that is in some way group-related which may give you a clue as to how you respond to group pressures?

How many of Asch's subjects caved in to group pressure? How many went along with the crowd rather than asserting what they believed to be the correct response?—75 percent. Three out of four agreed with the majority on at least one occasion. This contrasts with the control group, which did not include confederates giving wrong answers, where there was only a 5 percent error rate in matching the lines. There were, however, some important individual differences in how the subjects—the single exceptions—responded in the experimental groups. For example, of the 123 naive subjects, about 30 percent nearly always yielded, while another 25 percent remained entirely unaffected by the wrong choices of the rest of the group. Many of the subjects who bowed to group pressure began to have doubts about themselves with respect to eyesight, judgment, understanding instructions, and even mental capacities. Indeed, even those subjects who did not conform to the group expressed doubts about themselves, although most of them eventually decided that it was the group (and not they) that had a problem. It is also interesting to note that all who yielded to group pressure underestimated the extent to which they went along with the group. We are, apparently, swayed by group opinion more than we may care to believe or remember.

How Important Is Group Size as an Influence Variable?

Madison Avenue advertising psychologists have known for a long time that if they can create the impression that "everyone" is buying their brand-new, improved deodorant or automobile, a great many more people are likely to buy their products. And politicians, of course, are constantly reminding us of the vast numbers of people that, according to the "polls," will be voting for them. Large numbers of people engaging in somewhat similar behavior can have a significant influence on how any particular individual behaves. There is good reason for this. The more a group behaves one way and we behave another way, the more conspicuous and "different" we tend to feel. And the more our behavior is different from the prevailing group standards, the more likely it is that we will be socially ostracized in some way. What do you suppose would happen, for example, if you wore a pair of tattered jeans and a grubby T-shirt to a church service? Or if you spoke adamantly in favor of abortion at antiabortion meeting? Or against abortion at a proabortion meeting?

In fact, the results of a number of laboratory studies suggest that the size of a group, in terms of the majority–minority ratio, does not have to be very large in order to exert maximum influence. We can be influenced significantly by relatively few people. For instance, in Asch's original experiment,[98] a majority consisting of four people had as much influence on the naive subject as did a majority consisting of either eight or sixteen people. Subsequent research by Harold Gerard and his colleagues[99] and by Angelo Valenti and Leslie Downing[100] has shown that a group's influence on the behavior of particular member increases rapidly as the group size increases to five members, and then increases at a somewhat slower rate as the group increases to eight members.

Lesson: You stand a better chance of influencing another person in a group to agree with you point of view if you have the support of four to six others. But be careful—you also stand a good chance of being influenced if *you* are the exception.

Sometimes, however, a person in a group in not alone as a minority, but has the support of one or two others. This idea leads us to ask the following question.

Are We as Vulnerable to Group Pressure When Someone Supports Us?

The answer is no, we're not as vulnerable. Having someone in our corner makes it easier to stick to our guns. For instance, in a variation on the Asch experiment,[101] when one of the confederates was instructed to give the correct answer, the naive subject was far less apt to be influenced by the wrong answers of the rest of the group. In still another variation on the Asch experiment, Vernon Allen and Jerrold Levine[102] also set up the situation so that a confederate would agree with each naive subject. There was, however, a catch. Each of these confederates had an alleged visual problem and wore very thick, heavy glasses. (Remember, the task was to pick which of three lines matched the standard line in length, so a high degree of visual discrimination was required.) The findings indicated that even the support of a visually impaired person was enough to encourage the naive subjects to resist the pressure to conform and to respond using their own best judgment more often.

Stanley Milgram also noted, in his obedience research, that people are more inclined (or able) to resist when they feel supported. In one of Milgram's[103] experiments, for example, his subjects were exposed to the behavior of two confederates who simply refused to continue shocking the victim. One refused at 150 volts, the other at 225 volts. The effect of this behavior on the subjects was dramatic. While 65 percent of the subjects did exactly as they were told (i.e., they delivered the full 450 volts) when the confederates were absent, only 10 percent did so when the confederates were present. This is further evidence to suggest that once we see other people resist authority or group pressure, we seem more willing and able to resist also.

The question is, why are we better able to resist when we feel some support? There are a number of possible explanations. First, we don't have to feel so alone and vulnerable. Second, the presence of other people who do not agree with the majority or who resist authority reduces the likelihood of rejection for deviation.

(And even if we are rejected, we know we'll have company.) Third, there is definitely something confidence-boosting about knowing for sure that our point of view or feeling is shared by someone else.

A question that gets raised with increasing frequency these days is usually along the following lines.

Are There Sex Differences in Influenceability?

The old idea that women allow themselves to be engulfed easily by the tides of group fads and peer pressures, while men are more able to stand firm, is just that —an old idea. Times are changing and so, too, is the antiquated notion that females are supposed to be dependent, passive, and conforming. Surveying the data on this issue, psychologists Alice Eagly[104] found no solid evidence for this old idea. Instead, she found that the results pointed to several principles that are applicable to both sexes. For instance, when a person has a high personal investment in a situation, the opinions of others do not easily influence either a man or a woman. But when both men and women find themselves in unfamiliar or ambiguous circumstances, they are more "suggestible."

Eleanor Maccoby and Carol Jacklin[105] concluded from their comprehensive evaluation of the relevant literature that men and women are equally susceptible to persuasive communications. They also found that in face-to-face interactions where there is social pressure to conform to a group judgment, there are usually no sex differences in susceptibility.

Reflections

Some research you can do on your own: Keep your eyes and ears open to who seems most influenceable in groups. Who stands up to social pressure? Do you note any differences between men and women in this regard? What are your *own* biases when it comes to this issue? In what way do you suppose your biases shape your preconceptions of how men and women behave in group situations?

It is clear that a group can have a strong influence on its members. And sometimes it is an essentially negative influence. Which brings us to a process knows as groupthink.

GROUPTHINK: HOW PEOPLE CAN INFLUENCE EACH OTHER TO MAKE BAD DECISIONS

Ordinarily, groups can be a helpful medium within which to focus the thinking of many minds on a single issue as long as critical thinking remains intact and freedom of expression is allowed, people in groups can influence each other in positive ways that encourage constructive decisionmaking and creative solutions to problems. But groups don't always function like this, and you can no doubt think of instances to verify the idea that group thinking is sometimes *bad* thinking and can result in bad (and sometimes sad) decisions.

Irving Janis,[106] attempting to understand how and why group processes sometimes go awry, made an intriguing historical analysis of four major American policy decisions that turned into embarrassing fiascoes: our failure to be prepared for the surprise attack on Pearl Harbor, crossing the 38th parallel in the Korean War, the "Bay of Pigs" Cuban invasion in 1961, and our escalation of the Vietnam War. (Our aborted attempt to free the American hostages in Iran in April 1980 may be another of those fiascoes, but history has yet to make its final decision about that.) According to Janis, these four policy blunders may have been made because the members of the groups responsible for them became so concerned with maintaining a group atmosphere of congeniality and mutual acceptance that they failed to evaluate critically the information on which they based their decisions. They were, as Janis put it, victims of *groupthink.*

Janis hypothesized that groups subject to groupthink dynamics have three rather specific characteristics: (1) There is a strong sense of group cohesiveness —a strong "we-feeling," you might say; (2) the group is insulated from other, more balanced information authorities; (3) the group leader tends to actively promote his or her own preferred solution to the problems confronting the group. You can see how these characteristics reflect the popular image of a conspiracy: an insulated, tightly organized, cohesive group, and a leader with a plan. (The Watergate scandal comes to mind here.) Instead of carefully weighing the pros and cons of a decision, considering the alternatives, raising critical questions, examining moral issues, and so forth, a group subject to group think has an overriding concern with a consensus, which makes it vulnerable to committing serious errors. When group members stop trying to influence each other in the usual ways (raising questions, challenging, critically analyzing), then perhaps the groupthink process is taking over. Ordinarily, the symptoms of group think can be detected as various combinations of the following behaviors:[107]

1. There is the illusion of invulnerability, which tends to create a false sense of optimism and encourages extreme risks. ("No one can touch us—of course we can do it.")
2. There are efforts to rationalize the group's actions in order to discount warnings that might lead members to reconsider their assumptions. ("John doesn't know what he's talking about. We wouldn't be doing this if it weren't in the best interests of all concerned.")
3. There tends to be an unquestioned belief in the group's inherent morality, which sways the group away from a consideration of the moral or ethical consequences of their decision. ("We're doing this for the good of the people; no one can say we haven't done the right thing.")

4. There are stereotyped views of enemy leaders as too evil to justify genuine attempts to negotiate, or as too weak or stupid to stop whatever risky attempts are made to defeat their purposes. ("There's no way those dumbbells will ever understand what we're talking about—let's go on in do what we need to do.")
5   There is strong internal pressure on group members to conform to the group norm and not dissent. ("Mary, you're the only one who seems to question this decision. Why don't you try to see it the way we do and stop rocking the boat?")
6. Individuals begin to self-censor ideas and thoughts that deviate from the consensus of the group. ("I'm not sure I agree with the direction I see the group taking —but maybe it's the right one. Guess I'll just shut up and not cause a ruckus.")
7. There is usually an illusion of unanimity about the group decision, which is partly the result of the pressure to conform that members feel. (Publicly: "Yes, I agree. This is a good plan." Privately: "This will never work. Why are we doing it?")
8. Frequently, self-appointed mind guards emerge—these are group members who work actively to protect the group from deviant ideas or information that threatens the group's cohesiveness. ("You know, Fred, you really annoy me with your questions about what we're doing. We're all together on this—relax a little.")

The surprise attack on Pearl Harbor by the Japanese on December 7, 1941 is probably as good an example as any of how the influence process can go awry when group members get caught up in groupthink dynamics. For example, three top-level groups—the command of the Pacific fleet in Hawaii, the Army and Air Force command in Hawaii, and the President's war council of policy-makers in Washington—all believed that Pearl Harbor itself would not be attacked. This is not so alarming. What is alarming is the fact that, as a consequence of cracking the Japanese secret code, voluminous information was collected, all of which pointed to the strong possibility that Japan was preparing for a massive attack on some unknown location. On December 3, the U.S. military commands learned that Tokyo had ordered diplomatic missions all over the world to destroy their secret codes, and, in addition, it was learned that Japanese carriers were "blacked-out"—radios silent, locations unknown. In spite of all this information, all three responsible groups were unconcerned about a possible surprise attack.

According to Janis's analysis, this was in part the result of groupthink, which encouraged members of these groups to think alike. As a consequence, alternative points of view weren't developed, because no one seriously questioned the existing line of thought. Admiral Kimmel in Hawaii had a devoted, highly cohesive group of advisors. Inasmuch as they were consistently loyal and supportive, Kimmel felt free to soothe their anxieties and even to express his own doubts. In fact, the day before the attack, he voiced concern about the safety of the U.S. Pacific fleet, but one of his staff reassured him that the Japanese could not possibly be able to proceed in force against Pearl Harbor when so much of their strength was concentrated in their Asiatic operations. Another staff member told him that nothing more needed to be done. You can probably sense how this kind of cohesiveness can create powerful group norms that are difficult to deviate from.

The Vietnam War provides another example of groupthink dynamics, but with a different emphasis. Admiral Kimmel at Pearl Harbor had a highly cohesive group—no dissenters to put up with. This was not true for President Lyndon Johnson and his inner group of advisors, who were nearly unanimous in supporting the Vietnam war policy. However, Secretary of Defense Robert McNamara argued against escalating the Vietnam conflict and presented impressive facts to the Senate about the ineffectiveness of bombing raids. President Johnson expressed heated anger and declared that McNamara was playing into the enemy's hands. Here a powerful leader's need to stifle dissent set the stage for an all but unanimous, highly cohesive group to groupthink its way into one of the great tragedies of our time. Shortly thereafter, McNamara was eased out of the government.

Reflections

Would you like to see an actual example of what can result from a groupthink process? Consider the following memo written for, and distributed to, employees of the National Labor Relations Board, regarding what they should do in the event of an enemy attack.[108] Could any process *but* groupthink account for its contents?

National Labor Relations Board
Washington, D.C.
Administration Bulletin

TO: All Employees

SUBJECT: Post-Attack Registration of Federal Employees

Civil Service Commission instructions require that government agencies remind all employees annually of their responsibilities under the Commission-operated registration system.

In the event of an attack all National Labor Relations Board employees should follow the procedure outlined below:

If you are prevented from going to your regular place of work because of an enemy attack, or if you are prevented from reporting to an emergency location:

Go to the nearest Post Office, ask the Postmaster for a Federal Employee Emergency Registration Card, fill it out and return it to him.

He will see that it is forwarded to the office of the Civil Service Commission, which will maintain a registration file for your area. When your card is received, the Civil Service Commission will notify us and we can then decide where and when you should report back for work.

Another important reason for mailing your Registration Card as soon as possible is that it will enable us to keep you on the roster of active employees and enable us to forward your pay. Even though you complete your Registration Card promptly, it may be a while before you are put back to work. In the meantime, you would be expected to volunteer your services to the Civil Defense authorities.

Approved for issuance:
C.S.W.

Suggestions for Ways to Avoid Groupthink

Janis himself was among the first to admit that his groupthink ideas should be regarded more as hypothetical possibilities than as established facts about why some groups make bad decisions. Although it is certainly true that groups can make poor decisions even when groupthink dynamics are *not* involved, the probability of bad decisions seems to increase when groupthink processes are generated.

There are ways which Janis has suggested to short-circuit the groupthink syndrome before it gets started. They can be summarized as follows:

1. The leader should encourage each member to be a critical evaluater and to feel free to question and criticize without fear of punishment.
2. The leader should be impartial and not impose preferences and expectations when the group starts.
3. It is helpful to have several policy-planning groups established to work on the same problem, each arriving at independent evaluations.
4. Group members should be encouraged to discuss their differences outside the main group and get independent evaluations.
5. Outside experts should be brought in from time to time to give their impartial judgments.
6. After reaching a tentative consensus, it would be helpful to have a separate meeting during which members are both encouraged and expected to express any residual doubts.

The essential idea is to discourage the sort of early member cohesion that may inhibit a group's natural critical processes and that may interfere with a careful look at all the factors that need to be taken into account prior to making a decision.

Lesson: A leader's influence—whether in classroom, industry, business, or government—can be strong and pervasive, although more so with some group members than with others. In leadership positions, we would be well advised to softpedal our own ideas at the outset, in order to encourage broader and more diversified group participation during the planning and development phases of decision-making.

IN PERSPECTIVE

Like it or not, we are indeed vulnerable to influence—some of us more or less so than others. If you're too vulnerable, you may be what others refer to as wishy-washy; if you're hardly vulnerable at all, you may be seen as rigid or inflexible. Most of us, however, are probably somewhere in between—a healthy place to be, since we are able to see things in new ways, change our minds, and generally be flexibly adaptive.

We are not influenced, willy-nilly, by just anyone. *Who* is doing the influencing (the source) makes a big difference. For example, if a person is attractive (physically and/or psychologically), believable, trustworthy, and somewhat similar to us in basic attitudes and values, we are more apt to be influenced by that person. Not all people will have all of those traits, but the more they do have, the greater the impact they're likely to have on us. If you want to sell ideas, used cars, real estate, shoes, or perhaps yourself, then you should start by highlighting those personal and physical qualities that help people to see you in your best light. As we saw in Chapter 1, how people see each other determines how they will respond to each other. People influence each other more when their response to each other is positive, and how we present ourselves as a *source* of influence can make a very big difference in whether people respond to us negatively or positively.

It is also true that *what* a person says (the message) and *how* it is said can have a significant impact on others. Deciding whether to use a one-sided or a two-sided approach, considering the most effective order for presenting your ideas, choosing between fear-arousing and logical appeals, deciding whether to draw conclusions, determining what to do if you and your audience are far apart—these are all important facets of the message package that need to be weighed and evaluated. How do you decide what to do? Some hints: (1) A one-sided approach is effective with those who already agree with you, but presenting both sides (or however many sides there are) will probably be more effective when people may not agree with you. (2) Time is the important factor to consider when deciding which side to present first. When people have a lot of time to mull things over after hearing both sides of an issue in rapid order, they will usually be influenced more by what they heard first. On the other hand, they will be more influenced by what they heard last when they have to make up their minds in a hurry. (3) Generally, moderately fear-arousing messages with specific directions have more impact than logical appeals. (4) Drawing conclusions is a good idea, but don't go to such extremes that you discourage further thinking. (5) The farther apart you and your audience are on basic issues, the more resistance you can expect to encounter. This is a tough problem to handle. About all you can do is underscore your credibility and try to reduce the discrepancy.

Whom we're trying to influence (the audience) is a critical part of the influence package. Knowing something about the audience can help you tailor your message to a particular person or group, which can increase both their understanding and your impact. Self-esteem and intelligence are two important audience variables that affect how people respond to you. When taking these variables into account, it is best to use moderate approaches—rather than highly logical or extremely fear-arousing ones, to keep the message relatively simple and straightforward, and to acknowledge other points of view. Generally, it's a waste of time trying to influence people when they're in a bad mood. Either try to create a happier frame of mind—not easy to do—or wait for a more congenial emotional moment. When thinking about how to approach an audience in order to achieve maximum influence, remember that if you push people too hard, they will tend to resist when their personal freedom is threatened. Many plans and ideas have gone down the drain because certain parents, bosses, and teachers have tried to force-feed unpalatable madates to unwilling children, employees, and students.

Influence strategies can be derived from any one or a combination of six social power bases, which include: reward power, coercive power, legitimate power, referent power, expert power, and informational power. Of the six, the use of coercive power is probably least effective, because it requires the most surveillance and causes the most alienation. You may force people to change their behavior through the use of some kind of muscle, but their basic attitudes may remain unswervingly the same as they always were. Usually, you are apt to touch more people and to have a more lasting impact if your influence attempts make use of positive reward in your own role as a "legitimate" source, in your projection of the kind of person (referent) you are, in the expertise you reflect, and in the information you have at your disposal. Perhaps a way of summarizing this is to suggest that if you want to maximize your influence, work on being a decent human being, praise honestly and genuinely, be sure you know what you're talking about when trying to convince others, and recognize that there really are points of view other than your own.

Whether we hope to influence people to listen to our ideas or to buy our product, we must first of all, as salespeople like to say, get our foot in the door. There are basically two ways to do this. One is to make a very small request—one that is easy to fulfill—and then to ask for something more substantial. Generally, we find it easier to respond to a larger request once we've compiled with a smaller one, because we tend to want to behave in a manner that is consistent with our self-perception as a giving person. A second way—a variation on the first—has been dubbed the door-in-the-face approach. The psychology behind it is basically this: Ask for something so huge to begin with that any subsequent smaller request seems almost a relief by comparison. It's common tactic used in labor negotiations. And it usually works.

A guilty conscience is the enemy of confidence, and when confidence is missing, so too is one's capacity to resist being easily influenced by the opinions of others. When we feel guilty, we're more inclined to do what others want us to do, because we feel that we have less right to say no—a vulnerable way to feel.

It is rather clear in research that people generally tend to be more influenced by others when they see themselves in subordinate positions to those in authority. In fact, people can be influenced (when in subordinate–authority relationships) to the point of being irrationally obedient, and they can end up behaving destructively toward others. A case was made for the idea that obedience to authority —whether rational or irrational—may be *learned* behavior, in the sense that one does what an authority person wants because one has learned to *trust* authority, or to *fear* authority, or to do what is asked because of learned *expectations* for obeying authority.

Groups can have an incredibly powerful influence on individual behavior. Generally speaking, the more people who oppose us on a given issue, the more difficult we find it to hold our ground. We're less susceptible to influence, however, when we feel that we have a person or two (or more) supporting us. There is, indeed, strength in numbers. Courage, too.

When a group falls into a groupthink mode of thinking and interacting, its members no longer feel free to give each other the sort of honest and, sometimes, critical feedback that is necessary for sound decision making. Members of a group in the midst of groupthink dynamics (tightly organized, highly cohesive, explicit leader opinions about what should be done) cease to influence each other by raising questions, challenging, or critically evaluating and, thereby, reduce the possibility of considering all the alternatives that may be available. Encouraging group members to consider all the options and to feel free to question and criticize without fear of retribution are among the ways to avoid groupthink dynamics and encourage healthy, positive expressions of interpersonal influence.

We influence and are influenced all the time. And we're not always aware of it. In this chapter, we have looked at some of the ways in which the influence process works, so you can have a greater awareness of how and why it works the way it does. Whether you are a teacher trying to influence your students to learn as much as possible, or an administrator trying to get positive results from your staff, or a person immersed in a social world where wheeling and dealing go on in both high and low places, this awareness may help you in two ways: (1) It may assist you in being a better and more effective *influencer* in matters that are important to you, and (2) it may help you to recognize when someone is trying to influence you, so you can exercise more consciously your options to resist or concede.

REFERENCES

1. R. E. Nisbett and L. Ross, *Human Influences: Strategies and Shortcomings in Social Judgement,* Englewood Cliffs: Prentice-Hall, 1979.

2. E. Young, "Casual Clothes are the Death of a Salesman," cited in *Psychology Today,* August 1979, p. 29.

3. S. Chaiken, "Communicator Physical Attractiveness and Persuasion," *Journal of Personality and Social Psychology* 37 (1979): 1387–1397.

4. T. F. Cash, P. J. Begley, D. A. McCown, and B. C. Weise, "When Counselors Are Heard But Not Seen: Initial Impact of Physical Attractiveness," *Journal of Counseling Psychology* 22 (1975): 273–279.

5. A. P. Goldstein, *Psychotherapeutic Attraction,* New York: Pergamon Press, 1971.

6. L. Luborsky, M. Chandler, A. H. Auerbach, J. Cohen, and H. M. Bachrach, "Factors Influencing the Outcome of Psychotherapy: A Review of Quantitative Research," *Psychological Bulletin* 75 (1971): 145–185.

7. R. Barocas and F. L. Vance, "Physical Appearance and Personnel Adjustment Counseling," *Journal of Counseling Psychology* 21: (1974): 96–100.

8. J. Mills and E. Aronson, "Opinion Change as a Function of Communicator's Influence," *Journal of Personality and Social Psychology* 1 (1965): 173–177.

9. C. Hovland and W. Weiss, "The Influence of Social Credibility on Communication Effectiveness," *Public Opinion Quarterly* 15 (1951): 635–650.

10. T. R. Husek, "Persuasive Impacts of Early, Late, or No Mention of a Negative Source" *Journal of Personality and Social Psychology* 2 (1965): 125–128.

11. W. J. McGuire, "The Nature of Attitudes and Attitude Change," in G. Lindzey and E. Aronson (Eds.), *The Handbook of Social Psychology*, Vol. III, 2nd ed., Reading, Mass.: Addison-Wesley, 1969.

12. E. Walster, E. Aronson, and D. Abrahams, "On Increasing the Persuasiveness of a Low Prestige Communicator," *Journal of Experimental Social Psychology* 2 (1966): 325–342.

13. E. Walster and L. Festinger, "The Effectiveness of 'Overheard' Persuasive Communications," *Journal of Abnormal and Social Psychology* 65 (1962): 395–402.

14. H. W. Simons, N. N. Berkowitz, and R. J. Moyer, "Similarity, Credibility, and Attitude Change: A Review and Theory," *Psychological Bulletin* 176 (1970): 1386–1392.

15. T. C. Brock, "Communicator–Recepient Similarity and Decision Change," *Journal of Personality and Social Psychology* 1 (1965): 650–654.

16. E. Aronson and B. Golden, "The Effect of Relevant and Irrelevant Aspects of Communicator Credibility on Opinion Change," *Journal of Personality* 30 (1962): 135–146.

17. C. I. Hovland, A. Lumsdaine, and F. Sheffield, *Experiments on Mass Communications*, Princeton: Princeton University Press, 1949.

18. P. G. Zimbardo, E. B. Ebbesen, and C. Maslach, *Influencing Attitudes and Changing Behavior*, 2nd ed., Reading, Mass.: Addison-Wesley, 1977, pp. 56–62.

19. R. A. Jones and J. W. Brehm, "Persuasiveness of One-Sided and Two-Sided Communications as a Function of Awareness There are Two Sides," *Journal of Experimental Social Psychology* 6 (1970): 47–56.

20. N. Miller and D. Campbell, "Recency and Primacy in Persuasion as a Function of the Timing of Speeches and Measurements," *Journal of Abnormal and Social Psychology* 59 (1959): 1–9.

21. H. Leventhal, J. C. Watts, and F. Pagano, "Effects of Fear and Instructions on How to Cope with Danger," *Journal of Personality and Social Psychology* 6 (1967): 313–321.

22. J. M. Dabbs and H. Leventhal, "Effects of Varying the Recommendations in a Fear-Arousing Communication," *Journal of Personality and Social Psychology* 4 (1966): 525–531.

23. H. Leventhal and P. Niles, "Persistence of Influence for Varying Duration of Exposure to Threat Stimuli," *Psychological Reports* 16 (1965): 223–233.

24. R. I. Evans, R. M. Rozelle, T. M. Lasater, T. M. Dembroski, and B. P. Allen, "Fear Arousal, Persuasion, and Actual vs. Implied Behavioral Change: New Perspectives Utilizing a Real-Life Dental Hygiene Program," *Journal of Personality and Social Psychology* 16 (1970): 220–227.

25. I. L. Janis and S. Feshbach, "Effects of Fear-Arousing Communications," *Journal of Abnormal and Social Psychology* 48 (1953): 78–92.

26. H. Leventhal, "Findings and Theory in the Study of Fear Communications," in L.

Berkowitz (Ed.), *Advances in Experimental Social Psychology,* Vol. V, New York: Academic Press, 1970, pp. 119–186.

27. C. I. Hovland and W. Mandell, "An Experimental Comparison of Conclusion-Drawing by the Communicator and the Audience," *Journal of Abnormal and Social Psychology* 47 (1952): 581–588.

28. D. E. Linder and S. Worchel, "Opinion Change as a Result of Effortfully Drawing a Counterattitudinal Conclusion," *Journal of Experimental Social Psychology* 6 (1970): 432–448.

29. C. I. Hovland and H. A. Pritzker, "Extent of Opinion Change as a Function of Amount of Change Advocated," *Journal of Applied Social Psychology* 54 (1957): 257–261.

30. P. Zimbardo, "Involvement and Communication Discrepancy as Determinants of Opinion Conformity," *Journal of Abnormal Social Psychology* 60 (1960): 86–94.

31. C. I. Hovland, O. J. Harvey, and M. Sherif, "Assimilation and Contrast Effects in Reaction to Communication and Attitude Change," *Journal of Abnormal and Normal Psychology* 57 (1957): 244–252.

32. E. Aronson, J. Turner, and J. M. Carlsmith, "Communication Discrepancy as Determinants of Attitude Change," *Journal of Abnormal and Social Psychology* 67 (1963): 31–36.

33. A. R. Cohen, "Some Implications of Self-Esteem for Social Influence," in C. I. Hovland and I. L. Janis (Eds.), *Personality and Persuasibility,* New Haven Conn.: Yale University Press, 1959.

34. I. Silverman, "Self-Esteem and Differential Responsiveness to Success and Failure," *Journal of Applied Social Psychology* 69 (1964): 115–119.

35. D. E. Hamachek, "Dynamics of Self–Other Perceptions and Their Relationship to Leadership Style," *Humanitas: Journal of the Institute of Man* 14 (1978): 356–366.

36. P. G. Zimbardo, E. B. Ebbesen, and C. Maslach, *Influencing Attitudes and Changing Behavior,* 2nd ed., Reading, Mass.: Addison-Wesley, 1977, pp. 59–60.

37. M. Zillner, "Self-Esteem, Reception, and Influenceability," *Journal of Personality and Social Psychology* 15 (1970): 87–93.

38. H. Leventhal, "Findings and Theory in the Study of Fear Communications," in L. Berkowitz (Ed.), *Advances in Experimental Social Psychology,* Vol V, New York: Academic Press, 1970.

39. W. J. McGuire, "Theory and Structure of Human Thought," in R. Ableson, E. Aronson, W. McGuire, T. Newcomb, M. Rosenberg, and P. Tannenbaum (Eds.), *Theories of Cognitive Consistency: A Source Book,* Chicago: Rand McNally, 1968.

40. A. H. Eagly and S. Warren, "Intelligence, Comprehension, and Opinion Change," *Journal of Personality* 44 (1976): 226–242.

41. I. L. Janis, D. Kaye, and P. Kirschner, "Facilitating Effects of 'Eating-While-Reading' on Responsiveness to Persuasive Communications," *Journal of Personality and Social Psychology* 1 (1965): 181–186.

42. M. Galizio and C. Hendrick, "Effect of Musical Accompaniment on Attitude: The Guitar as a Prop for Persuasion," *Journal of Applied Social Psychology* 2 (1972): 350–359.

43. R. Norman, "When What Is Said Is Important: A Comparison of Expert and Attractive Sources," *Journal of Experimental Social Psychology* 12 (1976): 294–300.

44. W. J. McGuire and D. Papageorgis, "The Relative Efficacy of Various Types of Prior Belief–Defense in Producing Immunity Against Persuasion," *Journal of Abnormal and Social Psychology* 62 (1961): 327–337.

45. E. H. Schein, "The Chinese Indoctrination Program Prisoners of War. A Study of Attempted Brainwashing," *Psychiatry* 19 (1956): 149–172.

46. M. T. Singer, "Coming Out of the Cults," *Psychology Today,* January 1979, pp. 72–82.

47. H. Cox, "Why Young Americans Are Buying Oriental Religions," *Psychology Today,* July 1977, 36–42.

48. J. Freedman and D. Sears, "Warning, Distraction, and Resistance to Influence," *Journal of Personality and Social Psychology* 1 (1965): 262–266.

49. W. McGuire and S. Millman, "Anticipatory Belief Lowering Following Forewarning of a Persuasive Attack," *Journal of Personality and Social Psychology* 2 (1965): 471–479.

50. R. Hass and K. Grady, "Temporal Delay, Type of Forewarning, and Resistance to Influence," *Journal of Experimental Social Psychology* 11 (1975): 459–469.

51. J. W. Brehm, *Responses to Loss of Freedom: A Theory of Psychological Resistance,* Morristown, N.J.: General Learning Press, 1972.

52. M. B. Mazis, "Antipollution Measures and Psychological Reactance Theory: A Field Experiment," *Journal of Personality and Social Psychology* 31 (1975): 654–660.

53. S. West, "Increasing the Attractiveness of College Cafetreia Food: A Reactance Theory Perspective," *Journal of Applied Psychology* 60 (1975): 656–658.

54. R. Driscoll, K. E. Davis, and M. E. Lipetz, "Parental Interference and Romantic Love: The Romeo and Juliet Effect," *Journal of Personality and Social Psychology* 24 (1972): 1–10.

55. S. Worchel and J. W. Brehm, "Effects of Threats to Attitudinal Freedom as a Function of Agreement with the Communicator," *Journal of Personality and Social Psychology* 44 (1970): 18–22.

56. J. W. Brehm and J. Sensening, "Social Influence as a Function of Attempted Implied Usurpation of Choice," *Journal of Personality and Social Psychology* 4 (1966): 703–707.

57. J. W. Brehm and A. H. Cole, "Effect of a Favor Which Reduces Freedom," *Journal of Personality and Social Psychology* 3 (1966): 420–426.

58. J. R. P. French and B. H. Raven, "The Bases of Social Power," in D. Cartwright (Ed.), *Studies in Social Power,* Ann Arbor, Mich.: Institute for Social Research, University of Michigan, 1959.

59. B. H. Raven and A. Kruglanski, "Conflict and Power," in P. Swingle (Ed.), *The Structure of Conflict,* New York: Academic Press, 1970.

60. T. V. Bonoma, "Social Psychology and Social Evaluation," *Representative Research in Social Psychology* 7 (1976): 147–156.

61. B. H. Raven, "The Comparative Analysis of Power and Power Reference," in J. R. Tedeschi (Ed.), *Power and Influence,* New York: Aldine-Atherton, 1974.

62. D. E. Hamachek, *Psychology in Teaching, Learning and Growth.* Boston: Allyn and Bacon, 1979, pp. 220–226.

63. D. E. Hamachek, *Encounters With the Self,* 2nd ed., New York: Holt, Rinehart and Winston, 1978, pp. 218–220.

64.   D. G. Pruitt, "Power and Bargaining," in B. Seidenberg and A. Snadowsky, *Social Psychology: An Introduction,* New York: Free Press, 1976.

65.   L. H. Strickland, "Changes in Self-Presentation in Need for Approval Scores," *Perceptual and Motor Skills* 27 (1968): 335–337.

66.   T. Falbo, "Multidimensional Scaling of Power Strategies," *Journal of Personality and Social Psychology* 35 (1977): 537–547.

67.   J. T. Tedeschi, *Perspectives on Social Power,* Chicago: Aldine, 1974.

68.   D. E. Hamachek, "Dynamics of Self–Other Perceptions and Their Relationship to Leadership Style," *Humanitas: Journal of the Institute of Man,* 14 (November 1978): 356–366.

69.   D. M. Kipnis, "Inner Direction, Other Direction, and Achievement Motivation," *Human Development* 17 (1974): 321–343.

70.   J. Z. Rubin and R. J. Lewicki, "A Three-Factor Experimental Analysis of Interpersonal Influence," *Journal of Applied Social Psychology* 3 (1973): 240–257.

71.   J. L. Freedman and S. C. Fraser, "Compliance Without Pressure: The Foot-in-the-Door Technique, ' *Journal of Personality and Social Psychology* 4 (1966): 195–202.

72.   P. Pliner, H. Hart, J. Kohl, and D. Saari, "Compliance Without Pressure: Some Further Data on the Foot-in-the-Door Technique," *Journal of Experimental and Social Psychology* 10 (1974): 17–22.

73.   M. Snyder and M. R. Cunningham, "To Comply or Not to Comply: Testing the Self-Perception Explanation of the Foot-in-the-Door Phenomenon," *Journal of Personality and Social Psychology* 31 (1975): 64–67.

74.   C. Seligman, M. Bush, and K. Kirsch, "Relationship Between Compliance in the Foot-in-the-Door Paradigm and Size of First Request," *Journal of Personality and Social Psychology* 33 (1976): 517–520.

75.   D. A. Bem, "Self-Perception Theory," in L. Berkowitz (Ed.), *Advances in Experimental Social Psychology,* Vol. VI, New York: Academic Press, 1972.

76.   R. B. Cialdini and D. Schroeder, "Increasing Compliance by Legitimizing Paltry Contributions: When Even a Penny Helps," *Journal of Personality and Social Psychology* 34 (1976): 599–604.

77.   R. B. Cialdini, J. E. Vincent, J. E. Lewis, S. K. Catalan, J. Wheeler, and B. L. Darby, "Reciprocal Concessions Procedure for Inducing Compliance: The Door-in-the-Face Technique," *Journal of Personality and Social Psychology* 31 (1975): 206–215.

78.   A. Cann, S. J. Sherman, and R. Elkes, "Effects of Initial Request Size and Timing of a Second Request on Compliance: The Foot-in-the-Door and the Door-in-the-Face," *Journal of Personality and Social Psychology* 32 (1975): 774–782.

79.   J. M. Carlsmith and A. E. Gross, "Some Effects of Guilt on Compliance," *Journal of Personality and Social Psychology* 11 (1969): 240–244.

80.   J. L. Freedman, S. A. Wallington, and E. Bless, "Compliance Without Pressure: The Effect of Guilt," *Journal of Personality and Social Psychology* 7 (1967): 117–124.

81.   D. T. Regan, M. Williams, and S. Sparling, "Voluntary Expiation of Guilt: A Field Experiment," *Journal of Personality and Social Psychology* 24 (1972): 42–45.

82.   S. A. Wallington, "Consequences of Transgression: Self-Punishment and Depression," *Journal of Personality and Social Psychology* 29 (1973): 1–7.

83.   R. B. Darlington and C. E. Macker, "Displacement of Guilt-Produced Altruistic Behavior," *Journal of Personality and Social Psychology* 4 (1966): 442–443.

84.   S. Milgram, *Obedience to Authority,* New York: Harper & Row, 1974, p. 4.

85.   S. Milgram, *Obedience to Authority,* New York: Harper & Row, 1974, p. 6.

86.   A. Elms and S. Milgram, "Personality Characteristics Associated with Obedience and Defiance Toward Authoritative Command," *Journal of Experimental Research in Personality* 1 (1966): 282–289.

87.   S. Milgram, *Obedience to Authority,* New York: Harper & Row, 1974, pp. 170–173.

88.   *New York Times,* November 25, 1969.

89.   M. C. Kelman and L. H. Lawrence, "American Response to the Trial of Lt. William L. Calley," *Psychology Today,* June 1972, pp. 41–45, 78–81.

90.   S. Milgram, *Obedience to Authority,* New York: Harper & Row, 1974, p. 8.

91.   S. Milgram, *Obedience to Authority,* New York: Harper & Row, 1974, p. 188.

92.   E. Erikson, *Childhood and Society,* 2nd ed., New York: W. W. Norton, 1963.

93.   G. Sereny, *Into that Darkness,* New York: W. W. Norton, 1974.

94.   W. C. Becker, "Consequences of Different Kinds of Parental Discipline " in M. L. Hoffman and L. W. Hoffman, (Eds.), *Review of Child Development Research,* New York: Russell Sage Foundation, 1964.

95.   R. R. Sears, E. E. Maccoby, and H. Levin, *Patterns of Child Rearing,* Evanston, Ill.: Row, Peterson, 1957, p. 301.

96.   D. E. Hamachek, "Removing the Stigma from Obedience Behavior," *Phi Delta Kappan,* March 1976, 443–447.

97.   S. E. Asch, "Opinions and Social Pressure," *Scientific American* 193 (1955): 31-35.

98.   S. E. Asch, *Social Psychology,* New York: Prentice-Hall, 1952.

99.   H. B. Gerard, R. A. Wilhelmy, and E. S. Connoley, "Conformity and Group Size," *Journal of Personality and Social Psychology* 8 (1968): 79–82.

100.   A. Valenti and L. Downing, "Differential Effects of Jury Size on Verdicts Following Deliberation as a Function of the Apparent Guilt of a Defendant," *Journal of Personality and Social Psychology* 32 (1975): 655–663.

101.   S. E. Asch, *Social Psychology,* New York: Prentice-Hall, 1952.

102.   V. L. Allen and J. M. Levine, "Social Support and Conformity: The Role of Independent Assessment of Reality," *Journal of Experimental Social Psychology* 7 (1971): 48–58.

103.   S. Milgram, "Liberating Effects of Group Pressure," *Journal of Personality and Social Psychology* 1 (1965): 127–134.

104.   A. Eagly, "Sex Differences in Influenceability," *Psychological Bulletin* 85 (1978): 86–116.

105.   E. E. Maccoby and C. N. Jacklin, *The Psychology of Sex Differences,* Stanford, Calif.: Stanford University Press, 1974.

106.   I. L. Janis, *Victims of Groupthink: A Psychological Study of Foreign Policy Decisions and Fiascoes,* Boston: Houghton Mifflin, 1972.

107.   I. L. Janis and I. Mann, *Decision Making,* New York: The Free Press, 1977.

108.   C. Peters and T. Adams, *Inside the System: A Washington Monthly Reader,* New York: Praeger, 1970, pp. 248–249.

Chapter 4

TOWARD DEVELOPING HEALTHY INTERPERSONAL RELATIONSHIPS

OVERVIEW

PROLOGUE

Unless you decide to live on an island for the rest of your life, interpersonal relationships will continue to be an important part of your daily existence. It can't be otherwise. We live in a social world, one that can be negotiated only by communicating with, and relating to, others, although how we do this varies widely from person to person. How we feel about ourselves, others, and life in general is affected, for better or worse, by how we manage our daily encounters and how we feel about the outcomes. The outcomes are not always predictable, which, among other reasons, is why interpersonal relationships can be risky. In one instance, the conduct and course of an interpersonal connection may leave us with a sense of joy, purpose, and gain, while in another instance, we may find ourselves left with a sense of sadness, confusion, and loss. If something can be gained, whether in an interpersonal relationship, or in the stock market, it can also be lost. It is the loss part that, whether for the person looking to make a friend or the investor looking to make a buck, makes the whole process on investing either one's self or one's money a bit risky. Reduced to its simplest components, an interpersonal relationship is a complex mix of two people who happen to be connected at a particular point in time. What grows out of this interpersonal merging depends not only on what is said, but on what *isn't* said; not only on the choice of words, but on the choice of *expression;* not only on what each person hears, but on what each person *thinks* he or she hears or *wants* to hear; not only on what actually happens, but on what each person *expects* to happen.

There is probably no such thing as a perfect interpersonal relationship, but there is such a thing as an improved one. Good relationships—healthy ones, if you will—are not easy to maintain. They may start out that way—healthy, positive, and so on—but the test of an interpersonal connection comes after the initial glow or newness of a relationship wears off and the two people involved in it begin to surface as the people they really are.

What do you want from your relationship? What sorts of behavior in yourself and in others interfere with the development of healthy relationships? What happens when people are not assertive enough to ask for what they want or, for that matter, when they're too aggressive? How does game-playing short-circuit healthy relationship development? Is it true that lack of self-love makes it difficult to love others? What steps are necessary for developing healthy interpersonal relationships?

This chapter is titled "Toward Developing Healthy Interpersonal Relationships" to emphasize the idea that a relationship is more of a journey than it is a final destination, more of an ongoing process than it is a finished product. Perhaps a way to begin this journey is to ask an important question.

WHY ARE INTERPERSONAL RELATIONSHIPS IMPORTANT?

Although many reasons for their importance can no doubt be listed, two in particular stand out. One, interpersonal relationships are important, because they allow us to stay in touch with ourselves as individuals by providing us with opportunities to get feedback and to compare ourselves with others. Psychiatrist Harry Stack Sullivan[1] referred to this as a process of "reflected appraisals." Early social psychologist C. H. Cooley[2] had this idea of interpersonal feedback in mind when he theorized his concept of the "looking-glass self," which suggests that our self-concept develops largely as a consequence of social interaction. And two, interpersonal relations are an important escape from the emotional and physical ravages of social isolation.

Let's look at each of these two underlying reasons more closely, beginning with the social comparison idea.

Being with Others Provides a Basis for Social Comparison

A major way to know what our emotions and attitudes mean and how to interpret them is by comparing them with those of other people. For example, it would be difficult for you to understand how angry the angry part of you really is unless you've experienced others' anger, or how happy the happy part of you is unless you've experienced others' happiness. Seeing how others behave and knowing what they feel in situations similar to our own helps us to understand our own behavior better. It is sometimes difficult to know whether we should laugh or cry, clap loudly or remain silent, or drink from the glass to our left or to our right, until we have some idea of how those around us are behaving.

It is this need for *social comparison* that frequently motivates us to seek the company of others when we are tense, afraid, or upset. This tendency was nicely demonstrated in a novel experiment by Stanley Schachter[3] as part of his research on why people affiliate. He divided a group of female college students into two equal groups. One group (the high-fear group) was told that, as part of an important scientific study, they would receive a series of extremely painful shocks. The other group (the low-fear group) was told that they would experience mere "tingles," would feel no pain, and, in fact, would enjoy the experiment. Then each subject was told that while the equipment was being set up, she could choose to wait for ten minutes or so by herself, or in a room together with other subjects. The question: Were there differences in the choices made by women in the two groups? Yes. Fully two-thirds of the subjects in the high-fear group chose to be with others, compared to only one-third of the low-fear subjects.

In a follow-up study with a different group of women, Schachter used the same fear-arousing technique (you'll get a painful shock), but this time he told one group of subjects that, while equipment was being set up, they could wait with others who were also taking part in this study or they could wait by themselves. A second group of subjects were told they could wait by themselves or with some students who just happened to be in the building. Not a single person in the second group chose to be with those who "just happened to be in the building," but fully 60 percent of those in the first group chose to be with people who were also waiting for the "painful shocks." (Of course, no one got shocked—that was simply the experimental condition to test people's choices for affiliation.) Thus, when anxious or frightened, most people—women, in this case—tend to seek the company of others, particularly others going through the same thing.

Can the same be said of men? Indeed it can. Ira Firestone, Kalman Kaplan, and J. Curtis Russell[4] applied Schachter's basic experimental format to groups of men, each group being told that they would receive painful shots as part of a larger study. All the men were asked if they would prefer to be alone or with others while they waited their turn to be "shocked." Men in group A were told that if they desired, they could wait with some others who were in the shock study, and men in group B were told that if they chose, they could wait with some students taking part in an unrelated study. Fully two-thirds of the men in group A wanted to be with others who were in the same boat. And 45 percent of the men in group B chose to be with others who were part of the unrelated study.

It seems to be more true than not, as Schachter observed, for misery to love miserable company. There apparently is something quite soothing about being with others when distressed. This is not difficult to understand. From the moment we are born, we learn to associate other people with feeding us when we're hungry, warming us when we're cold, caring for us when we're sick, and comforting us when we're frightened. If our early years were essentially positive, it's not hard to see how we could get psychologically hooked on the presence of other people through this involuntary conditioning process. Of course, not all people have such fortunate positive early experiences, which helps us understand why some people do *not* seek the company of others when distressed, troubled, or frightened.

Ordinarily, we prefer to be with those people who have had or are having somewhat the same sort of emotional problems or feelings as we are. Stanley Schachter's affiliation research indicates that what is important is not necessarily that others are in the same objective situation, but that they are having *somewhat the same emotional reactions* to the situation. This is the key. If, say, you and I have just finished a demanding 2-hour final exam and you feel as though your world is doomed and I feel that I've conquered a mountain, chances are very good that you will not be particularly interested in a breezy, chatty conversation with me over a cup of coffee. However, you will find great relief in discussing your doomed world with others whose personal planets are in a similar state of chaos.

Indeed, in tough situations, we not only want to be with others whose feelings are similar to ours, but, as Norman Miller and Philip Zimbardo[5] found in their research, we want to be with people whose personalities are somewhat similar to our own. Why? Primarily because we're inclined to believe that if people are too different from us, they will respond differently to the threat facing us, and we're reluctant to be with those who don't act the way we do.

Social science research[6, 7, 8] points strongly to the idea that the need to affiliate with others who are somewhat like us grows out of a natural desire to find out where we stand when we compare ourselves with them. This principle operates in large groups like Alcoholics Anonymous or Weight Watchers, or in smaller and, many times, less formal groups, such as those formed for divorced or widowed people, or singles groups for those looking for companionship. In our personal lives, we find evidence of this affiliation principle in our choices for friends, roommates, or spouses. We enjoy being with others with whom we have much in common, which is one of the reasons why friendships and marriages established on this basis can last a long time.

To summarize, being with others, particularly others who are more like than unlike us, provides us with a basis for social comparison. We can achieve at least two things: (1) greater *self-understanding,* as we have opportunities for seeing reflections of our own behavior mirrored in the behavior of others, whom we can see with greater clarity than we can see ourselves (it's hard to see your own picture when you're in the frame); (2) greater *self-acceptance,* as we can see that we're not so unusual or alone as we may have thought and that, of all things, others like us and accept us despite our shortcomings.

Reflections

During the next several weeks, you may find it interesting to pay attention to who it is that you seek out when you feel troubled or happy, as the case may be. What person or persons do you choose to be with? What do your choices suggest to you about how you compare yourself with certain others?

Our interpersonal relationships are important not only because they provide us with a basis for social comparison and the concomitant benefits of self-under-standing and self-acceptance, but also because of the following.

Being with Others Short-Circuits the Hazards of Loneliness

There is a vast difference between being alone and feeling lonely. Many of us can be by ourselves for long periods of time without feeling a sense of loneliness. Being alone is essentially a physical state, while loneliness is more a state of mind, a deeper sense of being disconnected and apart from others altogether. Vello Sermat's[9] research into the personality correlates of loneliness confirms what we know from personal experience: the kind and amount of social interaction each of us needs varies widely from person to person. Some of us, as we all know, are extroverted, outgoing, gregarious souls who seek out, reach out for, and peak on interpersonal connections—the more the better. Others of us are more introverted and private people who are happy, content, and productive, even though social contacts are minimal. I suspect that what makes a very large difference as to whether a person equates being alone with feeling lonely is whether that person *wants* to be alone or not. The point is, each of us has our upper limit. That upper limit varies greatly from person to person, but once it is reached, the effects of loneliness—that sense of feeling socially isolated—are somewhat the same for all of us.

What are the effects? Consider the reflections of Indiana University Dean W. Carl Jackson, a man who prided himself on his "self-sufficiency," who, at age 55, successfully completed a 51-day solo voyage across the Atlantic Ocean in a 30-foot ketch. As he described it:

> I found the loneliness of the second month almost excruciating. I always thought of myself as self-sufficient, but I found life without people had no meaning. I had a definite need for somebody to talk to, someone real, alive and breathing.[10]

It is apparent that, although Dean Jackson's capacity and personal desire for separateness were great, he had reached his upper limit. He was no longer experiencing the peace and quiet of solitude, but rather, the pain and anguish of isolation. There is a similar account of the effects of being socially isolated in the daily log kept by Admiral Richard Byrd, who, in 1933, voluntarily spent 6 months completely alone in a South Pole weather station that was inaccessible from the main base he commanded. After only 24 days of solitude (I say "only" advisedly; I realize that, for some, *4* days may seem like a very long time), Byrd began to write of his "brain-cracking loneliness." A small excerpt:

> This morning I had to admit to myself that I was lonely. Try as I may, I find I can't take loneliness casually, it is too big. . . . I sometimes ask myself: where am I? What am I doing here? I discover myself straining, as if trying to hear something in a place where no sound could possible exist.[11]

Dean Jackson and Admiral Byrd's experiences in being absolutely alone were extreme (Byrd did have radio contact), but they are good examples to show that even those who choose to be alone feel the pain of social isolation after a given period of time. They survived for lots of good reasons: they were tough, hardy individuals, they had certain activities they had to take care of which distracted them from their loneliness, and perhaps too, they are sustained by the certainty that their lonely vigils would eventually end. They had something to look forward to, the knowledge of which can be emotionally nourishing when life appears empty and bleak.

There is evidence to indicate that there are a number of emotional and physical hazards associated with the long-term consequences of social isolation. For example, research[12, 13] shows that people who report feeling lonely much of the time are also more apt than nonlonely people to report feeling unhappy, empty, restless, and, in extreme cases, even suicidal. Psychiatrist James Lynch[14] documented an awesome list of potential medical hazards associated with loneliness. Consider some of his major findings:

1. People at every age who live alone have death rates two or three times higher than those of married people.
2. Compared to married men, the premature death rate (before age 70) for divorced men is double for heart disease, double for cancer of the digestive system, double for strokes, five times higher for suicide, seven times higher for cirrhosis of the liver, triple for hypertension, seven times higher for homicide, and ten times higher for tuberculosis.
3. The rate of every kind of cancer is higher for divorced men and women than for those who are not married—as much as five times higher.
4. Loneliness also affects recovery from illness; the more human contact there is, the better the chances for recovery. Lynch described the case of a 54-year-old man who had received the most intensive coronary care imaginable. He had no visitors the entire time. When it was clear that he was not going to survive, every effort was made to make him as comfortable as possible. He was in a deep coma; every muscle in his body was paralyzed by a potent drug; he was able to breathe only with the aid of a machine—and yet when a nurse held his hand and quietly comforted him, his heart rate changed.

It would be easy enough to implicate living alone as the cause of loneliness. This is not necessarily the case, although it is a factor. After analyzing data received from over 27,000 people who responded to their questionnaire related to loneliness, Phillip Shaver and Carin Rubenstein[15] found that people who live alone are not necessarily lonely, and that it is their mental outlook, not their living situation, that influences their psychological and physical health. The more often people said they *felt* lonely, regardless of their living situation, the more they said they were troubled by the nineteen various health problems mentioned in the questionnaires.

Reflections

Do you want to try an interesting experiment? For a specified period—you determine the amount of time—try behaving in a way that is different for you. If you're a people-person, reduce your social contacts, keep them to an absolute minimum. Get in touch with loneliness, if possible. It you're a more socially isolated person, make a strong effort to make contact with others—as much as possible. What does it feel like to move inside/outside yourself? What are the effects?

Whether the consequence of a mental attitude or a living condition, loneliness afflicts millions, usually for the worse. Death certificates read heart attack, cancer, or suicide; but coroners are missing the point. With no one to love or to love us, we tend to smoke, drink, brood, or simply cry ourselves into earlier graves.

It doesn't have to be that way, however. In an experiment with rabbits, Robert Nerem[16] found that petting, cuddling, and a little friendly conversation is good for the heart. He made this unexpected finding while feeding a group of rabbits high-cholesterol diets in preparation for an unrelated study. When he discovered that the rabbits did not built up as much fat as expected in the walls of their arteries, one of his colleagues mentioned that she had given them special attention, greeting and cuddling each four or five times a day.

Being the curious researchers they were, Nerem's team then fed high doses of cholesterol to two new groups of rabbits. One group was left unattended except at feeding time, while the other rabbits received some old-fashioned tender loving care (TLC) everyday for at least 1 hour. The results? The TLC rabbits developed only one-third as many fatty deposits as the others. The experiment was repeated three times and all the results were the same.

This fact is by no means final proof that versions of TLC will reduce heart disease among humans, but there are studies with humans that report findings consistent with that conclusion. Some examples:[17]

1. A 9-year study of 7,000 Californians found that among people with the most social ties—to spouses, friends, and religious and community groups—there were two to three times fewer earlier-than-expected deaths than there were among socially isolated residents. In both groups, heart disease was a primary cause of death.
2. According to a survey of men under stress from losing their jobs, the more supportive their affiliations with their wives, friends, and relatives, the lower the level of cholesterol in their blood.
3. People who own pets are more likely to survive the year following their first heart attack than are people without pets, presumably because of the positive emotional bonds between owner and pet.

I think you get the idea. Being with others, whether of the human or animal species, can be beneficial when we are feeling lonely. Social isolation can be stressful, and stress, particularly negative stress—the kind that leaves us feeling depressed, gloomy, and despondent—opens us wide to a variety of real or imagined aches, pains, illnesses, and emotional symptoms. Physician Hans Selye,[18] father of the stress concept, has expressed an idea for reducing the hazards of negative stress—loneliness being one kind, which he says involves the principle of "altruistic egoism." Simply put, it means *looking out for ourselves by being necessary to others, and thus earning their good will.* An interesting idea, one that involves both giving and receiving, both of which are notably absent—or at least unbalanced—in the life of a lonely person.

Reflections

You may want to be careful not to confuse egoism, which is looking out for oneself, with *egotism,* which is the ruthless and exclusive pursuit of one's own ends. Think about the most egotistical person you know. When's the last time you saw that person altruistically do something for others?

Relationships Are Important for Different Reasons for Different People

Our interpersonal relationships are important for many reasons, and these reasons vary greatly from person to person. To some extent, most of us have a certain need for acceptance and recognition from others and an even deeper need to be loved by certain special people. Again, these needs are differently expressed by different people. John has such a strong need for acceptance from others that he turns himself into a person whom others take advantage of because he can't (or won't) say no. Sally has such a strong need to feel loved that she ends up being a soft touch for any man with a smooth line. Robert has so little need for acceptance and recognition that he comes across as being standoffish and distant, even though he may not actually be so.

Our deeper needs to be with others have a great deal to do with how others perceive us. John may be seen as a nice guy, but weak and wishy-washy; Sally may be seen by men as a warm person but not as someone they necessarily respect; Robert may be seen as not only self-sufficient, but also very snobbish. What we put into relationships determines to a large extent what we take from them.

Developing an awareness of why our interpersonal connections are important to us is the first step toward developing healthy (or healthier) relationships. For example, if John were aware of how he uses other people's acceptance of him as, let's say, a substitute for his own lack of *self*-acceptance, then he would be in a better position to build himself up, and he wouldn't have to be so dependent on others' doing it for him. If Sally were aware of the extent to which she is controlled by her need to feel loved, she might grow to understand that she is needlessly sacrificing both self-respect and the respect of others by getting sexually involved too quickly and too easily. If Robert were aware of the idea that his lack of need for acceptance has to do with a deeper fear of rejection, then he would be in a much better position to work on why he's afraid of rejection. Doing so could spare him the prospect of walking down life's path—a lonely walk it would be—with the defensive attitude that he doesn't need others, and could enable him to live more fully, in the process.

Interpersonal relationships are important for at least two good reasons: (1) They are a means of learning who we are through a process of comparing ourselves with others; and (2) they are the only means we have for staying in

touch with our common humanity and avoiding the empty world of social isolation.

Good relationships—healthy ones—can help us achieve these goals. Sometimes, however, our relationships are not so good. Which leads us to ask . . .

WHAT INTERFERES WITH THE DEVELOPMENT OF HEALTHY PERSONAL RELATIONSHIPS?

A healthy relationship, like a healthy flower garden or a healthy body, doesn't
just flourish by chance or magic. It needs to be nourished, looked after, and cared
for. Sydney Jourard,[19] who spent his entire career studying interpersonal relationships, suggested that healthy personal relationships have the following characteristics:

1. The two people involved communicate authentically with each other and stay
   in touch with each other's perspectives.
2. Their demands and claims on each other are reasonable.
3. They are actively concerned about each other's growth and happiness.
4. Each treasures the other's freedom to be himself or herself and does not try to
   control the other.

These four basic characteristics associated with healthy personal relationships
do not always exist. The question is, why not? Let's consider some possibilities.

We May Underestimate the Changes We Have to Make in Ourselves

At first glance, the characteristics listed above seem like easy enough goals to
achieve. On the surface, it appears that it would be simple enough to stay in touch
with each other's perspectives, or to make demands that are reasonable, or to
treasure each other's freedom. These gestures give the appearance of requiring
only humble changes in our sensitivity toward, and attitude about, the other
person. However, when we think of these changes in terms of having to give up
some of our pet prejudices, or having to give up our inclination to be bossy and
authoritarian, or having to give up our secret ambition to change the other person
(usually in our own image), we're thinking about behavioral modifications that
involve deeper personality traits in ourselves.

It doesn't seem difficult at all to consider the possibility of making demands
that are reasonable or treasuring each other's freedom. These are things that we
can *do*. On a deeper level, however, they also mean being less bossy and authoritarian and less self-centered. These changes may be more difficult to accomplish
because they involve changing the way we *are*. I'm not suggesting that these basic
personality modifications are impossible, only that they are more difficult—and

maybe nearly impossible—to the extent that we focus primarily on platitudinous surface considerations.

For example, if someone advises you that a personal relationship you are involved in will very likely improve if you are more reasonable and if you stop trying to change your partner, you may, with every good intention, set out to be more reasonable and more accepting. Your effort may continue for days, even weeks. You may temporarily change the things you *do,* but as long as the person you *are* remains essentially the same, it is only a matter of time before you return to being the somewhat demanding, bossy person you were in the first place.

I'm reminded of a man I once worked with in therapy whose case illustrates the principle we're talking about. His problems were his unhappy marriage and his generally poor relationship with his two teenage sons. In his words: "I don't know what the hell is wrong, I do know that I've got certain ideas about how the house should be run and how the kids should behave, and I know my wife and kids don't always agree with me. It seems like every time I voice my opinion, someone takes issue with it and all hell breaks loose." The problem was not so much that he had "certain ideas" or "voiced his opinion," but that the way in which he did those things was reminiscent of the way a hard-nosed, authoritarian marine officer might run his platoon. As he learned more about how he was coming across to his family (and others in his life), he initially attempted to improve his relationships by being more fair, reasonable, and less demanding. At first, these attempts worked—his wife and sons applauded his efforts, and the relationships improved. But this condition didn't last. Slowly but surely he drifted back to his overly rigid, demanding ways, and his relationships became as alienating as they had been before. As he discussed his frustrations during one of our sessions, he said, "I don't know what's wrong. Just last week one of my sons asked me whether he should take geometry or physics next semester, and I told him he should make up his own mind about that. My wife asked me how much I thought should be taken from the savings account and put into checking, and I told her to use her best judgment. Hell, in the past I would've told each of them what to do and that would be that. Now I don't tell people what to do and things are like they always were—awful!"

My client stopped being a rigidly demanding person who went around telling others what to do and, as a substitute, he became a rigidly *undemanding* person who withheld his counsel even when it was asked for. *The person he always was surfaced in a new form.* Because the form was new, fresh, and different, he thought he was, too. The fact is, he was as inflexible and authoritarian in insisting that people do things their own way as he had been when insisting that things be done his way. (You may recognize that, via either route, things went his way —something he was unaware of.) His problems communicating with his family were not just the consequence of a lack of communication skills, but also a lack of knowledge about himself. As he came to understand himself more fully, he was able to see that it was his emotional make-up and not just the specific things he said that were causing problems. As he made adjustments in how he saw and felt about himself, the positive outcomes he began to experience in his personal relationships were a natural consequence of deeper changes in his own personality and self-image. As he became a less authoritarian person, his behavior became less authoritarian as well.

We may underestimate the changes we have to make in ourselves to improve personal relationships—not deliberately, but more because we fail to appreciate fully how deeply ingrained certain of our behaviors are. It seems generally true that each of us has his or her own prejudices and favorite ways of viewing the world generally, and ourselves and others specifically. Clinical and empirical research[20] points clearly to the fact that people do not change easily. Along this line, I'm reminded of a wry observation made by psychologist Gordon Allport,[21] who noted that "No person ever asks to be cured of his prejudice."

Implications: You are less likely to interfere with the growth of healthy personal relationships when you make realistic assessments of the changes you may have to make in yourself. There are two advantages to this process: (1) You may discover sooner what it takes, in yourself, to really make a relationship work or, (2) you may discover sooner that you simply do not choose to make all the changes that may be necessary in particular relationships, and you can be free to seek more compatible ties.

Reflections

Consider the relationship in which you feel personally involved at this time. Is it developing the way you would like it to? Do you see anything in yourself that may be standing in its way? Do you see any signs that you may be underestimating any changes you have to make in yourself? Do you wonder how your partner would answer these questions for you?

There is something else we may do to interfere with healthy relationships.

We May Overestimate the Changes We Want Others to Make

There is nothing potentially more hazardous to the development of healthy relationships than the preconceptions we sometimes have about how the other person is supposed to behave. In counseling sessions with both married and unmarried couples over the years, a complaint I've heard most frequently from one partner or the other is that he or she feels "trapped" or "smothered" by the relationship. People who feel that way no longer feel free. As one distressed, trapped wife said during a therapy session, "God, I feel like I'm not myself anymore. It seems like I've changed so much for him [the husband] over the past five years that I no longer know who I am. Isn't that awful? Is it so bad to want to feel free enough to be the person I am?" Hers is a familiar cry, one that is often the foreboding sign of a dying relationship.

You may recall from an earlier discussion in Chapter 3 that an elaborate theory has been developed in social psychology known as *psychological reactance*. [22] Its major premise is that people are more inclined to resist change when they feel they're being forced to change. A danger in overestimating the changes we think the *other* person should make is that we may underestimate the changes *we* need to make. When that happens, the focus on who needs to change, and how much, begins to get more and more one-sided, which inevitably leads one of the parties into feeling trapped, pushed, and more resistant than ever.

In G. B. Shaw's play *Pygmalion* (most of us know it better, in its musical form, as *My Fair Lady*), the main character, Professor Higgins, transformed an ignorant little flower girl, Eliza Doolittle, into an eloquent, beautiful woman. Eliza changed because she wanted to; Professor Higgins's expectations for her became her expectations for herself. He changed her not because he forced her to change, but because she *wanted* to change. There may be a lesson here. Could it be that some of us have problems with our personal relationships because we unwittingly try to play Professor Higgins with people who are perfectly happy being who and what they are?

Perhaps no professional has been more dedicated to the idea of personal freedom and its place in healthy relationships than psychologist Carl Rogers. In his book, *Becoming Partners,* [23] Rogers emphasized a new "person-centered" approach to personal relationships generally and marriages specifically, in which both partners work on granting each other greater personal freedom. In *Carl Rogers on Personal Power,* he suggested that:

> . . . each partner will need to grant the other more living space for outside interests, outside relationships, time alone—all the elements that enrich life. . . . Experiencing that greater freedom leads them to a more rewarding life together.[24]

It is a great temptation, it seems, to try to "fix" someone so that that person can live up to the elusive quality we call his or her "potential." If you sense yourself doing so and you see the other person resisting, you can be reasonably sure that you're being a Professor Higgins to an unreceptive student.

Implication: There is a basic principle we can extract from psychotherapy that applies equally well to everyday relationships: people are most apt to change when they're motivated to change, and they are most open to accepting our help when they ask for it.

Reflections

If you've ever been in a position where someone has tried to change you in a way you didn't want to change, what affect did his or her attempt have on you? How did you feel? Respond? Why did you change or why didn't you? Do you suppose the person you're most personally involved with right now feels you are trying to change him or her? If so, I wonder how that person feels about that?

Sometimes a hurdle to the development of healthy personal relationships lies not so much in the fact that we don't like others very much, but more in the fact that . . .

We May Not Like Ourselves Too Well

Lack of self-acceptance makes it more difficult to accept others. Research[25, 26, 27] has rather consistently shown that how we feel about others is pretty much a reflection of how we feel about ourselves. This is not a particularly new idea, but it is an idea with increasing support for its validity in human relationships. Indeed, the idea that respect for one's own integrity and uniqueness, love for and understanding of one's own self, cannot be separated from respect for, and love and understanding of, another individual, is at least as old as the Biblical injunction to "Love thy neighbor as thyself!"

When it seems as easy to find fault and flaws in what our neighbor is doing, this may be a stronger statement of how we feel about ourselves than it is about how we feel about the person next door. The negative characteristics we see in others are sometimes a projection of what we see in ourselves. It is a process of self-alienation, which is the other side of self-acceptance. Alienation results when we fail to acknowledge or to accept certain aspects of the self, which are then viewed as foreign or alien. People usually remain aware of their disowned capacities—they do not cease to exist—but they tend to rationalize their awareness of them by contending that they are part of someone else. When people do this, they quite literally *project* their alienated characteristics onto some convenient bystander, where they can view them with indignation and even contempt. For example, people who are burdened with suppressed anger are more likely to feel hostile toward other people (whose behavior, in their eyes, represents their own withheld feelings) than individuals who are more open to their anger and willing to admit that an inner rage does exist. Or, as another example, it frequently happens that people who are most threatened by their own sexual stirrings are the first to criticize, to moralize, and even to feel self-righteously indignant when they perceive other people behaving in sexual ways. On the other hand, people who accept their *own* sexual feelings are inclined to be more tolerant of sexual expression by others.

It seems to be generally true that we tend to despise in others those things we despise in ourselves. The more self-loathing we are, the more flaws we will find in others. Some people, it seems, are able to find some measure of self-acceptance only to the extent that they view others suspiciously, even contemptuously. It is as if they operate on a kind of psychological pulley system: it is only when they can put others down that they can feel themselves go up. On a small scale, these people are gossips who betray and distort facts to their own advantage or cynics who specialize in ripping apart and tearing down. On a large scale, we see these people in various institutions and organizations whose primary aim, it seems, is the ultimate destruction and demise of certain minority groups.

All in all, self-acceptance, which we might say is a lack of cynicism about the self, appears to be associated with accepting other people. Self-accepting people are inclined to view the world as a generally more congenial place than are self-rejecters; they are less defensive about themselves with others. Self-accepting people get back what they give—good feelings and positive reinforcement. Low-self-accepting people experience a quite different kind of feedback. And for good reason. If, for example, I don't feel very good about myself, then I'm not likely to think very highly of you. If I don't think well of you, you are not apt to think well of me, which will have the snowballing effect of reinforcing my negative feelings about myself. It is a cyclical process.

Implication: Coming to terms with the person within us seems to be a necessary prerequisite for coming to terms with the people outside us.

Shyness is sometimes an external expression of inner feelings of low self-worth. It is possible that the development of healthier interpersonal relationships is interfered with because. . . .

We May Allow Shyness to Stand in the Way

Shyness is the common cold of the American people. The symptoms range from feeling momentarily awkward to feeling persistently inept in social settings, from feeling uncomfortable in a social situation to feeling panicked by it. There are few among us who haven't had symptoms of this psychological cold from time to time. Philip Zimbardo[28] found that 80 percent of the 5000 men and women he questioned reported feeling shy at some point in their lives and that, of these people, 40 percent *presently* considered themselves to be shy. This translates into roughly four out of every ten people, or 84 million Americans. You may be interested to know that the shyness syndrome varies from culture to culture.[29] It is especially common in Asian cultures—Japan, Taiwan, Hawaii—where competition is intense, shame is a mechanism of social control, and youths are valued on the basis of their accomplishments. Shyness is less common among the Chinese, where cooperation is more important than competition, which reduces the possibility of individual failure. Shyness is also less common among American Jews and Israelis, which may result from a sense of being special, a sense of being chosen, and a great awareness of their place in the family group.

The major emotional behavior, or feeling, associated with shyness is anxiety, which is a vague, constant feeling of apprehension—as opposed to the kind of fear that is a response to a specific, real situation. As a group, shy people have a number of characteristic self-perceptions. For example, shy people tend to believe that they are different and/or inferior to other people. They may have a feeling that others are constantly evaluating them and that they must "perform" in just the right way to be accepted. They are less inclined to express either what they want or what they would like, and they tend to follow the lead of others, even though they may resent doing so.

Reflections

Are you shy? Below are ten statements that reflect how people feel in social situations. Which are true or false for you? First, indicate your responses and then check for what they mean at the bottom.

1.____I usually feel relaxed in unfamiliar social situations.
2.____I enjoy going to parties where I can meet new people.
3.____I find it easy to relax with other people.
4.____I usually go to social functions I'm invited to.
5.____Ordinarily, I'm calm and comfortable at social events.
6.____I tend to feel tense when I'm with people I don't know.
7.____I usually avoid situations in which I have to mix with others.
8.____I have an inclination to withdraw from other people.
9.____I find it difficult to be the first one to speak.
10.____I often want to get away from people.

A shy person would probably answer *false* to the first five items and *true* to the last five. The number of "shy" responses is an indication of how shy you may or may not be.

There are degrees of shyness. At one end of what we might call a *shyness continuum* are those people who feel more comfortable doing things by themselves than with others. Scientists, writers, forest rangers, anthropologists, and accountants might be examples of people who choose to spend much of their time alone. They are largely introverts, whose choices reflect preferences rather than fears. Like Henry Thoreau, they simply prefer the more solitary life of their own Walden Ponds.

The middle range of shyness contains the largest number of people who consider themselves to be shy. They feel uncomfortable and self-conscious in social circumstances, which makes it difficult and sometimes impossible for them to say what they think or do what they'd like to do. This middle range of shyness consists of people whose lack of self-confidence, poorly developed social skills, and easily triggered embarrassment combine to produce a reluctance to approach people. This form of shyness is probably best illustrated by the person who can't ask for a date, a favor, or faster service in a slow restaurant.

At the other end of the continuum are those individuals whose fear of others is a true people phobia (anthropophobia), whose feelings go beyond mere shyness into deeper feelings of dread and overwhelming anxiety. Feelings of paranoia are the extreme expression of this kind of fear.

Shyness research[30, 31, 32] indicates that presenting ourselves to others as shy can interfere with healthy personal relationships in at least four ways:

1. *It confuses others.* It's not hard to see how this can happen. A shy person is a withholding person. When an individual behaves shyly, others don't know if he or she is interested or bored, happy or sad, involved or indifferent. In the absence of very much verbal or nonverbal feedback, others may find it difficult to relate to him or her. (Which, to a shy person, may reinforce what he or she always thought was true—nobody likes him or her.)

2. *It leads to poor self-projection.* When a person witholds him- or herself too long and too often, others may come up with inaccurate perceptions of the kind of person he or she really is. More often than not, a shy person is considered to be bored, unfriendly, or even snobbish—far from how he or she really feels.

3. *It causes difficulties in being assertive.* Passive, quiet people have more trouble standing up for their rights. They get used and feel resentful about it, but tend to keep their feelings in. As a consequence, self-respect and respect from others dwindle.

4. *It makes thinking clearly more difficult.* This is particularly true in social situations where a certain amount of verbal give-and-take is both necessary and expected. When we are concerned primarily with how we're doing and whether we are successful, we may forget what we're doing altogether. Forgetting names and faces in social gatherings is an example of how thinking becomes more difficult when social anxiety is high. Who among us hasn't had that happen to him or her at one time or other?

Shyness can cause personal relationship problems, to be sure. On a more positive note, be assured that shyness is a learned behavior, and, as such, it can

©1966 United Feature Syndicate, Inc.

For some people, shyness can be a problem; for others, however . . .

be unlearned. If you see yourself as a shy person and want to change, you may find Philip Zimbardo's book, *Shyness: What It Is and What You Can Do About It* (Addison-Wesley, 1977) an excellent source of ideas and tips for dealing with problems related to shyness.

There is yet another thing that we may do that can stand in the way of healthy personal relationships.

We May Play Games that Keep Others at a Distance

The kind of games we are talking about here are not games like Monopoly, bridge, or checkers, but psychological games played both verbally and nonverbally and involving at least two players. Psychological games are not "fun" games, and when we play them, we usually feel worse for doing so. Psychiatrist Eric Berne introduced the idea of game playing in his best-selling book, *Games People Play,* in which he described a game as:

> . . . an on-going series of complementary ulterior transactions progressing to a well-defined, predictable outcome. Descriptively it is a recurring set of transactions, often repetitious, superficially plausible, with a concealed motivation; or, more colloquially, a series of moves with a snare . . .[33]

Berne used the word "game" in a serious way. He referred to the moves as *games,* because they are usually played by certain rules, although the rules are often poorly defined and seldom explicit. Nonetheless, the rules are there and they are unconsciously followed by the players involved. Psychological games have three specific components:

1. A recurring series of complementary transactions that seem plausible and even necessary on a social or conscious level
2. An ulterior transaction that carries the hidden (ulterior) message of the game
3. A predictable, well-defined outcome that concludes the game and is the real purpose for playing it in the first place.

Thus, psychological games refer to complex sets of transactions having predictable outcomes. Social games like bridge or Scrabble have predictable outcomes, too. Someone wins and someone loses. The predictable outcome of a psychological game is that both parties lose. People who play psychological games play to win, but, as underscored by Gisele Weisman,[34] people who play games as a way of life are not winners.

It's how we go about asking for what we want and how we go about the business of giving, receiving, and taking that make us either game players or people interested in being straight with others. If communication contains hidden meanings or motives or if manipulation is involved, the relationship is "game-y." Personal insecurities, unresolved fears, the need to feel "one up" on another person, the need to feel punished or self-righteous typically lead to game playing. Generally, the closer the relationship between ourselves and another person, the more powerful and intensive the effects of game playing will be.

Why do people play games in the first place? Berne[35] has suggested that there are at least four unconscious motivations for game playing:

1. Games help us to keep from facing up to what we may be afraid of, such as responsibility, competition, others' opinions of us, personal insecurities, deep intimacy, and so forth.
2. Games help us to pass time in relationships and to *be* in relationships without having to be too close.
3. Games help us get attention and recognition (referred to as "strokes" in Transactional Analysis language), even though we sometimes get negative responses.
4. Games help us "prove," again and again, that our view of ourselves and others (I'm OK, others are not, or others are OK, I'm not) is "right."

In his book, *Games People Play,* Berne labeled and described more than thirty-five games. Many more new games have been identified and described since the publication of his book.[36] It's not my purpose to describe each possible game (that would be a volume in itself), but rather, to cite some illustrative examples in order to recognize the basic principles involved in game playing.

Mine Is Better than Yours   This is probably the basic game of games, insofar as it symbolizes a raw power struggle. The idea is to feel superior by putting the other person down and thereby to feel at least temporary relief from a sense of not being OK. It's the old psychological pulley system—one person is up when the other person is down. We've all heard its primitive beginnings in the interactions of young children: "My bike can go faster than yours," says John to Robert. "So what, I can run faster than you," responds Robert. "Who cares, we live in a bigger house," answers John. "Well, we have a bigger car than yours," Robert replies. And so it goes. Someone else's is always a little bigger and better. *Mine Is Better than Yours* can become a full-fledged game when played between intimates. I have seen it happen time and again in working couples' marriages, in which one of the partners feels resentful or envious of the other's achievements. A dialogue between two such people goes something like this (perhaps for the fiftieth time):

She: *Spoken* "I think I'm going to get a 7 percent raise. They must like my work. I know I'm doing a good job. I was trying to remember what your last raise was."
      Unspoken, ulterior "I'm doing better in my work than you are."
He: *Spoken* "I'm glad to hear that. Gosh, it's about time. I remember it took only 6 months for me to get a raise."
      Unspoken, ulterior "Big deal, You got a bigger raise, but I got mine sooner."

She: "I don't know why you can't just forget about what you do for once."
He: "What are you talking about? I said I was glad to hear it. Besides, you didn't act all that thrilled when I got my promotion."

The payoff for both of them is that each feels put down, but each also feels a little superior to the other. As long as either one has a need to feel superior, the game will continue. It allows for interaction and some recognition from the other person (however negative it may be), and it permits them to be only minimally involved with each other's accomplishments and only minimally threatened. The one-upmanship keeps them together, but emotionally distant.

Uproar   This is a favorite game played between two people who are emotionally involved with each other, who may be too frightened to be really close, but too insecure to be really alone. Once it starts, a predictable set of transactions occur that typically climax in a loud fight. The outcome is always the same—angry withdrawal or yelling or crying or some combination to avoid closeness. That is the game's payoff—the avoidance of closeness, although neither person is aware of that.

Consider this example. To set the game up, either Jane or Bill provokes the other by doing something nonverbal like withdrawing or acting put off or irritated. When either partner gets "hooked" into playing, the game is under way.

For example, when Bill starts the game, the transactions might be like this:

Bill: (Comes home from work, barely says hello, and stalks off to the den to watch TV)
Jane: (After a few minutes, goes into the den)—"Can't you even say hello? I live here, you know."
Bill: "For heaven's sake, can't I have a little time alone without you accusing me of not paying enough attention to you?"
Jane: "All right then, go ahead and be alone if it's so damn important to you!" (Goes shopping, buys clothes she doesn't really need, and returns toting several packages)
Bill: (Explodes into a tirade about her careless spending habits. The game travels full circle when Jane stamps off crying and mad and Bill sleeps in the spare room.)

When Jane initiates the game, it might be something like this:

Jane: (Looks angry, irritated, and chews her gum loudly and aggressively)
Bill: "Now what's the matter?"
Jane: "Oh, nothing's the matter. I wish you'd quit bugging me."
Bill: (Withdraws by mixing himself a strong drink and disappears into the den)
Jane: (Bursts into an angry rage when he returns for another drink. She accuses him of being insensitive, then he accuses her of nagging—

charges and countercharges. The payoff comes when Jane accuses him of being a drunk and he accuses her of being a bitch. She bursts into tears; he mixes himself another drink. There is no further contact for that evening.)

Now I've Got You   In order for this game to work, one of the players has to be the persecutor while the other player is the victim. Let's look at an example of how this might work. After class, you and some other students get together for a bull session about the lecture you just heard. One of the students, Fred (someone you never did like very much) is rather quiet, and unlike the others, who enjoyed the lecture, you suspect that he probably didn't. So you get into a little dialogue with him that sounds like this:

You: *Spoken* "Hey, Fred, did you like the lecture?"
        Unspoken, ulterior "You dumb bunny, you're too thick to understand lectures."
Fred: *Spoken* "Not really. I don't know how the rest of you could get anything from it. There was no time to take notes, he went so fast."
        Unspoken, ulterior "I write slowly. It's my fault for not getting more from it. I need a good kick in the pants."
You: "Well, it's funny that you were the only one who didn't like it. What's wrong with you?"
Fred: "Why don't you get lost? Nothing's wrong with me."
You: "What are you getting uptight about? You're the oddball, not me."
        (Now I've got you.)

The *Now I've Got You* player is usually a person who is quick to pick up on other people's mistakes, errors, and shortcomings, and even quicker to point them out. On the surface he or she is motivated by a sense of interest and a desire to be helpful, but his or her ulterior motive is to be critical and punitive. The *Now I've Got You* player cannot play the game if the other person has no need to be criticized or punished. Fred, for example, could prevent the game from going on by simply saying, "No, I didn't particularly enjoy the lecture, but I know you and the others did."

Yes, but   This is a game that people play when they act as though they want our advice, but then proceed to shoot it down once they get it. A transaction that involves the *Yes, but* play might go like this:

James: *Spoken* "You know, I'm going to have a real problem getting this paper done by Monday. I don't know what to do. Any ideas?"
         Unspoken, ulterior "There isn't anyone who is going to tell me what to do."
Nancy: "Well, we don't have to go to the basketball game tonight."
James: "That's true, but we've planned on it all week."

Nancy:	"How about if we go to the library early in the morning?"
James:	"We could, but our dorm has basketball practice."
Nancy:	"Maybe we could hit the books hard all day Sunday and both of us could get a lot done."
James:	"That's an idea, but there should be *one* day a week for relaxation!"

And so it continues with one player suggesting all sorts of "Why don't you" options, which are systematically discarded with reasons why they won't work. The *Yes, but* player proves once again that no one can tell him or her what to do; and if you play along long enough, you may begin to feel stupid, which makes you the perfect partner for a successful game.

There are at least three other popular games that you should be aware of.

I'm Only Trying to Help   The key player is the "helper"—usually a person who functions best when in the one up position of rescuing secondary players, who are the "clients" or "patients," with unsolicited advice. When a secondary player criticizes the advice or wonders why it was given in the first place, the helper typically acts bewildered or hurt and says, in effect, "Well, I was only trying to help." The bewilderment and hurt are, in fact, the helper's psychological payoffs, which enable him or her to feel unjustly accused and self-righteously indignant. The primary goal of this player is to create dependent individuals, so that he or she can say, in various ways: "What would you ever do without me?"

See How Hard I've Tried   Some people, it seems, have lives that are programmed for failure. Unconsciously, they may actually enjoy the failure, because it is a way to get a sympathetic ear—a form of attention and recognition—as they lament their losses with, "Look how hard I've tried. No matter what I do, nothing works out." They may spend countless hours on projects only to have them rejected, or years developing relationships only to have them fall flat and be left alone in the end.

If It Weren't for You   This is one of the most common games played by married people, although it can occur in any emotional relationship between two people. Basically, it is a game in which person A blames person B for not being able to do something that person A wants to do but is *unconsciously fearful of doing in the first place.* Some examples of how this works: A middle-aged man blames his wife for holding him back and keeping him from recognizing his potential. Doing this enables him to avoid looking at his deeper fears of failure if he actually *were* to explore his potential. A husband says to his wife: "If it weren't for the fact that I had to support you, I would've gone further academically." So long as he can think in terms of "If it weren't for you," he may never have to look at the deeper sense of personal inadequacy that was his real reason for not applying to graduate school.

If you want an idea of whether or not you are playing games with someone, pay close attention to your feelings at the conclusion of any given relationship segment. If what you feel has an essentially negative coloration and, on top of that, seems repetitive and familiar, and if the segment concludes with either one or both of you feeling emotionally distant, then chances are good that you've just completed one of the many games that people play.

Reflections

Do you recognize any game playing in your own relationships? If you do, how would you describe what the games are doing or have done to the relationships? It has been argued that in certain relationships game playing is necessary to keep the relationship going on an even keel. How do you feel about that? Which of your relationships would you like to be gamefree? Why?

Concluding Overview

There are any number of ways that we can interfere with the development of healthy relationships. One way is to underestimate what *we* may have to do to make relationships work better, while at the same time overestimating what the *other* person needs to do. We may focus conveniently on what others need to change in themselves, while we comfortably overlook aspects of our own behavior that may be causing problems in the relationship. When we get too caught up in trying to "fix" the other person in order to fix the relationship, there is the high risk of that person feeling forced to change, which practically guarantees that he or she will *not* change. *Principle:* Change what you can in yourself. In declaring language and I-statements (which we discuss in Chapter 5), let the other person know what you would like, but be willing to allow him or her to be responsible for the changes.

Shyness gets in the way of healthy relationships because it is a dramatic expression of nonbehavior. It is difficult to relate to a nonbehaving person. Shyness is learned; as such, it can also be unlearned. There is a vast difference between a quiet introvert at peace with him- or herself and a shy person imprisoned by walls of fear.

Game playing interferes with open, honest, and intimate relationships between the players. It allows us to fill up time, get some attention, and reinforce the existing ideas we have about ourselves and others. People can stop playing games when they develop an awareness of what they are doing and when they *want* to stop the games.

Let's turn our attention now to an important final concept.

WHAT IT TAKES TO DEVELOP HEALTHY PERSONAL RELATIONSHIPS

A healthy relationship is like a good apple pie—it requires many ingredients blended together in just the right proportions to turn out right. Fortunately, there are many different ways of making a good apple pie, which helps explain why my grandma and yours can start out with different recipes, yet end up with equally fine results. Somewhat analogously, the same is true for forming a good relationship. There is no single recipe for accomplishing this, but what does seem to make a difference is the way in which the basic ingredients of patience, caring, commitment, and trust are proportioned and the care with which they are blended. Our grandmothers' chances of turning out good pies are probably increased if they begin with a sense of OK-ness not only about their baking ability, but also about the apples they're using. Similarly, we probably increase our chances of forming good relationships when we begin with a sense of OK-ness not only about ourselves, but about others as well.

Whether we're baking pies or forming relationships, the attitudes we start with can influence the final results for better or worse. We may be conscious of the idea that our attitudes about ourselves and others can influence behavior, but we're not always sure what those attitudes are. Which brings us to an important point when considering what it takes to develop healthy relationships.

An Awareness of How We See Ourselves and Others Helps

Awareness is a crucial concept, because it allows us to see more accurately how our self–other attitudes may be affecting our relationships with others. Each of us has a certain way of seeing ourselves and the world we live in. For most people, it's part of their "philosophy of life," largely unspoken and mostly unconscious. It's not that it has to be unconscious; it is more that way, it seems, because not many people have the know how to make it more conscious or what to look for as clues to what they believe about themselves and others. Before reading further, take a moment and complete the self–other perception inventory in Figure 4–1.

The self–other perception inventory may help to give you a general idea of how you see yourself and others. The first six statements are designed to give you a feeling for your own sense of OK-ness, and the last six are meant to give you a sense of your view of others' OK-ness, or lack of it, as the case may be. It is important to be aware of how we see ourselves and others, because it influences how much and in what proportions we mix and blend the basic ingredients that go into healthy relationships—patience, caring, commitment, and trust. As we discussed more thoroughly in Chapter 1, our perceptions dramatically affect our behavior. One person views the world as a jungle in which he or she is barely able to compete, where people are basically evil, dangerous, and not to be trusted; another sees the world as a friendly place inhabited by potentially congenial and trustworthy fellow beings with whom he or she can interact on an equal basis. It is not difficult to see that each of these individuals will have relationships that are qualitatively and quantitatively different from the other's.

FIGURE 4–1. Self–Other Perception Inventory

Directions: If you feel the statement on the left is one with which you agree strongly, circle the dot under number 1; a little less strongly, circle the dot under number 2. If you feel you're somewhere between the statements on the left and on the right, circle the dot under number 3. If you find that you more closely agree with the statement on the right, circle the dot under numbers 4 or 5, depending on the strength of your agreement.

1 2 3 4 5

1. I'm rather intelligent	. . . . .	I'm rather unintelligent
2. I'm emotionally strong	. . . . .	I'm emotionally weak
3. I do most things well	. . . . .	I do most things poorly
4. I'm reasonably attractive	. . . . .	I'm fairly unattractive
6. I feel worthwhile and adequate	. . . . .	I feel worthless and inadequate
7. People are basically nice	. . . . .	People are basically mean
8. People can be trusted	. . . . .	People cannot be trusted
9. People are wonderful	. . . . .	People are no damn good
10. Others can be counted on	. . . . .	Others can seldom be counted on
11. People are honest	. . . . .	People are hypocritical
12. Others are friendly	. . . . .	Others are self-centered

OK ◄─────────────────────────────────────► Not OK

Eric Berne,[37] along with Thomas Harris[38] and Muriel James and Dorothy Jongeward,[39] has helped us to understand that there are at least four ways of looking at ourselves and others. Each represents a basic "life position" that colors our self–other perceptions. Which represents your position? (Your responses to the Self–Other Perception Inventory may contain some hints.)

1. *I'm OK, You're OK* (Feelings of mutuality, trust, cooperativeness) This is a healthy position. It means, in effect, I like myself and I like you, too; I can be trusted and I can trust you, also. It's an attitude that helps people to be realistically accepting of themselves and others. It's a posture that says I'm not perfect, you're not perfect, but that's part of being human. I accept it in myself and in you. Let's get on with the business of living, working, and relating.

2. *I'm OK, You're Not OK* (Feelings of suspicion and lack of trust) Essentially, this is a position that means, I'm all right, but you need to be watched. It is held most commonly by people who feel victimized or persecuted. People with this outlook are predisposed to blame others for their problems and to find convenient scapegoats for their hostilities and suspicions. It is a posture suggesting that the world would be a whole lot better if others were more like me.

3. *I'm Not OK, You're OK* (Feelings of powerlessness and impotency) This is a position that means, in effect, I don't matter very much, but you do. People who feel this way tend to see themselves as generally inferior to others, and to see other people as generally more intelligent and able. When people have this attitude, they tend to withdraw, get depressed quickly, and look to others for advice and direction.

4. *I'm Not OK, You're Not OK* (Feelings of hopelessness and despair) Basically, this is a "going nowhere" position—one that means I don't count for much and you don't, either; I don't have much to give you and you don't have much to give me. Insofar as the thinking is negative and the risk is minimal, it is a loser's position. Little is ventured and little is gained.

Reflections

How do you see yourself—as an OK person? Not so OK? How do you see others —OK? Not OK? How willing would you be to say that you trust others to come through for you? (A reflection, perhaps, of your sense of others' OK-ness.) To what extent do you feel others would *want* to come through for you? (A clue, maybe, to your own sense of OK-ness.)

Our feelings about ourselves and others are very much interrelated. How I feel about you is affected by how I feel about myself and how I feel about myself is influenced by my feelings about you. However, our feelings about ourselves remain critical and important. Indeed, it may well be that healthy relationships with others are best accomplished when we have a healthy relationship with ourselves. Perhaps if more of us spent less time *looking* for the right person (spouse, friend, companion, colleague, etc.) and spent more time *becoming* the right person, our relationships would be longer lasting and more satisfying.

It takes something else to develop healthy relationships. You can refer to it as the ability and willingness to do the following.

Ask for What You Want in Positive Terms

More often than we may realize, we don't get what we want simply because we failed to ask for it in the first place. Each time this happens, the experience activates a kind of self-fulfilling prophecy. The working mechanism is simple: You imagine that something will (or will not) happen. Then, because of a natural tendency to fulfill the prophecy, you unconsciously set in motion those events that cause it to come true. And it frequently does. Some examples you may recognize:

John: "You wouldn't happen to have five dollars to lend me, would you?" Paul: "No, I'm a bit short on cash right now."

Mary: "You wouldn't like to take me to a movie tonight, would you?" George: "Not tonight. I'm really tired. Let's go another time."

Worker: "You don't suppose I could be considered for a raise, do you?" Boss: "Well, I think we'll have to wait and see. It doesn't seem quite time for that yet."

I think you get the idea. One of the reasons we may not get what we want from our various relationships is that we start out with negative expectations. And when our expectations are realized (the very expectations set in motion by our own behaviors and attitudes), we end up with negative feelings about ourselves and the other person.

You may wonder why it seems to be so difficult to start out with positive expectations. Why does it seem easier to say, "You don't suppose I could be considered for a raise, do you?" than to say, "I would like to be considered for a raise"?

Part of the difficulty, no doubt, goes all the way back to certain childhood experiences. How many of us can remember being told that we could ask for something at, say, Christmas, Hanukkah, or on a birthday, and then not receiving it? If this happens often enough, the quiet conclusion some of us reach is: "Why ask for what I want if I don't get it and, on top of that, why set myself up for disappointment by expecting something that I probably won't get anyway?" When we start out with negative expectations, there's no way to be disappointed. Hence, we may find ourselves saying things like: "You wouldn't have the time, would you?" or "I don't suppose you'd like to go to a movie tonight, would you?" Nothing ventured, nothing lost. Of course, nothing is gained, either.

On an even deeper level, the tendency to avoid asking for what we want may grow out of what has sometimes been referred to as *pleasure anxiety*—that is, the anxiety that results from the lessons we learned (some of us more so than others) while growing up that taught us that we must not ask for that which gives us pleasure. If either fate or the gods drop something pleasurable in our laps, then well and good, we can enjoy it, because we didn't ask for it. You can see what happens if we learn this lesson really well. Sooner or later, we may come to believe that the satisfaction of a need depends on the whim and the inclination of those who care for us. Eventually, this translates into: "If she only loved me, she would know what I want. I wouldn't have to ask." And, as a natural extension, "Because she didn't give me what I want, she doesn't love me."

Either way—stating what we want in negative terms or not stating what we want and hoping the other person will somehow know—we stand a good chance of losing out. If we're not getting what we want from our relationships, it may be that we're not asking for what we want in positive terms. Some examples of how to do this:

Teacher: "I would very much like us to work quietly for the next half hour so everyone can finish the assignment." Less effective—"You've been noisy all morning. How can anyone finish their work?"

Worker: "Since I've worked two weekends in a row, I would like Saturday and Sunday off on the next rotation." Less effective—"Since I've worked two weekends in a row, you don't suppose I could have Saturday and Sunday off on the next rotation, do you?"

Roommate: "I would appreciate it if the stereo could be kept down for the next hour —I've got a big test tomorrow." Less effective—"The stereo is always so loud around here!"

Reflections

Think about the way you ask for what you want. How do you do it? Directly? Indirectly? Do you start with positive expectations? Or are they more negative? Listen to yourself for the next several days, as you ask for things from others. Experiment a little: try asking for what you want in positive terms. Contrast that with a more negative approach. Listen to how others ask for what they want. What effect do the different ways of asking have on you?

Principle: When we want something, we have to ask for it. Being direct may help accomplish at least three things: (1) It opens the door for others to give us what we want because they *know* what to give; (2) it increases our chances of getting what we want; and (3) it makes us, not the other person, responsible for our behavior.

As we strive to develop healthy interpersonal relationships, we need to be aware of the different effects that assertive and aggressive behavior have on people.

Assertive Behavior Helps—Aggressive Behavior Hinders

Each of the situations below is followed by three possible responses. Choose the response in each instance that seems most like something you would probably say.

1. You've stood in line at the supermarket for 20 minutes waiting to be checked out, and you're in a very big hurry. A man steps in front of you with four items and says, "I hope you don't mind. This won't take long."
   ___a. "No, I don't mind. Go ahead." (You're boiling on the inside.)
   ___b. "Who do you think you are, mister? Go to the back of the line like everyone else."
   ___c. "I do mind, and I would appreciate it if you would wait your turn."
2. A coworker says to you, "You're really stupid to take on that extra assignment, when you're not even getting paid extra for doing it."
   ___a. "Well, you may be right." (Inside, you don't feel that way at all.)
   ___b. "It's none of your damn business what I take on—it's my choice, not yours!"

　　——c. "This is something I want to do, and I'd feel good if you could support my effort rather than belittle it."

3. For the third week in a row, your roommate violates an agreement between the two of you to take turns cleaning the place up.
　　——a. You feel increasingly resentful, but say nothing. You may even clean up when it's not your turn.
　　——b. You say, "The way you're willing to live is beyond me. Only a slob could exist like this. This place looks like a pigsty."
　　——c. You say, "We have an agreement about keeping the room clean on a shared basis. I would like it if you kept your end of the agreement."

The "a" choices in the three situations are essentially passive choices. They are the sorts of things a person might say or do who has strong feelings about a situation, but who keeps them locked inside. You're behaving passively when you give in to another person but feel resentful. It's these times when we say yes to something that we really do not want to do. It's a problem that psychologist Herbert Fensterheim and his wife, Jean Baer, view as so widespread that they wrote a book titled, appropriately, *Don't Say Yes When You Want to Say No.*[40] Passive responses do not facilitate healthy relationships, because when we keep the way we would really like to respond hidden, we reinforce the idea that we are powerless. And that feeds a sense of low self-esteem and resentment toward others, neither of which are fuel for good relationships.

The "b" choices are examples of aggressive responses. An aggressive response is essentially one that has the effect of hurting, humiliating, or deprecating others. It may be self-enhancing, but at someone else's expense. Robert Alberti and Michael Emmons[41] characterize an aggressive response as one that puts down the other person. An aggressive response may get us what we want in the short run, but the price we pay is negative feelings and ill will left in our wake, which, in the long run, may be paid back with vengeance. Those who rely on an aggressive (and frequently authoritarian) style in their relationship to others, whether parents with children, teachers with students, chairpersons with faculty, or husbands with wives (or vice versa), find out sooner or later that what they dole out eventually gets returned with interest. It is no surprise, for example, to find that aggressive, nagging parents have more problems with their children,[42] that cold, bossy teachers have more problems with student discipline,[43] that inflexible, demanding bosses and chairpersons have more difficulty controlling and motivating their employees or staff,[44, 45] and that nagging, aggressive spouses have more personal conflicts with their mates.[46] Once again we return to a basic truism about human nature: People don't like being pushed around. They may take it for awhile, but eventually, either through force or passive resistance, they will take no more. When we feel that someone is resisting us, this may be a sign that we're coming across as more pushy and aggressive than we may have thought and that, in order to correct the relationship, we need first of all to correct ourselves.

The "c" choices are illustrations of assertive responses. Basically, an assertive statement means: "This is how I feel" or "This is how I think" or "This is what I want." An aggressive statement is: "You're lazy." An assertive statement is: "I resent it when you don't pull your share of the load. I would feel a whole lot better if you'd be more cooperative." An assertive statement affirms what we want and how we feel. An aggressive response disaffirms the other person. Sharon Bower and Gordon Bower[47] have suggested that when you behave assertively, you can, among other things, practice any one of the following behaviors:

1.   *Speak up for your rights.* You do not let others take advantage of you, and you can say no without feeling guilty. You can say, "Sorry, you'll have to go to the end of the line," or "Please turn down the stereo," because you feel you have a basic right to be treated fairly.
2.   *Ask why.* When asked to do something that doesn't seem reasonable or enjoyable, you can ask, "*Why* do you want me to do that?"
3.   *Disagree.* You do not pretend to agree for the sake of keeping peace. Rather, you state your disagreement by grimacing, shaking your head, or stating your objections.
4.   *Ask for clarification.* When given directions you don't understand, rather than go away confused, you can say, "I don't think I follow you. Would you mind going over that again?"
5.   *Accept compliments graciously.* Rather than feel embarrassed or unworthy (or both) you can simply say, "Thank you for noticing," or "Yes, I like this outfit, too." Not only do you accept a positive comment, but you reward the complimenter for noticing.
6.   *Use feeling talk.* You can express your likes and preferences personally, rather than in neutral terms. For example, you can say (to a date), "I enjoyed being with you" or (to a teacher), "I got a lot from your class," rather than "This was a good evening" or "This class was interesting."
7.   *Talk about yourself.* When you do something interesting and worthwhile, you can let others know about it. A sense of timing and appropriateness are important. (However, be cautious not to carry on with self-talk too long, or you may run the risk of turning out like the man who, so the story goes, persisted in a long and windy discourse in an effort to impress George Bernard Shaw during a dinner party. As the evening wore on and Shaw's patience wore thin, Shaw turned to the man and said, "You know, between the two of us, I really believe we know all there is to know." "Really!" exclaimed the pedantic conversationalist. "Yes, you seem to know everything except that you are a bore," Shaw replied. "And I know that.")

Being appropriately assertive is a way of reminding ourselves that we matter, that what we feel and what we want are important. It is a simple and effective way to stay on good terms with ourselves, which is one of the best ways to remain on good terms with others.

IN PERSPECTIVE

Some foods, we know, are junk foods; although they may help fill us up, they contain a lot of empty calories, and we sometimes feel worse for having consumed them. Some relationships are like that; although they may help us to pass time, they may contain a lot of empty hours, and they aren't very healthy for us. On the other hand, there are foods available to us that are full of nutrients and vitamins that promote physical health. Analogously, there are relationships like this, too—they contain the kind of emotional nutrition which promotes psychological health, that special sense of well-being about ourselves and others. It's the kind of nutrition that derives from being with someone with whom we feel a mutual trust, respect, and liking. This is quite different from the empty calories derived from a relationship with someone toward whom we feel no trust, little respect, and zero liking. One adds to us, the other subtracts from us.

There is a relatively simple way to determine whether or not a particular relationship is healthy and good. Ask yourself the question: Does the relationship allow me to feel good about myself and the other person? If you want some sense of whether or not the relationship is something more than the average and everyday kind, then ask yourself: Does the relationship allow me to feel more enhanced and complete as a person? Basically, good relationships leave us with good feelings. Good relationships—healthy ones—do not have to be profound, although they can be and frequently are; but we can also have good relationships with people we know only casually. What counts is not so much the amount of time spent together or the depth of our self-revelations—although these may be important factors—but how we *feel* about the relationship or interaction.

All in all, our encounters with others are largely what we make of them and what we want them to be. Most of us have more control over the course and destiny of our relationships than we may realize. The old idea that what it takes to have a good friend is to be one may seem trite, but both research and common sense tell us it is true. Samuel Johnson once observed, "It is not within our power to be fond, but it is within our power to be kind."

The key to developing healthy interpersonal relationships is the way in which we communicate, which we discuss in Chapter 5.

REFERENCES

1.   H. S. Sullivan, *The Interpersonal Theory of Psychiatry,* New York: W. W. Norton, 1953.

2.   C. H. Cooley, *Human Nature of the Social Order,* New York: Scribner's, 1902.

3.   S. Schachter, *The Psychology of Affiliation,* Stanford, Calif.: Stanford University Press, 1959.

4.   I. J. Firestone, K. J. Kaplan, and J. C. Russell, "Anxiety, Fear and Affiliation With Similar-State Versus Dissimilar-State Others: Misery Loves Miserable Company," *Journal of Personality and Social Psychology* 26 (1973): 409–414.

5.   N. Miller and P. Zimbardo, "Motives for Fear Induced Affiliation: Emotional Comparison or Interpersonal Similarity?" *Journal of Personality* 34 (1966): 481–503.

6.   S. C. Jones and D. T. Regan, "Ability Evaluation Through Social Comparison," *Journal of Experimental Social Psychology* 10 (1974): 133–146.

7.   J. Suls and R. L. Miller (Eds.), *Social Comparison Processes*, Washington, D.C.: Hemisphere/Halsted, 1977.

8.   M. P. Zanka, G. R. Goethals, and J. F. Hill, "Evaluating a Sex-Related Ability: Social Comparison with Similar Others and Standard Setters," *Journal of Experimental Social Psychology* 11 (1975): 86–93.

9.   V. Sermat, "Some Situational and Personality Correlates of Loneliness," in J. Hartog and Y. Cohen (Eds.), *The Anatomy of Loneliness*, New York: International Universities Press, 1980.

10.   UPI, *Wisconsin State Journal*, September 7, 1978.

11.   R. Byrd, *Alone*, London: Neville Spearman, 1938, pp. 95–96.

12.   D. Russell, L. A. Peplau, and C. E. Cutrona, "The Revised UCLA Loneliness Scale: Concurrent and Discriminant Validity Evidence," *Journal of Personality and Social Psychology* 39 (1980): 472–480.

13.   V. Sermat, "Some Situational and Personality Correlates of Loneliness," in J. Hartog and Y. Cohen (Eds.), *The Anatomy of Loneliness*, New York: International Universities Press, 1980.

14.   J. Lynch, *The Broken Heart: The Medical Consequences of Loneliness*, New York: Basic Books, 1977.

15.   P. Shaver and C. Rubenstein, "Healthy Loners," research reported in *Psychology Today*, January 1980, pp. 27 and 95.

16.   R. Nerem, "Try a Little TLC," research reported in *Science 80* 1 (1980): 15.

17.   R. Nerem, *Science 80,* 1 (1980): 15.

18.   H. Selye, "On the Real Benefits of Eustress," *Psychology Today*, March 1978, 60–70.

19.   S. M. Jourard and T. Landsman, *Healthy Personality*, 4th ed., New York: Macmillan, 1980, p. 268.

20.   D. E. Hamachek, *Encounters with the Self*, 2nd ed., New York: Holt, Rinehart and Winston, pp. 69–110.

21.   G. W. Allport, *Personality and Social Encounter*, Boston: Beacon Press, p. 209.

22.   J. W. Brehm, *Responses to Loss of Freedom: A Theory of Psychological Resistance*, Morristown, N.J.: General Learning Press, 1972.

23.   C. R. Rogers, *Becoming Partners: Marriage and Its Alternatives*, New York: Delacorte, 1972.

24.   C. R. Rogers, *Carl Rogers on Personal Power*, New York: Dell, 1977, p. 52.

25.   L. A. Shepard, "Self-Acceptance: The Evaluative Component of the Self-Concept Construct," *American Educational Research Journal* 16 (Spring 1979): 139–160.

26.   D. E. Hamachek, *Encounters with the Self*, 2nd ed., New York: Holt, Rinehart and Winston, pp. 253–259.

27.   E. M. Berger, "The Relation Between Expressed Acceptance of Self and Expressed Acceptance of Others," *Journal of Abnormal and Social Psychology* 47 (1952): 778–782.

28.   P. G. Zimbardo, *Shyness: What It Is and What You Can Do About It,* Reading, Mass.: Addison-Wesley, 1977, pp. 13–14.

29.   P. G. Zimbardo, "Shyness—The People Phobia," *Today's Education,* January–February 1977, pp. 47–49.

30.   P. G. Zimbardo, *Shyness: What It Is and What You Can Do About It,* Reading, Mass.: Addison-Wesley, 1977. pp. 10–12.

31.   P. G. Zimbardo, P. A. Pilkonis, and R. N. Norwood, "The Social Disease Called Shyness," *Psychology Today,* May 1975, pp. 69–72.

32.   M. Girodo, *Shy? You Don't Have to Be!,* New York: Pocket Books, 1978, pp. 22–36.

33.   E. Berne, *Games People Play,* New York: Grove Press, 1964, p. 48.

34.   G. Weisman, *The Winner's Way: A Transactional Analysis Guide for Living, Working and Learning,* Monterey, Calif.: Brooks/Cole, 1980.

35.   C. M. Steiner and C. Kerr, (Eds.) *Beyond Games and Scripts; Eric Berne, M.D.,* New York: Ballantine Books, 1976, pp. 71–86.

36.   G. B. Barnes (Ed.), *Transactional Analysis After Eric Berne,* New York: Harper's College Press, 1977.

37.   E. Berne, "Standard Nomenclature," *Transactional Analysis Bulletin* 8 (October 1969): 112.

38.   T. A. Harris, *I'm OK—You're OK: A Practical Guide to Transactional Analysis,* New York: Harper & Row, 1967, pp. 37–53.

39.   M. James and D. Jongeward, *Born to Win: Transactional Analysis with Gestalt Experiments,* Reading, Mass.: Addison-Wesley, 1971, pp. 35–39.

40.   H. Fensterheim and J. Baer, *Don't Say Yes When You Want to Say No,* New York: Dell, 1975.

41.   R. E. Alberti and M. L. Emmons, *Your Perfect Right: A Guide to Assertive Behavior,* 2nd ed., San Luis Obispo, Calif.: Impact, 1974, p. 11.

42.   S. Fisher and R. L. Fisher, *What We Really Know About Childrearing,* New York: Basic Books, 1976, pp. 37–61.

43.   D. E. Hamachek, *Psychology in Teaching, Learning and Growth,* 2nd ed., Boston: Allyn and Bacon, 1979, pp. 395–400, 504.

44.   J. Hall, "What Makes A Manager Good, Bad or Average?" *Psychology Today,* August 1976, 52–55.

45.   D. E. Hamachek, "Dynamics of Self–Other Perceptions and Their Relationships to Leadership Style," *Humanities: Journal of the Institute of Man* 14 (November 1978): 355–366.

46.   H. A. Bowman and G. B. Spanier, *Modern Marriage,* 8th ed., New York: McGraw-Hill, 1978, pp. 221–249.

47.   S. A. Bower and G. H. Bower, *Asserting Yourself: A Practical Guide for Positive Change,* Reading, Mass.: Addison-Wesley, 1976, pp. 4–5.

Chapter 5

THE PSYCHOLOGY AND ART OF GOOD COMMUNICATION SKILLS

OVERVIEW

PROLOGUE

Of all those qualities we can point to that permit us to assume the lofty position we enjoy above all other life forms, the ability to communicate is probably our crowning achievement. It enables us to translate what we are thinking, feeling, and sometimes only sensing into a verbal or nonverbal language that connects us with other people. It makes our encounters with others possible. On the other hand, when communicating is done badly, either through blunders on the *sender's* part or errors on the *receiver's* part, some of our encounters with others are impossible—at least in the sense of anything productive or worthwhile growing out of them. Verbal communication between people is a complex and sensitive process. What I thought I said may not be at all what you heard. In fact, what you "heard" may have been greatly influenced (usually unconsciously) by what your eyes saw in my face and posture, considerations which may have been quite outside the range of my awareness at the moment. In any verbal exchange between two people, there is communication going on simultaneously on two levels. On one level, there is the cognitive aspect of the message, in terms of what is said, while on another level, there is the emotional component of the message, in terms of *how* it is said. These two communication channels are not always in harmony with each other, which is why (among other reasons) we're able to sense that some people are hostile and vindictive, even though they may say friendly, warm things, or that still others are hypocritical and self-centered, even though they present themselves as loving and altruistic. When there is too great a difference between how we *feel* about something—ourselves, another person, an idea —and what we *say* about it, others may say that we're confusing. When there is too large a gap between what we *say* and what we *mean,* others may conclude that we're ambiguous. When *what* we say does not square with *how* we say it, others may see us as inconsistent. With all of these hazards to interpersonal exchange lurking about, it may seem to you a good idea to cease communication altogether—or at least to limit it drastically. A worthy idea perhaps, but a flawed one. There is no such thing as not communicating. We all know from experience that another person's refusal to talk to us is a quite powerful communication. We cannot *not* communicate. Our deliberate efforts to withhold ourselves from encounters with others are no less interpersonal exchanges than our conscious decisions to reveal ourselves to others.

Our capacity to communicate is both a bane and a blessing. It can be used to drive individuals or groups farther apart, or it can be the essential vehicle for bringing people together in a spirit of mutual regard and understanding. Our purpose in this chapter is to try to understand this process better. What gets communicated nonverbally? How does it get communicated? Why is it that others may feel confused and uncertain about what we say when we feel so clear about it ourselves? What does it take to be a good sender? A good receiver? Why does it seem so risky to ask for what we want? What is the difference between destructive and constructive confrontation? These are just a few of the questions we'll try to answer in the pages ahead. Let's first of all turn to the most basic question of all.

WHAT IS HUMAN COMMUNICATION?

On the surface, this seems a simple question deserving a simple answer. Not so. As we have seen in previous chapters, nothing involving human behavior lends itself to either simple answers or easy solutions. This is surely true for the issue of human communication.

In the broadest sense of the word, communication can be defined as the *sharing of experience,* and to some extent all life forms are capable of this. What makes human communication unique and superior is humankind's advanced ability to create and use symbols, for it is this ability that enables us, as linguist Robert Goyer put it, to "share experiences indirectly and vicariously."[1]

We could easily enough get bogged down in trying precisely to define communication. (Communications expert, Frank Dance,[2] for example, came up with ninety-five definitions of communication in his review of the literature.) As we explore ideas and research related to communication in this chapter, I'd like to suggest a working definition for human communication: *the process of making verbal or nonverbal contact and creating a meaning for two or more people.* It is a process that goes on either intentionally or unintentionally, and it hap-

©1968 United Feature Syndicate, Inc.

No one ever said that human communication is simple or easy.

pens between two people in face-to-face interaction or in larger group interactions.

Our communication with each other involves basically two kinds of information. On the one hand, there is *cognitive* information, which is concerned primarily with tangible data and facts about each other and the surrounding world, while on the other hand, there is *affective* information, our transmission of feelings and emotions.

There are any number of ways to convey such information—through spoken words, voice tone and inflection, facial expression, body movements, gestures, even moments of silence. Thus, the way we communicate with each other takes place nonverbally, as well as verbally. Since *what* we say is more subject to our conscious control, verbal communication is used primarily to convey cognitive information. And since our nonverbal communication is less likely to be censored or monitored by conscious process, we tend to communicate a great deal about our feelings and emotions through this medium—more, usually, than we realize. Remember, these two modes of communication go on simultaneously, either on the same "wave length," or on different ones. When a sender transmits on two different frequencies, it is not difficult to understand why the receiver is confused about what a particular message really means.

Whether we're aware of it or not, we all seem to have an ability—some more or less than others—to extract meaning from the nonverbal aspects of communication. What we say is obvious. How we say it nonverbally is less so. Let's look at this dimension of human communication more closely.

NONVERBAL COMMUNICATION— THE LANGUAGE OF BEHAVIOR

Behavior has a language of its own, far beyond our words. Consider the following scenarios:

> Bob has an appointment to meet Charles at 9:00, and he finally arrives at 9:25. Their exchange is pleasant and friendly on the surface, but Charles feels angry and put down. Bob has unconsciously communicated that he considers neither the appointment nor Charles to be very important.

> Andrea is talking to Linda's date at a party. Their conversation is both innocent and trivial, yet Linda glares at them suspiciously. Their physical proximity and the way they are looking at each other suggest a strong mutual attraction.

> The instructor says he would be happy to talk to any student who has further questions after class. When class is over, he turns his back to the students, gathers his notes together, and puts on his coat. Although several students want to approach him, no one does.

> Maureen stops at the coffee shop, as she usually does before going to work. As she sits down, the waitress asks, "The usual?" Maureen nods yes. While she is enjoying her roll and coffee, a man takes a nearby seat and lights up a cigarette. Smoke circles in Maureen's direction and she glares disapprovingly at him. One puff later, the cigarette is put out as the man studiously avoids her eyes. Within a 5-minute period, Maureen sends two messages without uttering a syllable.

> José Lopez and Sidney Smith are at a social function, and it is important for them to get on friendly terms for business reasons. Each is trying to be warm and cordial, but they are both having problems. José, in typical Latin fashion, moves closer and closer to Sidney as they speak, which Sidney misinterprets as pushiness. Sidney keeps edging away; this is miscommunicated to José as aloofness. The nonverbal languages of Latin and American cultures are more difficult to learn than their spoken languages.

In each of these instances, we see the subtle power of nonverbal communication. The only language used throughout the history of humanity (in evolutionary terms, vocal communication is a relatively recent phenomenon), it is the first form of communication we use and learn. We use this preverbal language, consciously and unconsciously, every day to tell others how we feel about ourselves and them. Anthropologist Ray Birdwhistell[3, 4] was one of the first to note how we use body language in communication, and he coined the term *kenesis* to refer to this process. And an important process it is. For example, it has been estimated that in a normal conversation between two people, only one-third of the meaning is communicated on a verbal level, and nearly two-thirds is communicated on a nonverbal level.[5]

Few of us are fully aware of how much we all depend on nuances of body movement in our conversation or conscious of the hidden rules that determine how we communicate in that language form. Yet we know instantly (at least we have some good hunches) whether the person we're talking to is a caring individual or trustworthy or sincere or phony.

There are five major channels over which we transmit nonverbal signals. One has to do with our personal space and the way we manage it, protect it, and project it, while the other four channels are reserved for messages we send with our faces, eyes, voices, and body movement gestures. Although each of these five channels is subject to a certain amount of emotional interference and personal static, on the part of the receiver and the sender, the sum total of these signals is usually strong enough either to confirm or to refute the words we hear.

Let's look more closely at each of these major expressions of nonverbal communication.

The Bubble Around Us—Personal Space and What It Means

We are indebted to Edward T. Hall[6] for alerting us to the many ways in which we tend to use physical space in our interactions with others (called *proxemics*). Whether we're aware of it or not, each of us has a kind of "bubble" around us that serves to define what Robert Sommer[7] has termed our *personal space*. This bubble tends to expand or contract depending on where we are, whom we are with, and the circumstances. In crowded public places like, say, elevators, our bubbles tend to get rather small. We get a little tense, hold ourselves more stiffly, and thereby communicate to others a strong desire not to intrude in their space and not to touch or be touched. Walking along the street, our bubble expands slightly as we move in and out of a group of strangers, taking care not to have too much physical contact. At home, in a restaurant, at meetings, with a loved one, our bubble keeps changing as it adjusts to the changing flow of interpersonal activity.

Professor Hall[8] has observed that most Americans—at least white middle-class ones—use four major *distance zones* for communicating in their business and social relations: intimate, personal, social, and public.

1. *Intimate distances* vary from actual physical contact to a distance of 6 to 18 inches and are used for our most private activities—caressing, making love, comforting, protecting, and the like. At this distance, we're overwhelmed with sensory inputs—touching, body heat, breathing, body odors, all of which make the involvement very intense. This distance says that I care for you, or at least that I want to be close to you.
2. *Personal distances* generally range from 1½ to 4 feet or so. There may be some physical contact, but not necessarily. It's the most comfortable spacing used by people in conversation. This distance says that I like you (perhaps only at that distance, however), or it might say I'd like to know you better.
3. *Social distances* are somewhere between 4 and 12 feet and are commonly found between people who work together, between those conducting business transac-

tions, or among people at a social gathering. It's a distance that says let's not get too personal, I want to be cordial and polite, but no more than that.

4. *Public distances* usually go beyond 12 feet and are used by teachers or speakers at public gatherings. At this distance, it isn't necessary to acknowledge someone we would rather avoid, and interpersonal exchanges are more formal and impersonal. It is a distance that says let's not worry too much about personal relationships, but let us focus instead on what needs to be done.

The space we put between ourselves and others is one of those outer signs of inner feelings that may reflect important nonverbal cues about how we're feeling about others and how others may be feeling about us. Albert Mehrabian's[9] research, for example, suggests that we unconsciously stand closer to people we like than to people we don't like. There is also evidence[10] to indicate that we tend to move closer to people whose approval is important to us, but we remain more distant from people whose opinion we don't care about. Moreover, the chances are fairly good that we will find ourselves drawing physically closer to people we *expect* will like us, while on the other hand, we keep our distance from those who we expect will *not* like us. What happens when someone breaks into our personal space without an invitation? As Vladimir Konecni and his colleagues[12] discovered in their research, we usually resent it.

Reflections

When you enter a classroom setting, where do you ordinarily sit? Up front? Near the back? In the middle? Think about it—what do you suppose that your choice of a seat communicates about you? What does it say nonverbally to others? Or to put it another way, what would you like it to say? Read on to find out what research has uncovered about this.

Where people sit in a room, particularly as this relates to a classroom setting, turns out to be a rather strong nonverbal statement about their desire to take part in or be left out of discussions. Mele Koneya[13] found that students who talked a lot tended to prefer front and center seats, while the quieter students sat more often in the back. This finding is consistent with Hall's distance–zones categories, which suggests that whether or not a person wants to be more personally involved with others will be reflected to some extent by the size of the personal bubble he or she puts around herself.

What can we conclude from this? At least two possibilities come to mind: (1) The personal space between us and a particular person may communicate how we feel about that individual—for example, we feel attracted and draw closer, or we feel repulsed and pull away; or (2) our personal space may communicate, in a more private, internal way, how we feel about ourselves—we feel essentially positive about ourselves and are able to draw closer to another person, or move further away, depending on all the circumstances involved; or we feel essentially negative about ourselves, which may cause us to freeze our personal space so that it is no longer a flexible bubble, but a protective shell that keeps us from others regardless of the circumstances.

Reflections

What sort of personal space do you keep between yourself and others? How do you feel when you're physically close to someone? How large is your bubble? Whom do you allow to get inside it? I wonder what would happen if you deliberately expanded the size of your personal space over the next couple of days? Would it be worth trying to see how your encounters with others might be affected?

The Silent Language of Facial Expressions

Each face, it seems, has its own particular and unique message. Some faces, to be sure, are more expressive than others, but each in its own way serves as a kind of emotional billboard flashing hints of what may be happening on the stage of the inner person. Each of us learned a long time ago that reading facial cues with reasonable accuracy was necessary for understanding and predicting the unspoken feelings of those around us. Doing so has a certain emotional survival value, because it helps us to know when to approach or when to avoid someone, when to reach out or when to stay put. Statements such as "It was written all over his face" or "If looks could kill" speak eloquently of the emotional significance we give to facial expressions.

Intuitively, you may suspect that similar facial expressions seem to convey similar emotional states in different people, even though these people may represent different races or cultures. Your intuitions are correct. In fact, as long ago as 1872, Charles Darwin[14] theorized that such expressions are part of our basic biological inheritance and are innately determined. In addition, he speculated that since various facial expressions are universal, they will always be associated with a specific emotional state; that is, we will frown when sad, smile when happy, and so on.

Darwin was right. Research shows that all peoples of the world understand a common language for facial expressions, at least for such basic emotions as anger, sadness, happiness, surprise, disgust, and fear. Paul Ekman and his associates[15, 16] conducted a series of studies in which they showed photographs of facial expressions depicting each of the six emotions just mentioned, to people in five literate cultures, from four language groups—they were from Japan, the United States, Brazil, Chile, and Argentina. The findings were quite clear-cut; despite large cultural differences between them, people in different countries showed a high level of agreement as to the emotion reflected in each picture. Even more impressive support for the universality of facial expressions was found in Ekman and his associates' studies of people from isolated regions of New Guinea.

In spite of only limited contact with people from other cultures, the responses of New Guinea subjects were similar to those of other, less isolated cultures. All in all, this is strong evidence for the idea that various facial expressions are interpreted in much the same way all over the world. Although we don't know why these expressions are universal, or why certain facial expressions are associated with particular emotions (why don't we frown when happy or smile when angry?), we do know, as Ekman put it, ". . . that all human beings share the same neural programming, which links facial muscles with particular emotions."[17]

This does not mean that the language of facial expressions is capable of transmitting only six different emotions. Rather, our emotions can occur in many combinations. For example, we can feel happy and sad at the same time—and thus, perhaps, ambivalent—or we might feel anger along with fear. Since each of these emotions can vary in intensity, you can see that there are an endless number of possible variations.

A word of caution: What we see isn't always what is actually felt; the facial expression doesn't always match the inner feeling. We all know examples of this. John is fearful and anxious, but he laughs and smiles as though nothing is wrong; Mary is burning with anger, but her controlled poker face keeps it hidden from others; a salesman smiles sweetly and sincerely, masking his true opinion about the product he's trying to sell us. We can err in our interpretation of the silent language of facial expressions for three different reasons: (1) a person may show an expression that is different from what he or she really feels, or (2) an individual may inhibit overt facial expressions and give us little to go by, or (3) we may simply be remiss in spotting the cues available to us.

You can sometimes spot facial deception by looking carefully for inconsistencies. For example, people feigning surprise may raise their brows and open their eyes wide, but their mouths fail to drop open. Timing is another clue to whether a response is staged or fake. Ordinarily, genuine emotional responses appear on the face very quickly. For example, if you tell a joke and there's a delay between its conclusion and the other person's hearty response, you may have reason to doubt the sincerity of the laughter. (And maybe the worth of your joke.)

The Language of Eye Contact: Meaning and Implications

When you look at someone and then look away, you make a statement. If you hold the glance a second longer, you're making a different statement. If you hold it for two seconds, the meaning of the statement changes again. In practically every interpersonal situation, there is what Julius Fast[18] has called a *moral looking time*—the amount of time that we can hold someone's gaze without being accused of being rude, aggressive, or intimate.

In an elevator, for example, the moral looking time is only milliseconds. You look at the floor, the ceiling, the floor buttons, anywhere, it seems, but into the eyes of fellow passengers. The moral looking time is somewhat longer on a crowded bus, and still longer out on the street. There we may catch someone's eye as we walk toward him or her, but usually a definite uncomfortable feeling results if a glance is held for more than 3 seconds.

Why is this so? Why does prolonged eye contact between us and other people —particularly those we know only slightly or not at all—cause us to feel uneasy? The answer seems to be very closely associated with the idea that eye contact is a strong statement of our involvement—minimal or intense—with another person. Communications research[19, 20] rather clearly points out that if the person we're talking to happens to be someone we like or love very much, then we are more inclined to have (to *want,* even) longer and more intense eye contact with that person. It is as if our eyes were saying without words, "I want to be involved with you. I'm not afraid to be involved with you."

Intuitively, most of us seem to understand that the duration and intensity of eye contact can be a strong, nonverbal statement regarding how we feel about a particular person at a particular moment or how the other person feels about us. For example, studies by Chris Kleinke and his colleagues[21] have shown that we are inclined to feel more positive about people who engage in a high degree of eye contact than about people whose eye contact with us is minimal. Martin Cobin[22] has verified that this is particularly true in public speaking situations; people prefer speakers with good eye contact, something many speakers appear oblivious to as they look straight ahead, forgetting people on either side of them, or as they read from notes without looking at the audience. Of course, not only can a speaker's eye contact or lack of it affect his or her audience, but the audience's eye contact can also affect the speaker. Jon Blubaugh[23] found that when an audience sends out negative nonverbal feedback—by not looking at the speaker, dozing off, and the like—it can adversely affect a speaker's fluency and cause him or her to do poorly with the rest of the presentation. However, when an audience maintains good eye contact with the speaker, it helps him or her to be more fluent, confident, and effective. There is, it appears, the potential for both reward and punishment in looking up and out at the listening audience.

Although we usually like people who are able to look at us better than we like those who look away from us, there are, as seems to be true with all human behavior, exceptions. For instance, Phoebe Ellsworth and J. Merrill Carlsmith[24] found that whether increased eye contact leads to a positive or a negative impression of another person depends on the situation and the circumstances. In one experiment, when subjects heard positive feedback from an interviewer who looked them directly in the eye, they rated that interviewer quite positively. However, in another experiment, subjects heard essentially unpleasant feedback from an interviewer who looked them directly in the eye; in this case, they rated the interviewer more negatively. We like it when a person looks at us, but not if he or she accompanies the look with negative feedback. (The roots of this attitude may be found in our childhood. Do you remember the intense and penetrating eye contact your parents made with you when scolding or criticizing you?)

How do you feel when someone stares at you? Ordinarily, people tend to feel uncomfortable and embarrassed.[25] Why? Well, it's a definite nonverbal communication, but we don't know what it means. It could mean that the starer sees us as terrific or kooky; not knowing makes us a little jittery. We may think the starer is a bit kooky, but thinking so doesn't help our jitters. On the other hand, field studies[26, 27] have shown that when we're eyed intently by someone whose purpose is clear and nonthreatening—a hitchhiker or a panhandler, for example, we remain relatively unaffected. In fact, we're more likely to comply with the request for money or a ride if the panhandler or the hitchhiker looks directly at us than if he or she doesn't stare at us at all. (If you're inclined to pick up hitchhikers, when was the last time you stopped for one who was looking up at the sky or past your car to the cars behind you?) When we're able to place a person's stare in a context of understandable behavior, then we can respond positively or negatively, rather than simply avoid it.

Some suggestions for using eye contact as a positive expression in nonverbal communication:

To help establish closer relationships with people who matter to you, hold their gaze as long as possible when you meet, say hello, and pass.

Look at the person to whom you're talking or listening—but don't stare unwaveringly; doing so will help communicate the feeling that you care and that he or she matters.

When in a position of having to give criticism, make your moments of eye contact of shorter duration. The person you're criticizing needs breathing room. Reduced eye contact may help to give him or her that breathing room and may also help him or her to hear you less defensively.

Maintaining eye contact may help you to increase your chances of being perceived as a truthful person. Research[28] shows that people are inclined to see us as less credible when we avoid eye contact. (Of course, if you really do find yourself stretching the truth, eye contact may indeed be difficult.)

When you want to create a warm business or social relationship with a person, but you are *not* interested sexually, limit the amount of time you look into that person's eyes while listening or talking. Michael Argyle's[29] research indicates that using short, intermittent gazes during conversation is an effective nonverbal way of communicating that the task is the important thing, not the relationship.

Reflections

You may find it interesting to do a little experimenting. Try different modes of eye contact with people you interact with during the next several days. Vary the intensity and duration of your gaze. How do people respond? What effect does it have on you? Under which condition is your communication improved?

Vocal Cues Can Leak Our True Feelings

Quite apart from what we say is the *way* in which we say it. Pitch, tone of voice, volume, and rate of speech are important vocal components of the overall message that can easily confirm or refute what the words are saying. For example, how often do we hear someone say, "I'm glad to meet you," and yet we have a deep sense that that person couldn't care less about meeting us. Or consider the simple statement: "I hate you." Depending on how it's stated, it may reflect anger or it may sound like a seductive come-on. Most people have this intuitive under-standing in common. That is, we may not be able to be terribly specific about why we feel that John is insincere when he says, "I'm glad to meet you," but we nonetheless are convinced that he doesn't mean it at all.

Communications research indicates that not only are we able to judge the intensity of emotions,[30] but we can also identify with high reliability at least four basic emotional expressions from vocal characteristics: positive feeling, dislike, sadness, and apprehension or fear.[31, 32] (You may be interested to know that much of this type of research is done by taking tape recordings and electronically filtering vocal cues from verbal messages. The filtering system eliminates the higher frequencies of recorded speech so that the words are unintelligible, but the vocal qualities can still be heard. Groups of people listen to these recordings and try to identify the emotional expression being conveyed. There is a fairly high amount of agreement as to the emotional meaning of a message—the *way* we say something.) So, when you say, "I hope you have a nice day" or "I'm glad to meet you," chances are good that the person to whom you are talking will have a good sense of whether or not you mean it. You can see that it is quite possible to convey negative attitudes toward another person while *saying* positive things.

How we talk and the way in which we present the vocal portion of our verbal message tend to suggest rather definite stereotypes. For example, speakers who increase the loudness and rate of their speech are viewed as more active and dynamic than those who speak softly and slowly.[33] Those who use more intona-tion, have greater fluency, and speak with more volume tend to be judged as more persuasive.[34] In still another study,[35] it was shown that black, Anglo, and Mexi-can-American adolescent girls evaluated speakers with a standard English accent more favorably than they did speakers with a Hispanic accent, suggesting certain ethnic stereotypes when it comes to vocal patterns. Psychologist Robert Kraut's[36] research supports what we may have suspected all along; when people answer our questions with short responses and long pauses, we're less inclined to believe them.

Keeping an ear tuned to *how* something is said and the *way* in which it is expressed is an excellent means of staying in touch with the emotional component of a message. this can work both ways for you. That is, not only can you tap into the deeper feelings of the person who is talking by listening for the way he or she is talking, but you can also pay attention to your own vocal qualities for clues about your own inner feelings. If you don't seem to know how you truly feel about a particular person, listen to your own voice for otherwise hidden clues. A client of mine, working through his ambivalent feelings toward his wife, gave me a good example of how to do this when he said:

> I wasn't sure how I felt about her. I thought I loved her, but I didn't know with the kind of certainty I wanted to have. Last night after dinner I told her I loved her very much. Somehow I "listened" to my voice. It didn't falter, there was no hesitancy, it seemed strong. I was able to look directly at her when I said it. A remarkable thing happened—I was more certain at that moment that I loved her.

It took more than this for him to know for sure, but it was a starting point and gave him something to look for in himself, regarding his true feelings. Notice how he also paid attention to the language of his eye contact.

There is one final and very rich source of nonverbal communication.

Body Language from the Neck Down: What It Can Say and What It May Mean

Our bodies are constantly communicating how we feel physically and emotionally, how we feel about ourselves and others, and how we feel about the situation we may be in at the moment. Have you ever: (1) noticed how much more slowly you tend to move and walk on days when you're tired or depressed; (2) found yourself slamming a door or throwing something when angry; (3) observed how you may tend to sit or stand closer to a person you like as you converse? Each of these is a small outer sign of inner fellings communicated through the language of behavior.

The fact that so many of us tend to agree as to the meaning of the six body expressions in Figure 5–1 suggests that our culture transmits rather effectively the idea that certain body postures and movements are associated with particular behaviors and emotional states. It's one of those things we learn unconsciously. As a consequence, we tend to receive and to transmit body language signals in a way that enhances our understanding of others and, at the same time, others' understanding of us. Remember, body language is not really subject to conscious control, and most of us intuitively sense that a person's deeper feelings—which may or may not match what he or she is saying—are expressed through body language. Some examples:

> Susan would like to be perceived as a warm and friendly person, but her basic fear of people and social circumstances keeps her enveloped in a large protective bubble that puts people at a distance. Consequently, others may see her as somewhat cold and aloof, not because of what she says—she *sounds* friendly enough—but because of body language cues that say, "Don't get close."

> John perceives himself as a tough sort of hombre; he says he is not the type to "get caught up in unnecessary emotional tangles." However, he constantly touches others with reassuring gestures, he extends his hand—literally—to those who need help, and

we may even see him trying to hide a tear when something affects him deeply. We hear what he says about the necessity of "being tough," but we know from his behavior that he's really an old softie at heart.

Being sensitive to body language signals is a good way to pick up clues to how another person feels about you. For example, watching what a person does with her upper body and how she orients her body in relation to you may suggest positive or negative feelings, or even a more neutral attitude. Albert Mehrabian's[37, 38] research in this area indicates that the kind of immediacy seen

FIGURE 5–1.   Nonverbal Expressions

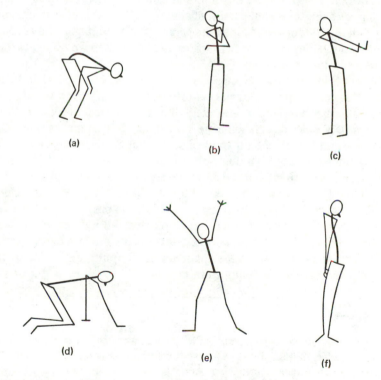

Reflections

Whether we realize it or not, we are constantly sending out body messages that convey outer signs of inner states. Consider the postures you see below. What does each of them say?*

(a)

(b)

(c)

(d)

(e)

(f)

Answers: (a) curious, (b) puzzled, (c) rejecting, (d) searching, (e) excited, (f) shy
*From: M. Argyle, *Bodily Communication,* New York: International Universities Press, 1975, pp. 273–275.

in the interaction between two people—its directness and intensity—is very much a reflection of the feeling tone that may exist in the relationship. If a person likes you, he will unconsciously (although there are times when he may be quite conscious of what he's doing) orient his body so that the direction of his head, the position of his arms, the lean of his torso and shoulders are more squarely in line with you and tilted toward you. When a person combines this kind of body orientation with extended eye contact, he or she transmits a powerful message indeed. It may be a message that, with a smile and warm eyes, says, "I like you." Or it may be a message that, with a scowl and glaring eyes, says, "I don't like you" or "I'm angry." In general, a body orientation that is tilted toward you reflects positive feelings; a body posture leaning away from you may suggest more negative feelings.

There are other body language signs that may indicate liking or disliking. Gerald Clore and his colleagues[39] found that nonverbal behaviors most likely to be interpreted as positive feelings for another person included sitting directly facing another person, moving toward that person, and nodding one's head in agreement. Behaviors associated with more negative feelings included looking at the ceiling, cleaning one's fingernails, shaking one's head in disagreement, and playing with the ends of one's hair. If the person you're talking to shows a sudden interest in your ceiling or his or her fingernails, you may have reason to wonder about his or her interest in you.

You might think that if a person seems quite relaxed with you, then he or she likes you. Not necessarily. Mehrabian and Friar[40] found in their research that one is either very relaxed or hardly relaxed at all in relation to a disliked person, but only moderately relaxed with someone who is liked. This makes sense. If you don't like me and, on top of that, you feel somewhat hostile or angry toward me, your body language may communicate a kind of passive, even bored attitude around me. On the other hand, when we're around people we like, we're more likely to be only moderately relaxed. Why should this be? Well, we can only speculate about this, but perhaps it has to do with the possibility that we do not find it necessary to be rigid with tension or passive and indifferent when in the company of people who are pleasant to be with. Being moderately relaxed helps us to stay alert and responsive to the opportunities for putting something into the relationship and taking something from it.

Reflections

You may find it interesting to experiment with your own body language and to make a conscious effort to watch for the signals others may be sending in your direction. Next time you're around someone you don't particularly like, notice the way you place your body in relation to his or hers; notice your tension by deliberately relaxing yourself. Make an effort to be aware of what you do with your body when you're with a person you like. Where do you stand? Sit? What differences do you see in body language signals between people who like you and those who don't?

If you want an idea of how accessible people may be to your ideas or your point of view, watch what they do with their arms and legs. Marianne LaFrance and Clara Mayo[41] found in their review of research in this area that people more closed to us will tend to communicate nonverbally that attitude with folded arms and crossed legs. On the other hand, people who are more open to us reflect that openness with arms that may be at their sides or extended invitationally or simply placed on their laps. When a person closes his mind to you, he will usually telegraph his inner feelings by closing his body to you as well. There are many signs: body orientation shifts away from you, distance increases, eye contact is reduced, arms and/or legs tend to cross, and the palms of the hands tend to turn inward. These body signs do not necessarily occur together, nor do they automatically happen when a person feels closed to to you. The probability, however, of seeing some of the nonverbal expressions of the inner feelings is rather high. As a general rule, it is quite difficult to *feel* one way and yet *behave* another way. Consider, for example, the trouble you would experience if you were to try to behave in a warm, friendly manner to a person you disliked rather intensely. Or for that matter, consider the problems you would experience being cold and distant to a person you liked very much. It is not easy to imagine carrying off either one of these poses very successfully—at least not for any sustained length of time.

Touch is a powerful nonverbal message. For example, if someone asks you for a favor and at the same time reaches out and touches you, do you think this might influence how you respond? If you're like many people, you are more likely to grant the request under these conditions. Chris Kleinke[42] found that a much higher percentage of male and female shoppers were willing to give a dime for a phone call to a female stranger when she touched them while making her request (51 percent) than when she did not touch them (29 percent). When you want to convey warmth, touch can say many things: "I like you"; "I really mean it"; "You're a likable person."

Reflections

Are you a toucher? How do you feel when someone touches you? When you touch another person? If you're not a toucher, maybe you could experiment a little. Touch people as you talk to them. Look for the effect it has on them and on you. What does touching another person or being touched by another person say to you nonverbally?

It may come as no surprise to you to hear that men and women have somewhat different reactions to the implications and meanings of touching, particularly between the sexes. Communications researcher T. Nguyen and his colleagues[43] asked a large group of college students what a pat, a squeeze, a brush, and a stroke meant when directed to different parts of the body by someone of the opposite sex, and they found that women discriminate among body parts more than men do. As a group, men seem less aware of the variety of meanings and implications conveyed by touching. (Lest we fall into the trap of stereotyping all men as insensitive, indiscriminate touchers and all women as noble practitioners of the art, let's remember that these research findings point only to a general trend; there are many individual male and female exceptions.)

Toward Understanding and Using Body Language to Enhance Communication

Body language signals can be a help or a hindrance. They help us when they reinforce and underscore what we say and what we want to convey; they hinder us when they replace or contradict our verbal message. If you tell Janet that you've had a really nice time, as you're walking away with your back to her, you can be sure that your words fall on deaf ears. Now it could be that you really have had a nice time and are simply oblivious to how your behavior contradicts your words. It might be, though, that you've had a rotten time, and you are simply trying, for whatever reason, to cover that fact up. The solution to contradictory body language signals and verbal messages caused by lack of truthfulness is to aim for—risk is probably a better word—greater honesty. If, as you turn to leave, you tell Janet that you're disappointed that the evening hasn't turned out better, there is a congruency between your words and your behavior that leaves no doubt as to what you really mean. (In fact, Janet now has something definite to respond to, which is the risk you take in being clear.)

It frequently happens, however, that we simply are not aware of how the language of our behavior contradicts or replaces a particular verbal message. The issue, then, is not lack of honesty, but lack of awareness. So if you want to feel closer to others and want others to feel closer to you, it might be helpful to keep the following research-based ideas and behavior possibilities in mind:

> Nonverbal signals are picked up as a behavioral package, each contributing to the final meaning a person gives it.[44] A person may greet us with a warm smile, but if he or she extends a limp hand of welcome and looks away, we may wonder about the sincerity of the smile. Be cautious about assigning too much meaning to a single gesture. Rather, look for the overall pattern. All forms of expression—verbal, postural, facial, and cultural, as well—must be considered.

> Be sensitive to the space you keep between yourself and others; generally, too great a physical distance keeps others psychologically distant, also. Make an effort to allow the distance between yourself and others to be consistent with your inner feelings.

> We typically look at another person's face first of all. Practice letting your face express what you feel inside. The face is a great message board.

> Eye contact is an invisible bridge between people that can help make for better interpersonal connections.

> The invisible bridge can become a more tangible bridge through the language of touch.

If you would like to be perceived as being as friendly as you feel, reach out and touch people more often.

If you happen to be a male and you suspect that the women you've known have always been pretty good at reading your behavior, your suspicions can be confirmed by research.[45, 46] Not only are women generally better than men at reading behavior, but they are also better at sending nonverbal signs about their own inner feelings. Men have a lot to learn from women with regard to being open to their own and others' emotional messages.

People tend to assign more weight to others' nonverbal messages than to their verbal statements, because they know intuitively that body language is less subject to conscious control. (Perhaps this is why Dane Archer and Robin Akert[47] found, in their review of research, that nonverbal channels have up to thirteen times the impact of the verbal channel.)

Perhaps more than we realize, the emotional, social, and psychological boundaries of our relationships are determined by the nonverbal messages that we exchange. Research findings[48] point clearly to the idea that people who are adept at reading behavioral cues are more effective in their interpersonal relationships. It's another way to tune in to people, and it seems to make a difference for the better.

Reflections

Is this you? The other person? Watch for these body language signals that indicate resistance or anger, or anxiety or a general closed-off feeling:

Cold hands
Yawning (when not sleepy)
Foot tapping
Gum chewing
Tightened jaw
Tight shoulder muscles—
  "a chip on the shoulder"

"Fencer's posture"
  (presenting a side view
  instead of the full face)
Arms folded across the chest
Hunching forward (by a woman
  to minimize breasts and the
  pelvis)

These signs may indicate more positive, open, warm feelings:

Shoulders down
Full exhalations
Pelvis at ease, not
  retracted
Hands warm and receptively
  open, not clenched

Full-face attitude in
  conversations
Direct eye contact
Free and loose movement
Frequent smiling

You may learn a great deal about your own and others' inner feelings by listening to the language in these behaviors.

Caution: There Are Cultural Differences

Culture is a guiding factor in body language in terms of meaning. As pointed out by Michael Argyle,[49] when North Americans pull on their earlobes, it's usually a sign of boredom. If an Italian male does this, it may mean he's attracted to a woman. A man in Georgia smiles at everyone. Although constant smiling is considered quite normal in Georgia, a man in Massachusetts smiling at everyone may be asked, "What's so damn funny?" Paul Ekman[50] has observed that Tibetans greet their friends by sticking out their tongues, something that you and I might do for quite different reasons. Norms about public displays of emotion vary from culture to culture. Ekman noted, for example, that when Japanese and American viewers watched the same emotion-packed film, Americans more openly expressed negative emotions on their faces than did the Japanese. North Americans traveling abroad are sometimes startled to see how close to one another Latin and Mediterranean men stand while talking and how often they touch one another. Edward Hall[51] has noted that Arabs sometimes feel estranged when interacting with Americans, because Americans tend to stay farther apart and to have less eye contact than Arabs prefer.

And so it goes. Different cultures—indeed, different subcultures within the main culture—give different meanings to both the expression and content of nonverbal communications. An awareness of this can help us to be better senders and receivers of body language signals.

Responding to people nonverbally is one way to impact and influence communication. Responding to people verbally is another way. Which brings us to an important aspect of human communication.

THE VERBAL RESPONSE STYLE WE USE MAKES A DIFFERENCE

The verbal response style we use does make a difference, and that difference is most clearly seen in the effect it has on others. The difference is essentially positive or negative and it can clearly affect the course and tone of our relationships.

When we communicate, we do more than simply exchange verbal and nonverbal information. We also convey messages that tell others how we feel about them. Communications researchers Evelyn Sieberg and Carl Larson[52] suggest that we do this through our use of *confirming* and *disconfirming* responses. As they define a confirming response, it is "any behavior that causes another person to value himself more." Confirming responses can be found in the following:

John: "Wow! That was a hard exam—one of the hardest I've taken in any college course so far. Sure hope I get at least a C."

Dave: "Man, you said it. That was a toughie."

or

Mary: "I'm so proud of my teammates. We were down by fifteen points in the final quarter and came back to win by one point!"

Peggy: "Yes, you and the whole team worked hard together and it paid off. I yelled myself hoarse!"

You can see that both Dave and Peggy responded in a way that not only confirmed what John and Mary said, but on a deeper level confirmed John and Mary as persons.

A disconfirming response, on the other hand, is one that Sieberg and Larson say causes "people to value themselves less." In that sense, two examples of disconfirming responses follow:

John: "Wow! That was a hard exam—one of the hardest I've taken in any college course so far. Sure hope I get at least a C."

Dave: "Well, you might think so, but I think a ninth-grade high school student could've handled it."

or

Mary: "I'm so proud of my teammates. We were down by fifteen points in the final quarter and came back to win by one point!"

Peggy: "Well, I don't know if there's that much to gloat about. The other team got pretty tired and that's why you caught them at the end."

You can see that Peggy and Dave's responses not only rejected the content of what John and Mary said to them, but, by implication, their responses reject John and Mary as persons. Another kind of disconfirming response is also possible. For example, to John's remark about a hard exam, Dave could say something like: "I think I'll go see a movie. Want to come?" This remark has the same impact as would a fourth possibility: complete silence. Both of these response possibilities are disconfirming because neither of them encourages the listeners to feel good about themselves or the interactions. If we grant Dave and Peggy the best of all positive motives, *it may well be that neither one of them consciously intended to be disconfirming or negative.* They could be like many people who simply lack an awareness of either the response style they are using or its effect on others. We are not talking now about those moments when we may consciously want, or need, to be disconfirming or negative. When we are so, we know what we're doing, and we're usually not surprised at the consequences—people pull away, clam up, get angry, attack back, and so on; you no doubt have experienced all of these behaviors as either the giver or the receiver.

Our purpose here is to become more aware of the response options available to us in order to facilitate better interpersonal communication. Confirming and disconfirming responses are somewhat generic labels describing fairly broad categories of behavior. Let's turn our attention to five rather specific response possibilities and relate them to the confirming–disconfirming framework we've just talked about.

Five Interpersonal Responses: Their Effects and Consequences

Some years ago, Carl Rogers and F. J. Roethlisberger[53] conducted a series of studies on how people communicate with each other in face-to-face situations. They found that there were five basic categories of interpersonal responses that made up about 80 percent of the verbal exchanges between individuals. The other 20 percent cut across many individualized responses that were not used frequently enough to be put in a category and, in that sense, were not particularly important.

Reflections

Read each situation described below and then rate the five responses for each from 1 to 5. A rating of 1 indicates the response with which you feel most comfortable, and a rating of 2 reflects your next choice for a response you might make, and so on through 5, which is the response with which you feel least comfortable.

1. *Young woman*: "I don't know what I'm going to do about my relationship to Richard. He continues to see other women even though he says he loves me and wants to get married, and then he lies when I ask him if he's dating anyone else. I feel like I love him and hate him at the same time."

   ____How have you answered him when he's talked about marriage?

   ____Maybe you can't make up your own mind about marriage and he's trying to force the issue.

   ____It seems strange that you would love someone who treats you that way.

   ____Sounds like you're sitting between two equally strong feelings and you don't quite know which is the right one.

   ____I think I know how you feel—I've felt that way myself.

2. *Sixth-grade boy*: "My parents never let me do anything. My mother hollers at me; my dad spanks me. My stupid sister gets to do whatever she wants and I don't think it's fair."

   ____Aren't you being unfair yourself by saying your parents *never* let you do anything?

   ____What are some things you would like to do that you feel your parents are against?

   ____Sounds like calling your sister stupid is a way of expressing you anger.

   ____It's not much fun when you feel the rules are unfair, is it?

   ____You feel that your parents have one set of standards for your sister and another set for you, is that it?

Situation 1:   (1) P, (2) I, (3) E, (4) U, (5) S
Situation 2:   (1) E, (2) P (3) I, (4) S, (5) U
The next several paragraphs will explain what these symbols mean.

From their observations of individuals in a variety of settings—at work, at home, at parties, at conventions, and so on—Rogers and Roethlisberger found that five responses kept emerging in the following order of frequency from most to least used: (1) *evaluative,* (2) *interpretive,* (3) *supportive,* (4) *probing,* and (5) *understanding.* In addition, they found that if a person uses one particular response category as much as 40 percent of the time, then other people see that person as always responding that way. It's one of the ways that people tend to stereotype one another. It's also another example of how little information it takes for us to pigeonhole each other, particularly *if we are not aware that this is what we're doing.*

Each of these five response categories is associated with a particular intent or purpose:

Evaluative (E): a response which indicates that we have made a judgment about the goodness, rightness, or appropriateness of another person's situation. It is a response that frequently tells the other person what he or she ought to do (3-E and 1-E above).

Interpretive (I): a response which indicates that our intent is to tell the other person what his situation really means, or how and why he feels as he does. It is more of an attempt to interpret the underlying meaning of a situation, rather than to tell the listener directly or indirectly what he ought to do about it (2-I and 3-I above).

Supportive (S): a response which indicates that our purpose is to reassure, to support, and to help the other person to know that she's not alone with her problem. It is not a response designed to talk a person out of her feelings; rather, it allows her to have them and not to feel so alone in the process (5-S and 4-S above).

Probing: a response which indicates our intent to get more information and to provoke more data-gathering discussion about the issue at hand. It is a response that says, in so many words, let's find out more about it (1-P and 2-P above).

Understanding: a response which reflects our intent to understand correctly what the other person is saying and how he or she feels about the problem. It's a response known as paraphrasing—that is, putting the essence of what the other person says into one's own words, but without changing the original meaning or being judgmental or evaluative (4-U and 5-U above).

How did you rate the responses to the two situations in the *Reflections* exercise above? What do your ratings suggest about how you respond to people? Your responses to only two situations can by no means be used as conclusive evidence about your response style, but perhaps you can see some tendencies.

Actually, the five response categories are neither good nor bad in and of themselves. What makes any one of them bad is its overuse or inappropriateness. If a person tends to use primarily evaluative or interpretive responses, that person runs a high risk of turning others off. Evaluative and interpretive responses are more likely to be viewed as disconfirming behaviors, and most of us prefer not to feel disconfirmed (judged, labeled, avoided). On the other hand, supportive, probing, and understanding responses are more apt to be perceived as confirming behaviors, and feeling confirmed (acknowledged, accepted, heard) is something most of us enjoy.

Does this mean that there is no place for evaluative and interpretive responses? Not at all. They are both necessary and appropriate, but it depends on the timing and context of their use. Remember, these are the two responses that tend to be used most frequently in human interactions. This means that they are usually used too frequently at the *beginning* of human relationships, when their effect on others can be to cause defensiveness. Evaluative and interpretive responses are most appropriate, can be most helpful, and can be most facilitating when used in developed relationships in which two or more people know, trust, and care about each other. If I have just met you and soon thereafter I say, "I know I'm a bit radical in my political beliefs, but I'm trying to temper them somewhat," and you respond either evaluatively, with a statement like, "You shouldn't have gotten so radical in the first place; then you wouldn't have to back down," or you respond interpretively, saying something like, "You probably got your radicalism from listening to too much left-wing rhetoric" then chances are good that I will spend more of my time arguing against you than revealing myself to you. On the other hand, if you and I have a relationship that has existed for some time and we know something of each other's values and preferences, and we like and trust each other, then occasional evaluative and interpretive statements may deepen both the discussion and the relationship. The idea that trust is a necessary prerequisite for being able to hear evaluative and interpretive comments less defensively is pointed out time and time again in clinical literature.[54, 55] When we know that another person has our best interests in mind, then we're in a better spot to hear an evaluative or interpretive remark as a facilitating comment or as constructive feedback, rather than as a personal attack. Whether on a first date, in the first week at school, or at the first staff meeting, evaluations and interpretations are usually better left unspoken.

If you're really interested in keeping lines of communication open, establishing mutual trust, and deepening a relationship, then using understanding, probing, and supporting responses can be helpful, facilitating ways to confirm the other person and to build rapport. An understanding response is a way of letting a person know that you're listening to both the content of what's being said and the feeling accompanying it; a probing response lets a person know that you want to know more and, on a deeper level, that he or she is worth knowing more about; a supportive response is a way of saying that you care and that you hope things will get better.

Each of these five major response categories plays an important part in human communication. Aim for a balance in your efforts to improve your communication skills. When we overuse a particular response category, we run the major (and perhaps deserved) risk of being stereotyped as a certain kind of person. The constant evaluator may be viewed as judgmental and authoritarian; the perpetual interpreter may be seen as an intellectual bore more interested in advertising his or her superiority than in finding a broader base of commonality with others; the constant supporter may be perceived as so indiscriminately positive and helpful that we wonder whether he or she is that way more for his or her own needs than for ours; and the always understanding soul may be viewed as empathic and warm, but perhaps too wishy-washy to be deeply involved with. A vast review of research by John Wiemann and Philip Backlund[56] shows clearly that people with flexible communication skills are more successful and competent in their interaction with others than those who are more rigidly locked in to a narrow range of responses.

Reflections

Experiment a little. Try using just a certain kind of response in your next several interactions. What happens when you're essentially evaluative or interpretive or understanding? Check yourself out with the persons you've talked to at the completion of your experiments. How do they feel about the interaction? About you? How do *you* feel?

INTERACTION BEHAVIORS AND EFFECTS ON COMMUNICATION

Whether we are aware of it or not, each of us has a particular way or "style" in which we interact with certain other people. The style we use at any particular time may be influenced by the person we're talking to, by our mood at the moment, by the current circumstances, or most likely, by some combination of all three possibilities. Most people are not aware of the way in which they interact with others—in terms of knowing what they're doing and being conscious of the consequences of what they're doing. We interact this way, we respond that way, but without really knowing what we're doing, why we're doing it, or where we learned to do it in the first place. It is outside the scope of this book to deal very much with the origins of our interaction behaviors, but perhaps we can become aware of what we're doing and why we're doing it.

John Narciso and David Burkett[57] observed in their experiences and clinical studies that most of us have learned three basic forms of behavior, which we use in conducting interpersonal transactions between ourselves and other people in the world. The extent to which any one of them is used varies widely from person to person. We learn to *defer,* to *demand,* and to *defect,* any one of which can be a prominent, and sometimes dominant, part of a person's mode of communication. Let's consider each of them.

Deferring Behavior: I Cancel Me for You

This is typically a behavior that most of us learn at an early age, when we are taught to do what other people expect us to do. It is necessary and important to learn this behavior, as it teaches us that we cannot always have our own way and that there are times when we have to give up what we may want to do. One basically "gives in" to the other person in order to avoid something negative and to get something positive.

When one person defers to another, it means that he or she is giving up what *he* or *she* wants in deference to what *someone else* wants. A way of looking at it:

Deferring Behavior M̶E̶/YOU

Here we cancel our desires for those of someone else. However, when an issue between two people is relatively insignificant and one person accepts the suggestion of another, it is not what we would call a deference interaction. It is when both partners find themselves in disagreement over an issue that is *significant* to them that we are most apt to see deference behavior. It is when one person submits to the other, but feels angry and resentful, that a deference interaction has taken place. When an interaction leaves you—and only you—with the feeling that your own preferences or wishes have been cancelled, then this may be a sign that you've just deferred to another person's demands.

Demanding Behavior: I Cancel You for Me

This is another behavior that's learned at an early age. At the same time that we're taught to defer by the adults in our lives, we pick up ideas about how to use demanding behavior by watching and imitating those who are telling us what to do and how to do it. It is a behavior that, quite literally, demands something of another person without any particular sensitivity to that person's position or wishes.

When one person demands something from another, he or she is trying to get what he or she wants by negating what *someone else* wants. You can look at it this way:

Demanding Behavior ME/Y̶O̶U̶

When this happens the other person's desires get cancelled. There are numerous examples of this behavior in relationships between parents and children, teachers and students, bosses and workers. One person demands what he or she wants— no options, no negotiations—and the other person defers. When both people demand something from each other, you know what typically happens—arguments, bickering, sometimes angry words, until one person gives in to the other. Or, a person can take refuge in another kind of behavior.

Defecting Behavior: We Both Get Cancelled

When a four-year-old goes off to his room and pouts because his mother won't let him watch any more television, it is an example of defecting behavior, which, too, has historical roots in childhood, and, like deferring and demanding behaviors, it carries over into adult transactions. One person gives another person the silent treatment; another person slams the door and stalks off, vowing, "I'm never going to talk to you again." Still other people withdraw into tears, or anger, or self-pity, and whatever hope there was for communication is severed.

When one person defects by withdrawing in various ways from further communication, that person, in effect, cancels both parties because nothing further can be accomplished. It looks like this:

Defecting Behavior   ~~ME/YOU~~

Each of these three interaction behaviors is sufficiently self-centered to block healthy, open communication. And for good reasons: a constantly deferring person may be so concerned about being liked that he undersells himself in order to buy acceptance; the always demanding person may be so concerned about getting what she wants that she oversells herself in order to have control; the perpetual defector may be so consumed by his own lack of self-worth (or perhaps his inflated sense of it) that he feels inwardly too weak (or too above the effort it would take) to confront troublesome issues. Whatever the reason, each is a losing interaction, because in each case at least one person gets cancelled.

I don't mean to suggest that any one of these behaviors is as simple or as pure as it may seem to appear here. These are complex behaviors that ebb and flow in various combinations during the course of our interactions in everyday life. Whether they stand out as stark expressions or are reflected in subtler tones of verbal exchange, their effect is to interfere with better communications. Remember, we're not always aware of the interaction behavior we're using, much less its effect on others. Being more conscious about *what* we're doing is the first step to making better choices about *how* to communicate more effectively.

Reflections

Think about how you tend to interact with others. Do you see yourself as a deferring, demanding, or defecting person? Which kinds of interactions bring out which kind of behaviors in you? Who do you defer to? Demand from? Defect from? Watch yourself in the laboratory of your day-to-day living, and see what you can learn about your interaction behaviors.

Narciso and Burkett have introduced another option for behaving in interpersonal relationships.

Declaring Behavior: No One Gets Cancelled

When we use declaring behavior, we are simply stating what we would like to happen, rather than demanding that it happen, or deferring automatically to the other person, or defecting before anything can happen at all. A declaring statement is one in which we make clear and explicit what we want, in a positive manner. More than that, it involves a willingness to listen to the other person's point of view, and if necessary, to negotiate the differences. You can easily recognize a declaring statement, because the speaker expresses what he or she wants in the first person singular. Consider an example: Suppose you would like to see a certain movie on a certain night with a friend. You have at least three options: (1) You can declare your preference: "I would like to see the double feature at the drive-in with you tomorrow night," or (2) you can use a more deferring approach: "Would you be interested in going to the drive-in double feature tomorrow night?" or (3) you can use a demanding approach: "I think we should go to the drive-in double feature tomorrow night."

At first glance, it may seem that the demanding behavior sounds like a declaring approach. Not so. Although the demander speaks in the first person and expresses what he or she wants to happen, he or she also speaks in terms of what the other is supposed to do—namely, go to the movies. In that sense, he assumes responsibility for the other person's behavior, which is characteristic of demanders. When we declare what we wish to happen, we are simply assuming responsibility for our own behavior and leaving it up to the other person to assume responsibility for her own behavior. He or she may say, "I'd like to see it too, but tomorrow night isn't a good time for me. I think I could make it Saturday night." It's at this point that some negotiation is in order, and unless we've made a demanding statement in the guise of a declaring statement, we'll be open to different options. Statements are made in the first person singular, channels of communication are kept open, and no one gets cancelled; these are the important features of declaring behavior.

You may see the trap that is sometimes built into the deferring approach— "Would you be interesting in going to the double feature tomorrow night?" The deferrer declares only by inference. The question technique automatically makes the other person responsible for the decision. The trap is triggered when our reply to the question is something like, "No, I don't think I'd like to go; I'm really pretty busy," and the other person then says, "You never want to do anything I want to do " When the other person only acts as if he or she is open to a choice, but gets mad when the choice doesn't go his or her way, we can be fairly certain that what sounded like a deferring question was really a disguised demand.

Using more declaring statements in our interactions is not a magical communication cure-all, but it is a way of making our connections with others more clear and direct. It is also risky. Rather than putting ourselves in the role of a "reactor" waiting for someone else to make the first move—so we can safely agree or disagree, support or attack, we put ourselves in the role of "actor," in the sense that we put what we want on the line. This is not to say that deferring, demanding, and even defecting behaviors are never necessary or appropriate. Human behavior is seldom a matter of black and white choices. Most of the time, we reside in a shady gray area and have to take into account the moment, the person, and the circumstances. At times, it's wiser to defer because a confrontation may be counterproductive at the moment. And then there are times when we have to make certain demands, because under the circumstances, negotiations are neither possible nor appropriate. There may even be instances when defecting behavior —leaving the scene—may be the wisest course, particularly when the person we're talking to is hopelessly beyond reason. Even then, however, we can declare what we want to happen—"I want to finish talking this through"—rather than simply exit with no explanation.

I-Statements Can Be Facilitating—But Be Careful

By definition, *I* is a pronoun used to refer to the one who is speaking or writing —I am fine; I am here; I have a new car. (It can also be used as a noun to refer to someone aware of possessing an individual identity—It is I.)

Sometimes, however, *you* statements are unknowingly used by the speaker to disguise the *I*. By definition, *you* is a pronoun used to refer to the one or ones being addressed; it is the pronoun of the second person singular or plural—"You are the one I would like to see," or "You are the ones I would like to see." The pronoun *we* can also be used to disguise an I-statement. We hear this all the time. Consider an example. You're talking to one of your friends after class and you ask him or her the following question, "In what ways do you think the study of communication skills will help you to be a better teacher?" He or she replies, disguising I with you, "Well, when you know more about basic communication skills, it enables you to speak with greater clarity, because you're more aware of how to present your ideas," or disguising I with we, "Well, when we know more about basic communication skills, it enables us to speak with greater clarity, because we're more aware of how to present our ideas."

In the first instance, it sounds as though the speaker is talking *for* the person who asks the question. And in the second instance, it sounds like the speaker is talking either for the person who asks the question or as a representative of an entire population of students. Do you have some feeling for how much more impersonal and distancing a disguised I-statement can be? Consider how an undisguised I-statement response to the same question sounds "Well, when I know more about basic communication skills, it enables me to speak with greater clarity, because I'm aware of how to present my ideas." Do you have a sense of how much more clearly, directly, and personally the response comes across? When you think about it, using the pronoun I when speaking for ourselves acknowledges a simple truism: No two people ever see the same event in quite the same way. When we use I-statements, it allows us to place the responsibility for a perception (idea, point of view, opinion) on the right person—ourselves.

I-statements can be helpful in another way, too. They can help us to stay tuned to our own inner world of feelings, so that we might evaluate and judge others less (turn-offs) and do more to reveal ourselves. Let's say, for example, that you do something that elicits a feeling of frustration in me. One way of responding to you would be to say something like, "You're really inconsiderate." Right away I judge and label you, which may prompt you to say, "No, I'm not!" Many arguments begin in exactly this way. One person says to another, "You're inconsiderate," "You're a slob," or "You're clumsy," the other person denies it, both get defensive, and communication goes haywire.

Another way I can respond to my feelings of frustration is to say something like, "I really feel frustrated with you." It won't make much sense for you to say, "No you don't." I'm simply revealing to you an inner feeling, which is something undeniable in me. As such, it is not something you can refute. However, if I should slip a you-statement in on top of the I-statement ("I really feel frustrated with you when you're so inconsiderate"), the door is again open to a defensive rebuttal and a communication breakdown. Thomas Gordon[58] characterizes a good I-statement as a " ... factual report without editorial characterization."

If you're interested in improving your interpersonal communications, I-statements may help in the following ways:

1. They heighten a sense of interpersonal trust and closeness insofar as you are able to reveal more of yourself to others.
2. You talk *to* people rather than for them or at them.
3. You stay in touch with your own inner feelings.
4. You avoid labeling, judging, and evaluating the other person's behavior.

Speaking in I-statements is not always appropriate. There are times when using more impersonal and general you-statements or we-statements is both necessary and suitable. Teachers need to generalize, politicians have to represent and speak for many people, chairpersons may have to keep communications formal and impersonal, in order to focus on tasks rather than personalities *Rule of thumb:* When your aim is to develop a less formal and more personal connection between yourself and another person, I-statements can help.

Reflections

I wonder what you would discover if you made a conscious effort to speak in more I-statements for the next week or so. Try it out. What effect does it have on others? On you? Why do you suppose it's so difficult for most people to use I-statements?

It may seem an easy enough task to express ideas, opinions, and personal perceptions in declaring sentences and I-statements, but what happens when we begin to tap the deeper layers of our psychology, known as feelings? Let's turn our attention to another idea.

THE VERBAL EXPRESSION OF FEELINGS: IMPORTANT BUT DIFFICULT TO ACHIEVE

For better or worse, our feelings about ourselves and others are important aspects of everyday living. Psychiatrist Willard Gaylin has defined *feeling* as simply "our subjective awareness of our own emotional state."[59] We may not always know what our feelings are, and we may even mislabel the feelings we think we have, but our private inner worlds are usually seething with rich and varied emotions related to our intra- and interpersonal lives.

It is on the feeling level of our lives that we are most vulnerable to attack and most susceptible to being misunderstood; because of these possibilities, it is the level on which we are most prone to experience pain. Hence, our difficulty in expressing inner feelings.

Most people don't start out being guarded about their feelings and cautious about expressing them, but because of too many hurtful experiences en route to growing up, they end up that way. Some examples you may recognize:

1. Four-year-old: "Mommy, I feel so sad that Spot died."
   Mother: "We'll get another dog, dear. You shouldn't feel sad."
2. Five-year-old: "I hate Tommy. He's always hitting me!"
   Father: "You don't hate him—that's not nice."
3. Six-year-old: "I don't like spinach. I don't want to eat it."
   Mother: "Sure you like spinach. Eat it—it's good for you."
4. Eight-year-old: "Ow, my knee hurts—look, it's bleeding."
   Father: "Oh, come on now, it doesn't hurt that much."
5. Twelve-year-old: "I feel so dumb in school, I'd like to quit."
   Parents: "Stop talking like that. You're not dumb at all."
6. Sixteen-year-old: "I feel so self-conscious and nervous when I have to get up in front of the class."
   Parents: "You shouldn't feel that way. Getting nervous won't help."

You get the idea. Sometimes well-intentioned parents, trying to protect their children (and maybe themselves) from hurtful, negative feelings, end up teaching them that what they're feeling isn't what they're feeling at all, which leads children either not to believe their feelings or to deny them in the first place, or that what they're feeling isn't all that big a deal, which, if repeated often enough, leads children to believe, at the very least, that their feelings are not important, or at the very most, that they themselves are not very important. This is a powerful form of schooling. If it is successful, then the children learn to associate the expression of inner feelings with being put down or turned off or misunderstood altogether. They then grow into guarded adults who have difficulty expressing inner feelings.

Other people may have problems voicing inner feelings, not so much because their feelings were squelched or ignored as they grew up, but because that sort of communication was simply not modeled on a verbal level by the significant people in their lives. Along this line, I'm reminded of a former male client of mine who, in the process of struggling with the problems he was having expressing his more positive, loving feelings toward his wife and children, observed:

> You know, I remind myself in a lot of ways of my own father, and I don't like the resemblance. I think he loves me, but I have to infer it; I think he is proud of me, but I have to guess it's true. I don't know either one of those things for sure. That's the hell of it, he never *said* any of those things. I never once heard "I love you or care about you or I'm proud of you," or anything like that. And here I am, just like him. I've got two kids, and I can't even remember the last time that I told either one of them directly that I really cared about them. For that matter, I can't really remember when the last time was I told my wife I loved her. Isn't that stupid. Here I don't like my father for the way he was in that regard, and I end up just like him.

This man is expressing a frustration that many people feel, from time to time, as they look back over their lives. They recognize in themselves negative behaviors that they originally saw in their parents, and they are surprised and dismayed to note the uncanny resemblance. It's the consequence of being immersed for years in a certain kind of emotional atmosphere and unconsciously absorbing—sponge-like—all of its aspects. If you have grown up in an emotional climate in which feelings were openly and freely exchanged, then chances are good that you have easy access to your feeling world. If, on the other hand, you have experienced an emotional climate in which feelings were neither encouraged nor expressed, then you may have more trouble in two ways: (1) knowing what your feelings are, and (2) expressing your feelings even when you do know. For some people, the inability to talk about and express inner feelings is not so much a reflection of low motivation or lack of desire to do so, as it is an indication of a lack of learning and opportunity to acquire the necessary skills for emotional communication.

I am not suggesting that, in order to be a good communicator, you always have to be on a feeling level. Sharing personal feelings, either about yourself or another person, is many times neither appropriate nor necessary. When your purpose in interacting with another person is to accomplish a task, complete a mission, or achieve a specific goal, then focusing on interpersonal feelings may be counterproductive. We can, however, invoke the same rule of thumb mentioned earlier: When your aim is to develop a more personal, perhaps even a more intimate relationship between yourself and another person, then more communication on a feeling level can be helpful. A word of caution, however. Timing is important when it comes to sharing your deeper feelings about yourself or the other person. Research[60, 61] indicates that if you get too personal or too deep too soon, you run the risk of scaring your listener off rather than drawing him or her closer to you. When deeper revelations come too soon in the relationship, they're apt to be viewed as either phony or attention-getting, which may leave your listener with a sense of being used and manipulated rather than confided in and trusted.

Self-Disclosure: An Avenue to Feelings and Better Communication

Not all topics involving feelings are difficult to talk about. How many of us, I wonder, have had someone say to us, "I want to be perfectly honest with you"? What this means, more often than not, is that he or she wants to be perfectly honest about us or another person, rather than about him- or herself. Consider, for example, the conversational pattern of several people you talk with rather frequently. Whom do they talk about? Themselves? Others? What is the usual focus of their communication? To what extent would you say that the following scale, suggested by psychologist David Johnson[62] (presented below in a somewhat modified form), reflects the way in which most people, including you, deal with feelings?

It is much easier to talk about others with a kind of "back-there-and-then" focus than it is to talk about ourselves with a more focused "here-and-now" emphasis. Showing some of yourself to another person, exhibiting some of your own feelings and attitudes about yourself and the other person, is not easy to do. It is generally both easier and safer for me to tell you how Kendall felt about Kim (back-there-and-then), than it is for me to tell you my present feelings about you or, more revealing, my present feelings about myself. Self-disclosure and honesty require courage. Not merely the courage *to be,* as theologian Paul Tillich[63] eloquently described it, but the courage *to be known,* to be perceived by others as we know ourselves to be. Sidney Jourard, whose self-disclosure research opened new doors to understanding interpersonal communication, has given us fresh insights into why self-disclosure can be a risky business. Why risky? Well, as Jourard put it ". . . you expose yourself not only to a lover's balm, but to the hater's bombs! When he knows you, he knows just where to plant them for maximum effect."[64]

LEAST SELF-REVEALING   *LEAST DIFFICULT TO DISCUSS*

1. I tell you how Kendall felt about Kim, neither person being present.
2. I tell you how Kendall feels about Kim, neither person being present.
3. I tell you my past feelings about Jim, who is not present.
4. I tell you my present feelings about Jim, who is not present.
5. I tell you my past feelings about you.
6. I tell you my present feelings about you.
7. I tell you my past feelings about myself.
8. I tell you my present feelings about myself.

MOST SELF-REVEALING   *MOST DIFFICULT TO DISCUSS*

The disclosure that we're talking about here is the sort of disclosure that allows our listener to: (1) know more about how we feel about ourselves, or (2) to know more about how he or she is affecting us. For example, let's say we are in an argument and I say to you, "I really feel you have a closed mind. I would like you to listen to my side and you just keeping yapping away. Why don't you shut up for awhile." Now I suppose I could say that I'm just telling you how I feel. But I'm not, really. What I am doing is characterizing good behavior in evaluative and judgmental terms, a practically guaranteed way to get a reactive and defensive reply from you. When I tell you that you have a closed mind or that you should shut up, I tell you nothing about myself. What you know—or think you know—about me has to be inferred from what I say and how I say it. You may have the sense that I'm frustrated or angry, but in your natural need to protect yourself and get back at me, it's not likely that how I feel will be very important to you. And the battle will continue. Now it may be that you *do* have a closed mind, that you *do* need to listen and stop yapping, that you *should* shut up for awhile. No matter how strongly I believe that those things are true, it is not likely that I will convince you to change by beating you over the head with judgmental evaluations of your behavior. From the way I express myself to you, you can easily conclude that I am trying to force you to change. You may recall from our discussion in Chapter 3 that it is precisely when people feel *forced* to change that they are most apt to be resistant and *least* apt to change.

We are apt to communicate better when we: (1) avoid evaluative and interpretive responses, (2) use declaring behavior, and (3) try to stick with I-statements that reveal something about ourselves rather than merely describe the other person's behavior. With this in mind, perhaps a better way of expressing what I said to you on the last page might be: "I really feel frustrated with you when you seem not to hear me. I would like you to listen to my side and I will try hard to listen to yours. I feel very unimportant when there doesn't seem much chance to express my opinion." Here the emphasis is on how I am feeling (frustrated, unimportant) and on what I would like to happen (us both to listen). Now you may still infer that I'm judging you or that I'm trying to coerce you to change, but if you do, then it is something that comes from inside *you*, rather than something *I* am trying to force on you from the outside.

Reflections

You may find it interesting for the next several days or so to pay close attention to how people talk when interacting with you. Note what their conversations focus on. How often do you hear self-revealing statements? How do you feel about those who are able to disclose themselves to you? Experiment with self-disclosure yourself. When you reveal your inner self to a friend or a loved one, how is the relationship affected?

It is easy enough to be self-disclosing when we feel happy, strong, psychologically grounded, and generally on top of things, but there is far more risk in revealing those parts of us where we feel more psychologically vulnerable. For most of us, there are certain areas that may well be referred to the following way.

Feelings that Are Difficult to Express

Ordinarily, the feelings that we find hardest to reveal to others are associated with characteristics that we consider to be personal flaws or emotional weaknesses. Although they vary from person to person, there are at least nine feeling states that seem particularly difficult to disclose to others. These feelings states are not presented in order of their difficulty of expression (that depends on the person), and they are followed by examples of possible self-disclosing I-statements and then examples of more evaluative and accusatory you-statements. Note how the I-statements *reveal* inner feelings and how the you-statements *conceal* those feelings by focusing on the other person.

1. *Feelings of being hurt or rejected*   (a) "I feel hurt and left out when I'm not included in the conversation." (b) "You constantly dominate the discussion and make others feel unimportant."
2. *Feelings of inadequacy*   (a) "I just don't feel like I'm good enough for you; I feel so far behind you in so many ways." (b) "You always act as though you're superior to everyone."
3. *Feelings of dependency*   (a) "I really get scared when I'm in touch with how much I need you." (b) "You never seem to need anything from me."
4. *Feelings of not being able to accept affection from others*   (a) "When you hold me I feel my whole body get tense; I want you close, yet I feel so uptight about the closeness." (b) "It seems to me that you want to be physical in some way all the time. Why can't you just talk without hanging on?"
5. *Feelings of guilt*   (a) "I feel just awful about lying to you; it's not something I like in myself." (b) "Why are you looking at me that way? It seems like you're always trying to make me feel guilty about every little thing I do."
6. *Feelings of shame*   (a) "I feel so embarrassed when I stumble over words while talking to you." (b) "You look at me so critically whenever I happen to use the wrong word."
7. *Feelings of helplessness*   (a) "Nothing I do about the situation seems to work. I feel defeated and powerless to change anything." (b) "You are as rigid and unbending as an iron post. Nothing anyone says seems to affect you."
8. *Feelings of passivity*   (a) "I have a tendency to let people step all over me; I feel more like a doormat than a person." (b) "You just barge in without considering how others are feeling; you don't give anyone a chance."
9. *Feelings of anger*   (a) "I really feel angry about what you've just said." (b) "You're so damned insensitive about the way you say things."

You may have a sense of why these feeling states are difficult to reveal to others. There is a certain risk involved in telling another person that we feel inadequate or guilty or angry, as the case may be. Self-disclosing statements are involving statements. They tend to draw people closer to us and vice versa. Two lovers are typically persons who have disclosed a great deal to each other, which helps explain why, if the relationship goes awry, there are frequently hurt and sometimes bitter feelings. It is as if each of them has invested a portion of themselves in the other person, only to find that it has been a bad investment. There is a sense that each is being betrayed by someone who was once regarded as completely trustworthy. It seems generally true that we can be hurt or disappointed by another person only as much as we have invested ourselves emotionally in that person. Self-disclosure is a form of emotional investment. Like investments in the stock market, the more we invest in another person or persons, the more there is to lose, which is the risk. On the other hand, we can end up a whole lot richer and better off, which is the gain.

Self-disclosing inner feelings just because you may want to be open or honest is usually not a good idea. Richard Archer's[65] review of self-disclosure research suggests that too much disclosure is probably just as symptomatic of personal problems as too little. Not only is the timing of a self-disclosing statement important to consider but, so, too, is its *appropriateness*.[66] Does it fit the content of the occasion? Is it relevant to the conversation? Is it likely to enhance the relationship and add to it, or is it likely to be more of a block and subtract from the relationship?

A working principle: When you would like someone to know you better, when you would like more from a relationship than superficial chatter, when you would like to encourage the other person to disclose more of him- or herself, then revealing more of the inner you in the form of self-disclosing I-statements may help you achieve your goals.

Expressing feelings is important, because it can enhance interpersonal communications, particularly when they involve relationships we would like to make closer and more intimate. Which brings us to an important question.

What Happens When Feelings Are Withheld?

The answer is: it depends. It depends on the nature of the relationship and what you want from it. If it is a somewhat casual or formal or business-related or professional relationship, and you both want to be less personally involved, then withholding deeper feelings is probably both desirable and appropriate behavior. If the doctor who gave you your last physical examination behaved in a brusque and cold manner, you may not care to take the time or to use your energy to let Dr. X know how you feel about that. If your roommate or loved one or good friend treated you in such a manner, you might feel a greater inclination to let that person know how you feel.

Generally, the more important a relationship is to you and the more you want out of it, the more necessary it is to share feelings openly and honestly. When feelings are withheld, relationships either become or remain superficial and unsatisfying. In a relationship with a casual acquaintance or colleague, communication that is more small talk or shop talk can be quite satisfying because *that is all we expect to give to it or get out of it.* In an emotional relationship with a loved one, small talk—at least as a steady diet—may be quite unsatisfying, because *we expect more from the relationship.* Sidney Jourard,[67] and Douglas Daher and Paul Banikiotes[68] have documented persuasive arguments for why and how mutual disclosure can be highly rewarding for two people who have emotionally invested in a relationship. Feelings are an important source of feedback; when they are not revealed, two people can easily end up misunderstanding each other's motives and responding to each other inaccurately. Consider this example.

Bill and Donna are driving home from a party they've just attended. During the evening, Bill noticed that Donna was spending what he considered to be an unusual amount of time with Steve, a single man whom neither one knew very well. At one point in the evening, while Donna was engaged in what seemed to be a lively conversation with Steve, Bill went over and wondered if she would like something from the snack table. Donna said no, because she had just been there with Steve. Bill felt himself burn a little on the inside, mumbled, "Oh, OK," and ambled over to another group. On the way home, the conversation between Bill and Donna goes something like this:

Donna:	"You seem awfully quiet. Is anything wrong?"
Bill:	"No, I'm just a little beat. It's been a long day. (Privately: "Hell yes, something is wrong. You spent the whole evening throwing yourself at what's-his-name!")
Donna:	"I looked for you shortly after you said something about the snack table, but I couldn't find you anywhere."
Bill:	"It must've been about the time I stepped outside for a minute; the stuffiness was getting to me in there." (Privately: "I'm surprised you could tear yourself away."
Donna:	"That fellow, Steve, I was talking to is an interesting person. Did you get a chance to meet him?"
Bill:	"No, I didn't. The evening went so quickly, there seemed to be a lot of people I didn't talk to." (Privately: "No, and the reason I didn't is because the two of you seemed too interested in each other to want to talk to anyone else!")

When they get home there is very little interaction between the two of them, and Donna senses that there is more to Bill's silence than merely fatigue.

Donna:	"Bill, you seem distant. Is something bothering you?"
Bill:	"Look, why don't you quit nagging me. I told you nothing's wrong!" (No more private thoughts. Now it's all beginning to surface.)
Donna:	"Well, you don't have to yell at me. You've been snarly all evening."

Bill:	"I'm surprised you even noticed me this evening!"
Donna:	"Well, for heaven's sake—what's that supposed to mean?"
Bill:	"It means you were so wrapped up in what's-his-name that it's a wonder you noticed anyone else was there."
Donna:	"Oh, come on, Bill, you talk to other women all the time and leave me standing around. The last party we went to, you spent the whole time flitting around with Sally Grimes—the biggest flirt in the crowd."
Bill:	"You distort time and facts like crazy. God, you go around goggle-eyed all night over some guy and that's supposed to be all right."

This goes on and on until they are too tired to argue any longer, and they go to bed tired, unresolved, and emotionally distant.

It frequently happens this way. Two people care for each other deeply, but they end up expressing more of their angry feelings than their caring ones. When two people cease being direct with each other, neither knows where the other is coming from, and both begin to operate more on the basis of assumptions than facts.

Bill, for example, assumed that Donna was involved with Steve probably much more than she actually felt herself to be. As a consequence, he felt rejected, unimportant, and jealous. He began to feel vulnerable, and feeling this way, he began to behave defensively. There are two primary ways for communication to take a defensive turn: (1) by withholding or distorting basic feelings ("Is anything wrong?" Donna asked. "No, I'm just a little beat," Bill answered), or (2) by attacking the other person rather than revealing one's own inner feelings ("You spent the whole time flitting around with Sally," said Donna. "You go around goggle-eyed," responded Bill.)

You may see in the example that Bill initially withheld his feelings because he felt hurt and vulnerable. When confronted a bit more, he felt the hurt (resulting from feeling rejected—a common cause of hurt) more intensely, and he externalized it by attacking Donna with snide remarks and judgmental statements. This hurt Donna, which triggered an angry outburst from her. Rather than being emotionally honest about themselves, their conservation escalated into an emotional attack on each other as persons. Could it have been prevented? Probably, but it would require a quite different exchange. Let's go back to where it started and reconstruct it differently.

Donna:	"You seem awfully quiet. Is anything wrong?
Bill:	"Well, I feel quiet. I've felt kind of angry on the inside, ever since I asked you if you would like something from the snack table and you said you had just been there with Steve. I guess I was feeling jealous —in fact, I still am."
Donna:	"Gee, I feel bad about that. I sure didn't intend it to seem like I didn't want to spend time with you. I had a sense you were feeling

something, so I went looking for you about 5 minutes later, but I couldn't find you."

Bill: "I know. I went outside for awhile. I felt angry at you, but also angry at myself for feeling angry. Here I was behaving like a jealous teen-ager and I didn't like it. I sometimes feel that I get jealous too easily."

Donna: "I think I know how you feel. I had some of those same feelings two weeks ago at the party we were at when you were talking and laughing with Sally Grimes."

Bill: "You felt jealous about Sally Grimes? I had no idea. Well, maybe I did. You seemed somewhat withdrawn all the next day. I remember noticing that, but I wasn't sure why you were behaving that way."

Donna: "I think I was jealous, but I just didn't say anything, so how *could* you have known? Deep down, I guess I have the feeling that you'll find someone more attractive than I am, and I get jealous."

Bill: "Well, I know what you mean, 'cause I'm sure I was feeling that about Steve."

Here the focus is on revealing rather than attacking, disclosing *to* the other person rather than enclosing the self *from* that person. There is a certain risk factor, because disclosures can be misused or misinterpreted. For example, to Bill's disclosure that he was feeling jealous, Donna could have said, judgmentally, "Oh, come on now, that's silly. You don't have to feel jealous." Or she could have said defensively, "I was hardly doing anything to make you jealous. I was just talking to him, not necking with him." Either one of those replies could cause Bill to wish he hadn't said anything, but if the relationship is important and he wants to work it through, he will persist with nonjudgmental I-statements. He might say, "But I do feel jealous" or "It is not what *you* were doing, but something *I* am feeling in myself."

When feelings are withheld, particularly the more negative ones (anger, resentment, envy, jealousy, and so forth), they tend not to be forgotten, but rather, misplaced or displaced. For example, if we express anger directly at the person we're mad at, it helps to focus the discussion on the issue at hand. If we suppress the anger, it will invariably leak out in other ways, at different times, and in different situations. We may end up snapping at another person (displacing it), or getting disproportionately angry at the person toward whom we originally felt anger for some small incident two weeks ago (misplacing it).

If we withhold negative feelings, we withhold the very feedback that allows a relationship to grow, and to go beyond its present boundaries. Abraham Tesser and Sidney Rosen[69, 70] have shown that there seems to be a pervasive reluctance to pass on negative information or bad news to others. We don't want to hurt the other person, but mostly, we don't want the other person to dislike us. Hence, our inclination to remain quiet. Rosen and Tesser call it the *mum* effect.

However, when we're mum, the relationship suffers. For example, let's say that you're my good friend and that you've done something that makes me angry. If

I don't express this anger, then you have no way of knowing that what you've done has been disruptive to the relationship. If, on the other hand, I give you immediate feedback about how your behavior has triggered my anger, then you have at least two options: (1) you can continue to behave in that way, or (2) you can behave differently. The choice is yours. Without the feedback, there is no choice. With the feedback, you may choose to be different, because our relationship is more important than what you give up, or you may decide that the behavior is so important that you don't wish to change it. However it turns out, we can at least talk about it and, who knows, we may find a compromise that satisfies both of us.

Reflections

Think about a person in your life to whom you feel an emotional bond. Do you communicate your deepest feelings to that person? Can you let that person know when you are angry or hurt? Have you gotten into the habit of withholding feelings? Are you giving that person a chance to choose between behaving differently or not by giving him or her feedback that is immediate and direct?

In our ongoing encounters with others, we have probably all felt the need, from time to time, to directly confront certain people with the effects of their behavior. Which leads to us ask an important question.

WHAT IS CONFRONTATION AND WHEN SHOULD WE USE IT?

A basic communication skill is the ability to use confrontations appropriately and constructively. To tell another person that he or she is an awful individual and then to walk away with no further involvement is not confrontation. It is more a hit-and-run mission, with verbal assassination as its major goal. The kind of confrontation we have in mind here gives another person constructive feedback so that he or she *will behave less destructively.* Robert Carkhuff[71] has defined confrontation as "telling it like it is," by pointing out, for example, discrepancies between what a person says and how he behaves, how he says he is behaving and how he is actually behaving, or by calling attention to the obvious consequences of behaving in a self-defeating manner.

Confrontation is an invitation to self-examination, particularly when it originates in your concern for the other person and your willingness to involve yourself deeply in the relationship. A related primary rule of confrontation is: *Do not confront another person if you do not wish to increase your involvement with that individual.* When we confront without a willingness to be further involved, then we are only committing a verbal hit-and-run mission. It is something like a teacher telling a student that he (the student) has done very poor work, without making an effort to help him improve; it is like a parent telling a child to act her age, without attempting to develop the kind of relationship that may help the child to know *how* to act her age.

When should we confront? David Johnson[72] suggests that a decision of this kind is determined by two major aspects of the relationship:

1. The quality of the relationship. Generally, well-developed relationships can tolerate stronger confrontations.
2. The perceived ability of the person being confronted to use the confrontation constructively. It is generally better to avoid a confrontation, if the other person's anxiety is high or if his or her motivation or ability to change is low.

You can see that trust and motivation are necessary ingredients for a successful confrontation. If you don't trust me, you will quickly discard any attempt on my part to get you to look at the consequences of your behavior. The less well developed the relationship, the lower the trust level. If, for any reason, you're not motivated or ready to change, then my confrontation is only likely to make you defensive about what you're doing, rather than open to doing things differently.

Five Rules for Confronting Another Person Constructively

Confrontation is risky business; it means suggesting to another person that there may be better or more productive or more healthy ways of thinking or behaving; it means suggesting change—something that most individuals (including ourselves) are reluctant to do even when they perceive the best of intentions in the other person. So, in order to enhance the possibility of a confrontation resulting in positive outcomes, it may be wise to follow at least these five simple rules:

1. *Be sure the timing is right.* This is a tough one, but basically the idea is to try empathetically to put yourself in the other person's shoes. Is that person ready to listen? Can the relationship between the two of you tolerate a confrontation at this moment? Is there time to work through any fallout resulting from the confrontation?
2. *Stay current by focusing on here-and-now behavior.* This can be helpful, because it allows both you and the other person to use current and ongoing behavior as a kind of "data-base," which is less likely to be distorted or forgotten. My confrontation about something you did last week is not nearly as powerful as a confrontation about what's going on between us at this moment.
3. *Make an effort to state your feelings or observations tentatively rather than dogmatically.* It seems to be generally true that when people feel that someone is trying to force them to change or is trying to coerce them into a point of view, they tend to be more resistant. Suppose I confront you in the following way: "You always speak for longer than is necessary, and you seem insensitive to the

©1964 United Feature Syndicate, Inc.

Confrontations that are negative and judgmental can be disastrous.

opinions offered by others." Contrast that confrontation with this one: "I think I understand what you're saying, but I wonder if you may be overstating your point?" The first accuses and evaluates, while the second raises a question designed to encourage you to evaluate your *own* behavior. Ordinarily, we'll be more open to a confrontation that doesn't bulldoze us.

4. *Use descriptive statements.* The rule here grows out of J. L. Wallen's[73] suggestion to *describe* what we see as counterproductive behavior in another person, and to *describe* the impact it has on us. An example of this is Mary's response to Frank's sixth proposal: "Frank, I know you care for me, because I see signs of it in all the things you do for me. But when you push me so much to get married, I really feel frightened and I feel myself pulling away from you." Frank will likely be less defensive and more receptive to Mary's feelings than he would be if Mary had said: "Frank, you push, push, push, and I wish you would stop." (If Mary really *is* certain about never wanting to marry Frank, then this may be just the thing to say.)

5. *Focus on strengths rather than on weaknesses.* The psychology behind this rule is simple: Positive feedback is a far more effective motivational tool than negative feedback. In order to change, we need to know not only what we do that is wrong or inappropriate, but also what we can do that is better or more appropriate. Research studies by B. G. Berenson and K. M. Mitchell[74] have demonstrated that confrontations are far more apt to be successful when they point either to existing strengths or to those strengths that can be developed, than when they focus primarily on existing weaknesses. A weakness confrontation might go like this: "Ralph, the reason you may not be doing better in this course is because you never take notes, you seldom contribute to the discussions, and you probably don't study as hard as you should. Don't you think you should be more in-

volved?" A strength confrontation may go like this: "Ralph, I k
doing well in the course, and from what you've said, I know you
better. You made some contributions in the class discussion today th
keep the ball rolling. I've a hunch you can do more of that and I know I
good if you did. I bet you could put a whole lot more into the course than y
are." Honesty is an important part of a strength-focused confrontation. It's no
going to do any good to tell someone that he or she "helped keep the ball rolling"
if that wasn't really the case. Your body language or tone of voice will very likely
communicate how you truly feel, if your verbal message is inconsistant with your
inner feelings.

To summarize: Confrontation can be a helpful way to motivate a person to
examine the meaning and consequences of his or her behavior. It is generally best
to avoid confronting another person when: (1) you do not have the kind of
relationship in which trust has been established, or (2) you do not wish to be
further involved with that person, or (3) you sense that the other person, for
whatever reason, is emotionally unreceptive to a confrontation at this time.

Reflections

How would you distinguish between confronting a person and attacking him or her?
What behaviors do you think would be associated with each interaction? What
would you say is the most difficult aspect, for you, in confronting another person?

EGO STATES AND THEIR INFLUENCE ON COMMUNICATION

The idea of ego states is an outgrowth of the creative thinking of the late Eric
Berne, a psychiatrist who fathered a new approach to understanding human
personality and interpersonal communication called *Transactional Analysis*
(TA). It is an approach that focuses on an analysis of what people do and say
to one another as they engage in what Berne called *transactions.* An important
part of Transactional Analysis is known as *Structural Analysis,* which is, quite
literally, a study of the structure of personality. It is a way of analyzing our
thoughts, feelings, and behavior, based on the idea that each of us has three
different ego states. The way we send messages, or receive them, depends very
much on the ego state we happen to be in at a particular time.

How to Recognize the Ego States Within Us

As Berne[75] conceptualized them, each person has three ego states, called the
Child, the *Parent,* and the *Adult.* These are not roles; nor are they concepts like

o. They are, rather, "phenomenological reali-
an be directly observed in oneself and in others.
:ates as voices within us. When we pay attention
y tell which of the three ego states is dominant
ample, when we are in our *Child* ego state, we
's Friday—thank heavens," or "I wish I had a
er hope I get a good grade on that test," or "No,
ur *Parent* ego state, we may say things like, "I
should get started on the paper I have to write," or "Don't turn up the radio,
I have to study," or "I ought to exercise more," or "You're a good person." When
we are in our *Adult* ego state, we may say thing like, "How can I get my work
done so I can goof off tonight?" or "What are my options for solving my money
problems?" or "It seems to me that your question is very relevant," or simply,
"Why must it be done that way?"

According to Berne's theory of Structural Analysis, an individual's personality
can be schematically drawn as in Figure 5–2.

You may find it helpful in recognizing your individual ego states to familiarize
yourself with the particular behaviors commonly associated with each of them,
as follows:

The *child ego state* contains all the impulses and behaviors that come naturally
to an infant and a young child. It contains the recordings of early life experiences
and how we responded to them. When you are feeling and acting the way you
did as a child, you are in your child ego state. Indeed, when you feel yourself
behaving in a childlike way—laughing, giggling, romping, running, or perhaps
crying, pouting, or sulking—it very likely is your child ego state that is being
expressed. Actually, there are two sides to the child ego state, the *natural child*
and the *adapted child.* Your natural child is spontaneous and free—it is that part
of you that does what it wants to do just because it wants to do it. Your adapted
child, on the other hand, is that part of you that has learned to do what others

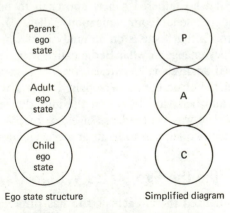

Ego state structure   Simplified diagram

FIGURE 5–2. Ego States Within Us

—usually beginning with parents—insist upon, which may have the effect of causing you to feel compliant or rebellious. Your adapted child, in other words, has learned that the world is made up of certain rules, regulations, and restrictions that may inhibit total spontaneity.

The *adult ego state* operates as an information gatherer and is not at all related to a person's age. It is that part of you which organizes and assimilates information, in order to seek solutions and solve problems. It functions by asking questions, assessing consequences, and figuring out ways to get things done. When you are dealing with current reality, gathering information, and thinking objectively, you are in your adult ego state.

The *parent ego state* is made up of the attitudes, behaviors, and values incorporated from external sources, parents or parent-figures being the primary sources of input. There are also two sides to the parent ego state. One side is the *critical parent,* and it shows up when you are instructing others in what to do and how to do it. The other side is the *nurturing parent,* which is reflected in your behavior when you're consoling or comforting or caring for another person. Outwardly, you parent ego state is expressed when you are behaving in critical or nurturing ways. Inwardly, it is experienced as old parental messages that continue to influence your inner child.

To summarize and simplify, your child is your feeling and intuitive side. It's that part of you that likes ice-cream cones and going to movies and having fun at parties. Your parent is made up of learned ideas about what is right or wrong, good or bad, moral or immoral, and about how you "should" or "ought" to act. It's the part of you that cares deeply for a loved one or admonishes a child for not looking both ways before crossing the street. Your adult is your data processing, "computer" side. It's the part of you that balances the checkbook and looks for ways to solve problems. To help you in developing your sensitivity to the particular ego state from which you or another person are communicating at any given moment, Figure 5–3 has been designed to give you some of the specific behavioral clues associated with each of them.

Ego State Transactions: Expressions and Outcomes

A way to understanding human communication is through an analysis of the kinds of transactions that go on between people, as they relate to each other from similar or different ego states. A transaction is an exchange between two people, consisting of a stimulus and a response between two or more ego states. Transactions can be simple, involving two ego states, or complex, involving three or even four ego states. It is an exciting and different way of looking at why and how we communicate with each other the way we do. By developing an awareness of the way that each ego state influences how we say things and the way we say them, we enhance our possibilities for communicating more accurately what we're thinking and feeling. For example, have you ever had the inner sense that when you talk with some people, you feel younger than you really are—more childlike?

FIGURE 5–3. Behavior Clues to Help Identify Which Ego State is Being Communicated

EGO STATES	COMMON VERBAL EXPRESSIONS	CHARACTERISTIC VOICE PATTERNS	BODY LANGUAGE CLUES
Critical parent	That's nice, bad That's cute, good You should	Judgmental Admonishing Critical	Points or wags finger Frowns, squints Feet apart, hands on hips
	You ought You never Be quiet, good	Condescending Loud Disgusted, sneering	Slaps, spanks Serious looking Arms crossed, closed posture
	Don't you Ridiculous You must	Scheming Comparing Demanding	Foot tapping Looks up in disgust Pounds table
Nurturing parent	*Uses words that are:* Reassuring Comforting Consoling Loving Supporting Nonjudgmental	Soft Concerned Soothing Encouraging Sympathetic	Arms open Palms outward Holds hands Hugs, holds, kisses Cradles Smiles Touches, strokes Nods approvingly
Adult	*Asks questions:* How What Where Who Why It seems to me Let's see what we find The solution is I wonder	Modulated Appropriate Corresponds to feelings Controlled, calm Straight Confident	Relaxed Stroking the chin Finger pointing to head area Looks up (as if in search of answers) Brow wrinkles when thinking Supporting head with hands Attentive
Natural child	I wish I want I hope I can't	Loud or quiet, depending on mood Laughs Cries Rages	Showing off Rolls, tumbles Walks freely, easily Posture open, ready to swing into action

FIGURE 5–3. Continued

EGO STATES	COMMON VERBAL EXPRESSIONS	CHARACTERISTIC VOICE PATTERNS	BODY LANGUAGE CLUES
	I won't	Giggles	Flops easily and comfortably on chair or floor
	Wow Gee Whoopee		Skips
Adapted child	*Compliant words:* Yes, OK, You're right I'll do it, I'm wrong *Defiant, rebellious words:* No, Make me, I won't, You're wrong, I don't care *Other expressions:* Help me, It's your fault, You'll be sorry	Annoying Repetitive Sweet Placating Angry Defiant Loud or soft Total silence	Showing off Pouting Fights aggressively or Withdraws timidly Chip on shoulder or Passive conformity Teary eyed Looking innocent

And have you observed yourself behaving more like a child when you're around certain people? Perhaps with some people you feel natural, free, and fun-loving, while with other people you feel subdued, obedient, and compliant. We've all felt these ways from time to time, and it may be a sign that our child ego state is activated and is responding to one person's parent ego state or to another person's child ego state. In other instances, you may notice yourself behaving in a somewhat protective and nurturing manner toward certain people, and you may feel older or wiser with these people. Now it could be that certain people we interact with tend to be more childlike in *their* behavior, so we behave somewhat more parentally around them. Or perhaps certain others feel quite parental toward us and we respond somewhat in kind. In other words, the ebb and flow of any given transaction between us and another person will depend on which ego state each of us is in at any given moment.

As originally delineated by Eric Berne,[77, 78] and further clarified and discussed by TA specialists Muriel James and Dorothy Jongeward,[79] Gisele Weisman,[80] and Graham Barnes,[81] *transactional analysis* is a way to understand the psychology of human communication by being aware of the ego states that are involved in transactions between people. There are basically three kinds of transactions—complementary, crossed, and ulterior, each with its own particular expression and outcome. Let's consider each of these.

Complementary Transactions (We're On the Same Track) A complementary or parallel transaction occurs when the message you send from a specific ego state elicits a more or less predictable response from a specific ego state in another person. It's the kind of communication between people that is direct, clear, and mutually reinforcing. A complementary transaction can occur between any two ego states. For example, two people may communicate parent to parent when expressing concern for someone, or adult to adult when exchanging information, or child to child or parent to child when living it up a little. We can communicate from any one of our three ego states to any one of the three ego states of the other person. You may get a better idea of how complementary transaction works by considering the examples in Figure 5–4.

You will recall from our discussion earlier in this chapter that nonverbal cues —facial expressions, body language, gestures, tone of voice, and so forth—all contribute to the final meaning of any transaction. We have assumed in the examples in Figure 5–4 that the exchanges are straightforward, in the sense that the verbal and nonverbal components are congruent. When there is congruency between *what* is said and *how* it is said, and when the responses are pretty much what is expected and appropriate, then we can say that the communication transaction is complementary. This does not, however, always happen. Sometimes, our message receives an unexpected or inappropriate response, and the lines of communication become what are called. . . .

Crossed Transactions (One of Us is Discounted) You're talking to someone, and his or her response to what you've just said causes you to feel angry, or maybe frustrated, or perhaps like not even wanting to talk anymore. What you've just experienced (and haven't we all) is a crossed transaction. It happens when we get an unexpected response from the person we're speaking to. For example, let's say you ask me what time it is (adult/adult), and I say to you, "You should buy a watch and then you'd know," (my parent ego state to your child ego state). What happens is that I give you an unexpected reply from an ego state different from the one you're addressing. It is at this point that communication frequently breaks down. One person feels hurt or misunderstood, and the conversation abruptly ends or, frequently, both people get defensive and argumentative. Crossed transactions create many problems and are a frequent cause of conflict between husband and wife, parents and children, teachers and students, boss and employees, and so forth. A crossed communication begins with one person initiating a transaction and concludes with an unexpected response from the other person. The initiator is often left feeling discounted. The examples in Figure 5–5 may help you to understand this process better.

You can see from the examples that crossed transactions are most likely to occur when the receiver responds in some kind of feeling way (anger, frustration, hurt) to something the sender has said. A way to uncross a crossed communication is to use one of the responses discussed earlier, such as reflective listening, or a probing response, or perhaps a supportive reply. Any one of these responses

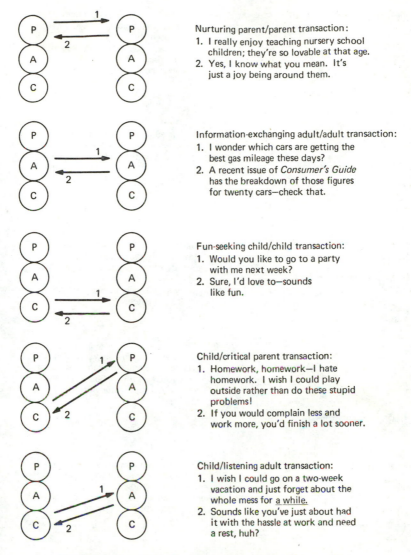

Nurturing parent/parent transaction:
1. I really enjoy teaching nursery school children; they're so lovable at that age.
2. Yes, I know what you mean. It's just a joy being around them.

Information-exchanging adult/adult transaction:
1. I wonder which cars are getting the best gas mileage these days?
2. A recent issue of *Consumer's Guide* has the breakdown of those figures for twenty cars—check that.

Fun-seeking child/child transaction:
1. Would you like to go to a party with me next week?
2. Sure, I'd love to—sounds like fun.

Child/critical parent transaction:
1. Homework, homework—I hate homework. I wish I could play outside rather than do these stupid problems!
2. If you would complain less and work more, you'd finish a lot sooner.

Child/listening adult transaction:
1. I wish I could go on a two-week vacation and just forget about the whole mess for a while.
2. Sounds like you've just about had it with the hassle at work and need a rest, huh?

FIGURE 5–4. Examples of Complementary Transactions

lets the receiver know we've picked up the *feeling* tone of what was said, which may help to uncross a crossed communication. For example, in the husband-wife transaction in Figure 5–5, the husband could uncross the transaction by responding to his wife's parental admonition with a supportive parental reply like, "I know check writing is no fun, and I'll make it a point to help out with it more in the future." This is his Nurturing Parent response directed at her critical parent reply. The chances are rather good that a reply of this sort will tend to sooth her ruffled feathers. Can you imagine what would happen if he were to reply, say,

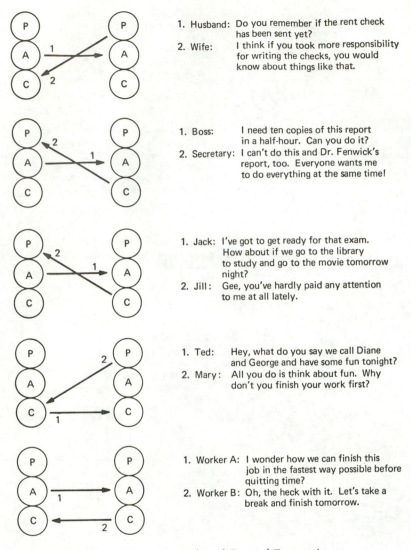

1. Husband: Do you remember if the rent check
             has been sent yet?
2. Wife: I think if you took more responsibility
            for writing the checks, you would
            know about things like that.

1. Boss: I need ten copies of this report
              in a half-hour. Can you do it?
2. Secretary: I can't do this and Dr. Fenwick's
              report, too. Everyone wants me
              to do everything at the same time!

1. Jack: I've got to get ready for that exam.
         How about if we go to the library
         to study and go to the movie tomorrow
         night?
2. Jill: Gee, you've hardly paid any attention
         to me at all lately.

1. Ted: Hey, what do you say we call Diane
         and George and have some fun tonight?
2. Mary: All you do is think about fun. Why
         don't you finish your work first?

1. Worker A: I wonder how we can finish this
             job in the fastest way possible before
             quitting time?
2. Worker B: Oh, the heck with it. Let's take a
             break and finish tomorrow.

FIGURE 5–5. Examples of Crossed Transactions

"Look, you do little enough around here as it is; the least you can do is write a few checks." (This response would be from his critical parent to her child, which would keep the communication crossed and a potential cause of problems).

There is still another kind of transaction, and it is more complex because it involves having to read between the lines of what is said in order to understand what is really meant.

Ulterior Transactions (There's a Hidden Message) On the surface, ulterior transactions appear to be open and complementary, but they contain hidden or ulterior messages. It's a frequent kind of communication between two people who are playing games with each other, who are fearful of being direct and open because they may not want to hurt the other person or to be hurt themselves. Ulterior transactions mask the *real* message, which is usually camouflaged by what looks like an adult-to-adult communication. For example, if Jim wants to ask Ann for a date but is fearful of coming right out and asking because he doesn't want to be rejected, he may ask questions like, "Do you spend all your time studying?" or "How do you fill your weekends?" or "I enjoy going to movies for relaxation—how do you relax?" We only call these ulterior transactions if there is another, unexpressed message that remains hidden. In Jim's case, if he doesn't come out with what he really wants, namely, to ask Ann to go to the movie with him, we will have to conclude that his real reason for the questions is to avoid the risk of directness. There are other examples of how ulterior transactions look and sound in Figure 5–6.

Ulterior transactions have a sometimes necessary and appropriate place in human communication. For example, in Jim's case, it seems altogether appropriate that he find something out about Ann's schedule and tastes before asking more directly for a date. It is when ulterior transactions are used more or less consistently as the major mode of communication that they cause problems. You can never know for sure whether the other person has an ulterior message in mind, but you usually do know for sure whether or not you do. How can you tell? When there's a difference between what you're really thinking or feeling and what you're actually saying, you may have reason to suspect a lurking ulterior message.

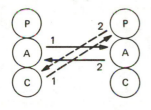

1. Teacher : The exam tomorrow will be very hard.
   (*Ulterior: You'd better study like you've never studied before or you'll flunk.*)
2. Student: How many questions will be on the exam?
   (*Ulterior: Do you think I have any chance of passing it?*)

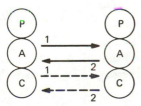

1. Barbara: Would you like to come in for a cup of coffee and some cake? (*Ulterior: Want to fool around a little before going home?*)
2. Joe: Yeah, coffee and cake sound good.
   (*Ulterior: Yeah, let's fool around.*)

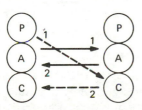

1. Jill: I just read that venereal disease was on the upswing, particularly among young singles. (*Ulterior: Don't get any funny ideas about making a pass.*)
2. Jack: Yes, I think I heard the same thing.
   (*Ulterior: Boy, you're no fun at all.*)

FIGURE 5–6.   Examples of Ulterior Transactions

To summarize: The three transaction modes we've just looked at are ways to understand what is happening in our interpersonal communications. Complementary transactions keep things going, because the interactions are more or less in line with what each of us expects from the other. Crossed transactions are disruptive, because the responses we get are unexpected and catch us off guard, triggering defensive replies. Ulterior transactions, particularly when carried to extremes, stand directly in the way of open, honest relationships, because we find ourselves reluctant to be too deeply involved with people who refuse to be straight with us.

Recognizing the Ego State in Your Response Style and Interaction Behaviors

Earlier, we talked about five major response styles that are available to us in terms of the sort of interaction pattern and language that we use in our everday communications. It may be helpful to consider the possible ego state corollary that seems to be naturally associated with each of these styles (see Table 5–1).

The ego state idea can be useful in helping us to understand better why we interact with others the way we do. This understanding may lead us to a greater consciousness and awareness about our communication patterns, which is the first step to changing those aspects of ourselves that may be causing communication problems. A former client of mine, a man working on improving what he considered lousy interpersonal relationships, said something toward the end of his therapy that illustrates well how this understanding can be used:

> I always wondered why I had so many problems relating to others. I just was not conscious of the fact that I was constantly evaluating others or demanding things from them, and in general behaving like that spoiled adapted child we've talked about, or the critical parent. No wonder people didn't like me. I wouldn't have liked me either. It's a whole new world for me since I've stopped being so damned bossy and rigid. I wish I had known what a lot of other people knew about me a lot sooner.

Well, now he does know. And he can make choices that allow him to step outside of his history of conditioned reflexes and be the person he wants to be when he communicates with others.

IN PERSPECTIVE

What is human communication? It is practically everything you can think of that we do. It is more than *what* we say, it is also *how* we say it. More than that, it is how we are behaving *when* we say it. In the final analysis, human interaction

TABLE 5–1.

RESPONSE STYLE	EGO STATE COROLLARY
1. *Evaluative*—judgmental about what is good, bad, or appropriate; many "you shoulds" are said	Critical Parent
2. *Interpretive*—telling others what their behavior "really" means and why they feel as they do	Critical Parent, when said critically or hurtfully, or Adult, when cited as information intended to be helpful
3. *Supportive*—an attempt to reassure and let the other person know he or she is not alone	Nurturing Parent
4. *Probing*—an effort to get information, to find out more	Adult
5. *Understanding*—reflectively listening, trying to understand more deeply the other person	Adult and Nurturing Parent (a combination of getting information and showing concern)
INTERACTION BEHAVIOR	
1. *Deferring*—giving in to the other person either because it is appropriate and necessary and we choose to or doing it even though we don't want to	Adapted Child
2. *Demanding*—literally demanding something from another person	Adapted Child, when screaming for own way, or Critical Parent when ordering others around or being overly aggressive
3. *Defecting*—leaving the scene, withdrawing, slamming doors, etc.	Adapted Child
4. *Declaring*—making it clear to the other person in I-statements what you want or would like to happen.	Adult and Nurturing Parent (a combination of giving information and doing it in a friendly, nonhostile way)

is a collage of spoken words, nonverbal gestures, and body postures that, for better or worse, allows us to communicate how we think and feel, and what we believe.

More so than we realize, some of our more significant communications are transmitted on a nonverbal level. The way we say things, the clothes we wear, the look on our face, our eye contact or lack of it—all of these factors interact with what is said on the verbal level and help to color others' interpretations of what we say. There is an important cultural factor in all of this, in the sense that different cultures (or subcultures within the main culture) may give different meanings to certain verbal and nonverbal messages.

How we respond to others in the course of our day-to-day interactions has a definite bearing on both the content of a communication and the feelings about it. If we constantly evaluate others, pretty soon there will be fewer and fewer people to interact with us. If we spend at least as much time listening, reflecting, and supporting, there will be more people seeking our company than we have time for.

Declaring what we want in nonjudgmental, nondemanding I-statements can be a very helpful way to keep communication going. It is a direct and open expression of where we are and what we want, which helps the other person know what to expect.

Self-disclosure is an important aspect of open communication. If I tell you something that reveals something about me as a person, it is possible for you to share something of yourself. Mutual sharing in a self-disclosing way not only builds relationships, but keeps them going. One of the reasons your best friend is your best friend is very likely because you are able to confide in each other things that are meaningful and personal. It is a way of investing in another person, and enhances a sense of belongingness, while reducing a sense of separateness.

Confrontation is frequently necessary, but it is a form of communication that needs to be handled carefully and skillfully. Ways of doing this have been discussed, but there are two basic rules of confrontation worth repeating here: (1) Don't confront unless you wish to be further involved with that person, and (2) don't confront if the other person—for any reason—seems not to be ready for it. Timing is crucial.

Being aware of the ego state that we may be in at a particular moment can help us to assess the effect we may have on others. If we communicate too much from a constant child state, we may unwittingly hook the parent state in others, which keeps us in a dependent role. If we relate too much from a constant adult state, others may consider us boring and unfeeling. If we interact too much from a constant parent state, we may find ourselves frequently feeling exhausted, because of the number of people we've unknowingly encouraged to be dependent on us.

Good communication—communication that is open, direct, honest, and facilitating—is the essential medium that keeps friends together, marriages alive, and relationships of all sorts growing. It's one of the core ingredients that go into making a good teacher, a good parent, a good friend, a good boss, or a good spouse good in the first place.

Happily, it's one of the most learnable skills around.

REFERENCES

1. R. S. Goyer, "Communication, Communicative Process, Meaning: Toward a Unified Theory," *Journal of Communication* 20 (1980): 4–5.

2. F. E. Dance, "The Concept of Communication," *Journal of Communication* 20 (1970): 201–210.

3. R. L. Birdwhistell, *Introduction to Kinesics* Louisville, Ky.: University of Louisville Press, Foreign Services Institute, 1952.

4. R. L. Birdwhistell, *Kenesics and Context,* Philadelphia: University of Pennsylvania, 1970.

5. L. M. Sielski, "Understanding Body Language," *Personnel and Guidance Journal,* January 1979, pp. 238–242.

6. E. T. Hall, *The Silent Language,* Greenwich, Conn.: Fawcett, 1959.

7. R. Sommer, *Personal Space: The Behavioral Basis of Design,* Englewood Cliffs, N.J.: Prentice-Hall, 1969.

8. E. T. Hall, *The Hidden Dimension,* New York: Doubleday, 1966.

9. A. Mehrabian, "Relationship of Attitude to Seated Posture, Orientation, and Distance," *Journal of Personality and Social Psychology* 10 (1968): 26–30.

10. R. Sommer, *Personal Space: The Behavioral Basis of Design,* Englewood Cliffs, N.J.: Prentice-Hall, 1969, p. 65.

11. A. Mehrabian, "Significance of Posture and Position in the Communication of Attitude and Status Relationships," *Psychological Bulletin* 71 (1969) 359–372.

12. V. J. Konecni, L. Libuser, H. Morton, and E. B. Ebbesen, "Effects of Violation of Personal Space on Escape and Helping Responses," *Journal of Experimental Social Psychology* 11 (1975): 288–299.

13. M. Koneya, "Location and Interaction in Row-and-Column Seating Arrangements," *Environment and Behavior* 8 (1976) 265–282.

14. C. Darwin, *The Expression of Emotions in Man and Animal,* (originally published, 1872), Chicago: University of Chicago Press, 1965.

15. P. Eckman, W. V. Friesen, and P. Ellsworth, *Emotion in the Human Face: Guide-lines for Research and Integration of Findings,* New York: Pergamon Press, 1972.

16. P. Ekman and W. V. Friesen, *Unmasking the Face,* Englewood Cliffs, N.J.: Prentice-Hall, 1975.

17. P. Ekman, "Face Muscles Talk Every Language," *Psychology Today,* September 1975, p. 39.

18. J. Fast "Eyes Have a Language of Their Own," *Family Health,* April 1979, pp. 23–25.

19. J. S. Efran and A. Broughton, "Effect of Expectancies for Social Approval on Visual Behavior," *Journal of Personality and Social Psychology* 4 (1966): 103–107.

20. C. L. Kleinke, F. B. Meeker, and C. LaFong, "Effects of Gaze, Touch, and Use of Name on Evaluation of 'Engaged' Couples," *Journal of Research in Personality* 7 (1974): 368–373.

21. C. L. Kleinke, R. A. Staneski, and S. L. Pipp, "Effects of Gaze, Distance, and Attractiveness on Males' First Impressions of Females," *Representative Research in Social Psychology* 6 (1975): 7–12.

22. M. Cobin, "Response to Eye Contact," *Quarterly Journal of Speech* 48 (1962): 415–418.

23.   J. Blubaugh, "Effects of Positive and Negative Audience Feedback on Selected Variables of Speech Behavior," *Speech Monographs* 36 (1969): 131–137.

24.   P. Ellsworth and J. M. Carlsmith, "Effects of Eye Contact and Verbal Content on Affective Response to Dyadic Interaction," *Journal of Personality and Social Psychology* 10 (1968) 15–20.

25.   P. Ellsworth, J. Carlsmith, and A. Henson, "The Stare as a Stimulus to Flight in Human Subjects: A Series of Field Experiments," *Journal of Personality and Social Psychology* 21 (1972): 301–311.

26.   C. L. Kleinke, "Compliance to Requests Made by Gazing and Touching Experimenters in Field Settings," *Journal of Experimental Social Psychology* 13 (1977): 218–223.

27.   M. Snyder, J. Grether, and K. Keller, "Staring and Compliance: A Field Experiment on Hitchhiking," *Journal of Applied Social Psychology* 4 (1974): 165–170.

28.   G. D. Hemsley and A. N. Dobb, "The Effect of Looking Behavior on Perceptions of a Communicator's Credibility," *Journal of Applied Social Psychology* 8 (1978): 136–144.

29.   M. Argyle, *The Psychology of Interpersonal Behavior*, Baltimore, Md.: Penguin Books, 1967, pp. 105–116.

30.   J. A. Starkweather, "Vocal Communication of Healthy Personality and Human Feelings," *Journal of Communication* 11 (1961): 63–72.

31.   A. Mehrabian, "Communication Without Words," *Psychology Today,* September 1968, pp. 53–56.

32.   W. F. Soskin and P. E. Kauffman, "Judgment of Emotion in Word-Free Samples," *Journal of Communication* 11 (1961): 73–81.

33.   J. R. Davitz and L. J. Davitz, "Nonverbal Vocal Communication of Feeling," *Journal of Communication* 11 (1961): 81–86.

34.   A. Mehrabian and M. Williams, "Nonverbal Concomitants of Perceived and Intended Persuasiveness," *Journal of Personality and Social Psychology* 13 (1969): 37–58.

35.   E. Ryan and M. Carranza, "Evaluative Reactions of Adolescents Toward Speakers of Standard English and Mexican-American Accented English," *Journal of Personality and Social Psychology* 31 (1975): 855–863.

36.   R. E. Kraut, "Verbal and Nonverbal Cues in the Perception of Lying," *Journal of Personality and Social Psychology* 36 (1978): 380–391.

37.   A. Mehrabian, "Orientation Behaviors and Nonverbal Attitude Communication," *Journal of Communication* 17 (1967): 324–332.

38.   A. Mehrabian, "Inference of Attitudes from Posture, Orientation, and Distance of a Communicator," *Journal of Consulting and Clinical Psychology* 32 (1968): 296–318.

39.   G. L. Clore, N. H. Wiggins, and S. Itkin, "Judging Attraction from Nonverbal Behavior: The Gain Phenomenon," *Journal of Consulting and Clinical Psychology* 43 (1975): 491–497.

40.   A. Mehrabian and J. Friar, "Encoding of Attitude by a Seated Communicator via Posture and Position Cues," *Journal of Consulting and Clinical Psychology* 33 (1969): 330–336.

41.   M. LaFrance and C. Mayo, *Moving Bodies: Nonverbal Communication in Social Relationships,* Monterey, Calif.: Brooks/Cole, 1978, pp. 108–111.

42. C. L. Kleinke, "Compliance to Requests Made by Gazing and Touching Experimenters in Field Settings," *Journal of Experimental Social Psychology* 13 (1977): 218–223.

43. T. Nguyen, R. Heslin, and M. Nguyen, "The Meanings of Touch: Sex Differences," *Journal of Communication* 25 (1975): 92–103.

44. P. Ekman, W. V. Friesen, M. O'Sullivan, and K. Scherer, "Relative Importance of Face, Body, and Speech in Judgments of Personality and Affect," *Journal of Personality and Social Psychology* 38 (1980): 270–277.

45. J. A. Hall, "Gender Effects in Decoding Nonverbal Cues," *Psychological Bulletin* 85 (1978): 845–857.

46. R. Rosenthal and B. M. DePaulo, "Sex Differences in Eavesdropping on Nonverbal Cues," *Journal of Personality and Social Psychology* 37 (1979): 273–285.

47. D. Archer and R. M. Akert, "Words and Everything Else: Verbal and Nonverbal Cues in Social Interpretation," *Journal of Personality and Social Psychology* 35 (1977): 443–449.

48. J. A. Hall, R. Rosenthal, D. Archer, M. DiMatteo, and P. L. Rogers, "The Profile of Nonverbal Sensitivity," in P. McReynolds (Ed.), *Advances in Psychological Assessment,* Vol. 4, San Francisco: Jossey-Bass, 1978.

49. M. Argyle, *Bodily Communication,* New York: Internationl Universities Press, 1975.

50. P. Ekman, "Facial Muscles Talk Every Language," *Psychology Today,* September 1975, p. 39.

51. E. T. Hall, "Proxemics—The Study of Man's Spatial Relations and Boundaries in L. Galdston (Ed.), *Man's Image in Medicine and Anthropology, Monograph Series No. 4,* New York: International Universities Press, 1963.

52. E. Sieberg and C. Larson, "Dimensions of Interpersonal Response," paper delivered at the annual conference of the International Communication Association, Phoenix, Arizona, April 1971.

53. C. R. Rogers and F. J. Roethlisberger, "Barriers and Gateways to Communication," *Harvard Business Review,* July-August 1952, pp. 28–35.

54. C. R. Rogers, *On Becoming a Person,* Boston: Houghton Mifflin, 1961, pp. 39–58.

55. T. J. Cottle and P. Whitten (Eds.), *Psychotherapy: Current Perspectives,* New York: New Viewpoints, a division of Franklin Watts, 1980.

56. J. M. Wiemann and P. Backlund, "Current Theory and Research in Communicative Competence," *Review of Educational Research* 50 (Spring 1980): 185–199.

57. J. Narciso and D. Burkett, *Declare Yourself: Discovering Me in Relationships,* Englewood Cliffs, N.J.: Prentice-Hall, 1975.

58. T. Gordon, *T.E.T.: Teacher Effectiveness Training,* New York: David McKay Company, 1974, p. 142.

59. W. Gaylin, *Feelings,* New York: Ballantine, 1979, p. 1.

60. R. L. Archer and J. A. Burleson, "The Effects of Timing and Self-Disclosure on Attraction and Reciprocity," *Journal of Personality and Social Psychology* 38 (1980): 120–130.

61. C. B. Wortman, P. Adesman, E. Herman, and R. Greenberg, "Self-Disclosure: An Attributional Perspective," *Journal of Personality and Social Psychology* 33 (1976): 184–191.

62. D. W. Johnson, *Reaching Out: Interpersonal Effectiveness and Self-Actualization,* Englewood Cliffs, N.J.: Prentice-Hall, 1972, p. 88.

63. P. Tillich, *The Courage To Be,* New Haven, Conn.: Yale University Press, 1952.

64. S. M. Jourard, *The Transparent Self,* New York: Van Nostrand Reinhold, 1971, p. 5.

65. R. L. Archer, "Self-Disclosure," in D. M. Wegner and R. R. Vallacher (Eds.), *The Self in Social Psychology,* New York/Oxford: Oxford University Press, 1980, pp. 183–205.

66. A. L. Chaikin and V. J. Derlegn, "Variables Affecting the Appropriateness of Self-Disclosure," *Journal of Consulting and Clinical Psychology* 42 (1974): 588–593.

67. S. M. Jourard, *The Transparent Self,* New York: Van Nostrand Reinhold, 1971, pp. 25–74.

68. D. M. Daher and P. G. Banikiotes, "Interpersonal Attraction and Rewarding Aspects of Disclosure Content and Level," *Journal of Personality and Social Psychology* 33 (1976): 492–496.

69. S. Rosen and A. Tesser, "On Reluctance to Communicate Undesirable Information: The MUM Effect," *Sociometry* 33 (1970): 253–263.

70. A. Tesser and S. Rosen, "The Reluctance to Transmit Bad News," in L. Berkowitz (Ed.), *Advances in Experimental Social Psychology,* Vol. VIII, New York: Academic Press, 1975.

71. R. R. Carkhuff, *The. Art of Helping,* 3rd ed., Amherst, Mass.: Human Resource Development Press, 1976, pp. 112–123.

72. D. W. Johnson, *Reaching Out: Interpersonal Effectiveness and Self-Actualization,* Englewood Cliffs, N.J.: Prentice-Hall, 1972, p. 160.

73. J. L. Wallen, "Developing Effective Interpersonal Communication," in R. W. Pace, B. D. Patterson, and T. R. Radcliff (Eds.), *Communicating Interpersonally,* Columbus, Ohio: Charles E. Merrill, 1973, pp. 218–233.

74. B. G. Berenson and K. M. Mitchell, *Confrontation: For Better or Worse,* Amherst, Mass.: Human Resource Development Press, 1974.

75. E. Berne, *Transactional Analysis in Psychotherapy,* New York: Grove Press, 1961.

76. E. Berne, *Transactional Analysis in Psychotherapy,* New York: Grove Press, 1961, p. 24.

77. E. Berne, *Beyond Games and Scripts: Selections from Major Writings,* Claude Steimer, Ed., New York: Ballantine, 1976, pp. 21–134.

78. E. Berne, *Games People Play,* New York: Ballantine, 1964.

79. M. James and D. Jongeward, *Born to Win: Transactional Analysis with Gestalt Experiments,* Reading, Mass.: Addison-Wesley, 1971.

80. G. Weisman, *The Winner's Way: A Transactional Analysis Guide for Living, Working, and Learning,* Monterey, Calif.: Brooks/Cole, 1980.

81. G. Barnes, (Ed.), *Transactional Analysis After Eric Berne: Teachings and Practices of Three TA Schools,* New York: Harper's College Press, 1977.

INDEXES

SUBJECTS

NAMES